Your
Practicum in
Psychology

SECOND EDITION

Your Practicum in Psychology

A Guide for Maximizing Knowledge and Competence

SECOND EDITION

Edited by
Janet R. Matthews and C. Eugene Walker

American Psychological Association • Washington, DC

Published by
American Psychological Association
750 First Street, NE
Washington, DC 20002
www.apa.org

To order
APA Order Department
P.O. Box 92984
Washington, DC 20090-2984
Tel: (800) 374-2721; Direct: (202) 336-5510
Fax: (202) 336-5502; TDD/TTY: (202) 336-6123
Online: www.apa.org/pubs/books
E-mail: order@apa.org

In the U.K., Europe, Africa, and the Middle East, copies may be ordered from
American Psychological Association
3 Henrietta Street
Covent Garden, London
WC2E 8LU England

Typeset in Meridien by Circle Graphics, Inc., Columbia, MD

Printer: Edwards Brothers Inc., Lillington, NC
Cover Designer: Naylor Design, Washington, DC

The opinions and statements published are the responsibility of the authors, and such opinions and statements do not necessarily represent the policies of the American Psychological Association.

Library of Congress Cataloging-in-Publication Data

Your practicum in psychology : a guide for maximizing knowledge and competence / edited by Janet R. Matthews and C. Eugene Walker. — Second edition.
    p. ; cm.
  Includes bibliographical references and index.
  ISBN 978-1-4338-2000-7 (alk. paper) — ISBN 1-4338-2000-5 (alk. paper)
  I. Matthews, Janet R., editor. II. Walker, C. Eugene (Clarence Eugene), 1939- , editor. III. American Psychological Association, publisher.
  [DNLM: 1. Psychology, Clinical—United States. 2. Ethics, Clinical—United States. 3. Internship and Residency—United States. 4. Psychotherapy—methods—United States. WM 105]

  RC467.7
  616.89'0071—dc23

                                2014046277

British Library Cataloguing-in-Publication Data
A CIP record is available from the British Library.

Printed in the United States of America
Second Edition

http://dx.doi.org/10.1037/14672-000

To my husband, clinical psychologist Lee H. Matthews,
who pushes me to be professionally active and supports me so I can be.
To my former students who repeatedly told me that the practicum course
was the most important aspect of helping them find their career passion
and who inspired me to keep teaching this course.
—Janet R. Matthews

To my father, Lewis G. Walker, and my mother, Olga Thresa Brioli
—C. Eugene Walker

Contents

Contributors

Amanda S. Cherry, PhD, Clinical Assistant Professor, University of Oklahoma Health Sciences Center, Oklahoma City

Jean C. Elbert, Department of Psychology, California State University, Northridge

Stephen R. Gillaspy, PhD, Associate Professor, University of Oklahoma Health Sciences Center, Oklahoma City

Kimberly E. Hiroto, PhD, Home Based Primary Care, VA Puget Sound Health Care System, American Lake Division, Tacoma, WA

Noel J. Jacobs, PhD, Associate Professor, University of Oklahoma Health Sciences Center, Oklahoma City

Janet R. Matthews, PhD, ABPP, Professor Emerita, Loyola University New Orleans, New Orleans, LA

Lee H. Matthews, PhD, ABPP, Department of Psychiatry and Behavioral Sciences, Tulane University Medical Center, New Orleans, LA

Bruce K. McCormick, PhD, Private practice, Shreveport, LA

Peter E. Nathan, PhD, Emeritus Professor, University of Iowa, Iowa City

B. Max Price, PhD, Private clinical practice, Oklahoma City, OK

Sara H. Qualls, PhD, Department of Psychology and Gerontology Center, University of Colorado, Colorado Springs

Morgan T. Sammons, PhD, Executive Officer, National Register of Health Service Psychologists, Washington, DC

Daniel L. Segal, PhD, Psychology Department, University of Colorado, Colorado Springs

Elizabeth Swenson, PhD, JD, John Carroll University, University Heights, OH

Timothy S. Thornberry Jr., PhD, Assistant Professor, Department of Psychology, Morehead State University, Morehead, KY

C. Eugene Walker, PhD, University of Oklahoma, Norman

Preface

This book is written for students who are entering their first practicum experience. Some of you reading this book are advanced undergraduate students; others are beginning graduate studies. When we collaborated on our first book for this course with a different publisher, we did it because we were tired of piecing together selected readings from various sources for our students. We wanted to have a single source for them. That first book taught us the variability of this first practicum experience. We found the book a reasonably good match with the needs of our courses, but some colleagues who teach similar courses did not. We then began to discuss more specifically what students were doing on the first practicum experience. This discussion resulted in the first edition of the current book about 9 years after our initial attempt. Although we were much happier with this new book than our previous one, we realize that it is now time to update some of the chapters, remove some topics, and add others.

Although we developed this book as a textbook, we do not view it in the traditional sense of that term. For us, each chapter is equivalent to a guest lecture that might occur in the seminar-style class that typically accompanies the assigned field placement. Depending on the location of the university, guest lecturers may not be readily available on certain topics of interest to students enrolled in such a course. By having those lectures in textbook form, students can revisit topics as they occur during the placement time. Because these lectures are essentially independent, there are several ways in which this book differs from a more traditional textbook. First, the voice is more variable than a classroom textbook. The authors are speaking from their individual perspectives on their area of expertise. Second, there is some minor repetition of information because of the nature of the subjects. It is important for students to hear certain topics in the different contexts. For example, many of the mental health professions described in the final chapter of the book are also mentioned in Chapters 1 and 3. Third, each chapter contains material that may not be specifically relevant to an individual reader or even a particular course format. As we evaluated practicum courses in various universities, we learned that students have quite different levels of interaction with clients and professionals during their first practicum. Some initial practicum experiences involve little or no direct client contact. They are mainly observational. In other settings, however, the practicum student may be expected to be a participant in group therapy sessions, be trained as a technician to administer simple paper-and-pencil tests, participate in team staff meetings, and have access to inpatient charts with notes by various health care professionals. Students in the latter type of placement may benefit from having information about medications mentioned in charts and staff meetings, samples of how to handle ethical dilemmas when interacting with clients at the placement, and a resource of what tests are used for specific purposes and populations.

Because of the variable nature of this course, students may find that they benefit from reading chapters in a different order from their placement in the book. As stand-alone presentations, this allows instructors as well as students to individualize their use.

As we noted in the preface to the first edition of this book, although graduate students preparing for a profession in psychology are certainly expected to adhere to the *Ethical Principles of Psychologists and Code of Conduct* of the American Psychological Association (2010), there is some variability of opinion among psychologists regarding whether undergraduate students who are mainly observers are held to a professional code of ethics. It is our view that students of psychology in applied settings should be held to the same code of ethics as professionals in applied settings. It is important for them to learn this material early in their career, just as they learn about research ethics in methods courses before actually conducting research. Those students who have a more active role in their first practicum often sign confidentiality agreements at their sites. Having a complete context for this expectation is part of the learning process for the practicum experience. Even students who are in an observer role may find themselves talking individually with patients. For example, students placed on an inpatient psychiatric unit may find themselves talking individually with patients in much the same role as psychological technicians. Reading about ethical issues that may arise as well as how to establish rapport provides them with a foundation to maximize this part of the learning experience.

The first four chapters and the final chapter in the book are intended to provide basic orientation information on the context of applied practicum settings. Some of the chapters in this book are designed to provide summary material from specific content areas. Depending on the student's background, these chapters may be read as a quick review or a summary learning experience. Chapters 5, 6, and 7 are noteworthy here. If it has been several years since you completed an abnormal psychology course, Chapter 5 provides a quick review. For other students, some of the material may be different from what was learned because of the variable nature of textbooks and instructional style. Undergraduate courses in tests and measurements are common but seldom required. Thus, for some students, Chapter 6 may provide the initial exposure to material that may be integral to the practicum site. Even those students who have had a beginning course in tests and measurements may find that their placement site uses specialized tests not typically emphasized in their course. Thus, this chapter may provide a general understanding of the tests being used. Chapter 8 covers material that may be part of an undergraduate clinical psychology course. Like tests and measurements, clinical psychology courses are not likely to be required. These courses may even be taken after the practicum experience because of the interest developed as a result of the practicum.

The chapters on special issues in working with children and with older persons are provided for students who may be working in agencies dealing with these age groups. The chapter on aging is new to the second edition. The chapter on working with children is reprinted from the first edition of this book. We were unable to locate the author for a revision of the material. Thus, some of the references are older than those in the other chapters. We believe, however, that the basic content remains solid, and we encourage students who are working with children to pursue further information on this topic. As you read these chapters, keep in mind that they are intended to be sources of basic information that you will need for your practicum experience. Often, you will find it useful to do further reading in areas of particular relevance to what you are doing. In such cases, a literature search via PsycINFO on your university library website, as well as a Google Scholar search, will uncover much information. Along this line, a useful glossary of medical terms and abbreviations may be found at http://www.jdmd.com/pdf/jdmd_glossary.pdf. You may find this useful in trying to read the charts and files on clients with whom you are interacting.

We thank all of our chapter authors for their diligence in sending us material and making revisions in a timely fashion. Special thanks to

Linda McCarter and Andrew Gifford of APA Books, who remained in contact with us throughout this process of writing and finalizing the necessary paperwork to bring this book to print.

Reference

American Psychological Association. (2010). *Ethical principles of psychologists and code of conduct* (2002, Amended June, 2010). Retrieved from http://www.apa.org/ethics/code/index.aspx

Your
Practicum in
Psychology

SECOND EDITION

Janet R. Matthews and C. Eugene Walker

What You Get From a Practicum

1

I f you are about to start your first practicum, or are in its early stages, you are on your way to an exciting adventure. Be prepared to experience many new things in the coming weeks. If you experience emotions ranging from anxiety to fear to excitement, you are not unique. Regardless of whether you have talked with other students who have already completed this course, most students taking their initial practicum find that the experience is quite personal. Thus, what you find frustrating, another student might find fascinating.

A Note on Terminology

The terms *practicum* and *internship* in psychology refer to education in settings in which students receive supervised training experiences in applied settings. These experiences

http://dx.doi.org/10.1037/14672-001
Your Practicum in Psychology: A Guide for Maximizing Knowledge and Competence,
Second Edition, J. R. Matthews and C. E. Walker (Editors)

are designed to supplement classroom learning. Psychology uses the term *practicum* to refer to such experiences earlier in the educational process and *internship* to refer to the yearlong applied experience required of some doctoral students. These practica are designed to provide building blocks for each other. Thus, the initial practicum tends to be the most basic. Less prior course work is expected, and therefore more supervision is needed. Once these basic experiences have occurred, combined with the related academic coursework, the student is ready for the full-time experience of the internship. Another term that undergraduate institutions sometimes use is *field placement*. Because other disciplines may use these words interchangeably, however, some universities may call an initial experience in an applied setting an *internship*, whereas others may call it *practicum* or *field placement* (Baird, 2012). For the sake of simplicity, we use *practicum* throughout this chapter.

Another set of interchangeable terms is *client* or *patient*. Although many psychologists today use the word *client* to refer to the recipient of their services, we were trained in medical centers and became accustomed to using the term *patient*. Because applied psychologists are now considered health care providers regardless of their practice setting, this term is also logical. Furthermore, an increasing number of people who seek psychological services expect their health insurance to pay for a significant part of the cost, and thus the term *patient* seems to be appropriate. Although some psychologists use *client* for outpatients and *patients* for inpatients, we use *patient* throughout this chapter to indicate the recipient of services regardless of the setting. For that matter, one psychologist recently noted that when he thought of *client*, "the thing that comes to mind is insurance agent!"

Before Starting—Consider These Ideas

There are some basic issues to think about before you even start your placement. Although they are covered in more detail later in the book, we'll introduce them here. First, think about your overall appearance—clothing, hair, and visible additions to your body. These topics are addressed in more detail in Chapter 3 (Matthews and Matthews) on getting started. Remember, you are now a trainee, not just a student in a class. Requirements for attire vary considerably from one placement site to another. A good strategy is to show up on the first day in conservative, professional dress. At that time, you can inquire about specific dress standards for your setting. Keep in mind that some sites will have specific rules.

Second, how should you handle the situation if you encounter a person you met at your practicum in a setting outside the practicum? For example, suppose you see him or her in the supermarket or on campus? Your initial thought may be that you would say hello but try not to have an extended conversation with the person. This seems like the polite response to the situation. However, consider what would happen if one of your friends happens to see the interaction and then asks you how you know that person. What will you say? Occasionally, this type of situation occurs, and you make the mistake of acknowledging the person and a friend asks you who they are. Your best response in this case is short, noncommittal, and probably not totally accurate. For example, you might say that you thought the person looked familiar but you are not sure why. Adult patients seem to handle these situations better than children. With children you meet through your practicum, you may find it easier to just smile, nod, and move away as quickly as possible. Some professionals tell their patients during treatment that, in the interest of confidentiality, they will not recognize the patient outside of the office unless the patient speaks first.

One of our former students faced a much more difficult situation of this type. She and her friends were in a crowded club. Dancing was a major activity there, with a crowded dance floor and people dancing with each other just because they were in proximity. She looked up at one point and realized that her dance partner was someone she had met at her practicum placement. She immediately excused herself, indicating that she had not realized the time and needed to return to her friends. These issues are explored as part of the discussion of confidentiality later in this chapter and in the chapter on ethics.

Third, although we talk about confidentiality in courses such as abnormal psychology, we do not typically talk about *your* confidentiality. What should you do if, while at your placement site, you are asked for personal information, such as your phone number or e-mail address, or if you are asked to "friend" someone on a social network? For most students, it seems obvious that you do not provide such information to an adult. Our students who have had the most difficulty with this issue are those who work with children. The children become attached to them and want to remain in contact through one or more of these venues. The response is still: "Do not provide personal information to patients or their relatives." It is important, however, to explain to the person that in your role as a trainee, you are not permitted to provide that type of information or to have contact with them outside the facility. You do not want the patient to think you are rude or insensitive.

In contrast, remaining in contact with the professional staff is certainly acceptable. Depending on the situation, they may be willing to write letters of recommendation for you as you make postgraduation plans. In other cases, you may be able to continue to work with them on research projects or other volunteer projects to gain additional experiences.

Competency Development

The practicum is different from service learning. In service learning, the focus tends to be on helping various community groups or agencies by providing extra hands for their work. There is often no specific academic prerequisite for such an experience. Service learning may occur in settings that are not psychological in nature. The idea is to give back to the community. The staff member with whom you work at the site may have no background in psychology. Even when service learning is part of a college course, there is not the expectation that the student will be gaining *competencies* as a result of the experience. The practicum experiences are intended to assist you to develop the core competencies that are considered part of clinical practice. The Association of Directors of Psychology Training Clinics developed an outline of competencies to help both you and your supervisors track the development of these needed skills. This outline was expanded after a 2002 national competencies conference (Hatcher & Lassiter, 2007).

One of the competencies associated with practicum is the development of *personal responsibility*. You will be expected to behave according to the American Psychological Association (2010) "Ethical Principles of Psychologists and Code of Conduct." During the practicum, you will be expected to learn how the words of this document translate into the core professional values demonstrated by psychologists. This includes behaving in a professional manner including your attire, behavior, and language.

Another competency you will develop during this initial practicum is *accountability*. In the traditional classroom setting, you were expected to come to class regularly, turn in assignments on time, and so on. However, you were not usually expected to let the professor know in advance when you would be missing class or possibly turning in a paper a bit late for a small penalty. The practicum site, however, is different. If something is going to cause you to be late or not come when you are scheduled to be there, you will notify the supervisor as soon as you are aware of the problem. Part of accountability is determining before such situations occur what method of contact the supervisor would prefer. Do you use voice messages, e-mail, or texting in such a situation? Accountability includes following the site's policies and procedures, which you learned in the initial training or orientation for that placement.

Another competency you will develop is *self-awareness*. This broad term covers both your own reactions and your impact on others.

Although you may feel you are following all of the rules you learned and applying them accurately to the situation, you may not be accustomed to paying attention to how all of these experiences are affecting you. This process is sometimes called *self-care*. Some aspects of self-care are more obvious than others. Are you getting adequate sleep, nutrition, and exercise? Reflecting on what is happening inside yourself may be a bit more difficult to evaluate. Determining your stress level is an important aspect of this process. Are you worrying about some of the patients when you are not at the placement? You will not be able to function effectively on your practicum if you do not take care of yourself. Another part of self-awareness is that you will start to reflect on the actions you have taken. You will no longer just respond in various situations but instead consider various reasons you chose to respond the way you did. You may look at your own stereotypes or biases as they relate to various characteristics of the patient.

During your practicum you will fine-tune both your *affective* and *expressive skills* to a new level of competency. On an affective level, you will learn to tolerate a wide range of emotions in others and respond in an emotionally mature way. You will also learn to handle situations in which the affect is ambiguous. On an expressive level, you will learn to organize your thoughts so that you express yourself in a coherent and cohesive way. You will also learn to express yourself clearly in nonverbal ways.

All of these competencies will help you move toward the development of a *professional identity*. You will be thinking like a psychologist rather than a student of psychology. You may find that as you do this, you will also want to start to join some professional organizations as a student member. Becoming part of one of more professional associations will allow you to expand on this gradual change in your self-view. Ask your professor to suggest appropriate associations for your educational level and interest.

How the Practicum Differs From Other Courses

The initial practicum experience may occur at either the undergraduate or graduate level. This chapter is intended to give you a broad view of what you can expect to learn and how to maximize that learning experience. In most of your previous education, you knew that you would be expected to develop knowledge of facts. These facts were covered in your books as well as presented by the professor. By contrast, during a practicum experience, you never really know what facts you will need to remember. It is unlikely that a staff member will indicate that something is important for you to remember.

Knowing the information is only the first step. What is more important during the practicum is how you apply that information to the current situation. Thus, one thing you will learn from your practicum experience is to think on your feet. You need to be flexible rather than rigid in approaching a situation with a solution in mind. This flexibility includes the ability to change course if you find that your initial approach does not seem to be working.

What Will I Be Expected to Do?

According to Falender and Shafranske (2012), "The practicum experience will engage and develop skills and knowledge that have been the focus of prepracticum coursework" (p. 255). If this initial practicum is on the undergraduate level or early in your graduate career, you may be doing more *observing* than actual *performing*. This is because your prepracticum coursework is likely devoted to theory more than actual skill development. Baird (2012) found that the initial practicum experience will involve either observation or informal interactions with patients for most students. Observing is a key part of your learning process and is quite different from merely reading about these activities. Remember that there is a difference between this type of observation and merely watching something. As Yogi Berra reportedly said, "You can see a lot just by observing." Even during informal interactions with the patients, whether in a waiting area of an outpatient setting, or on the unit of an inpatient setting, you will have the opportunity to learn and test your skills. Your observing will include both the verbal and nonverbal behavior of the patients. You will then mentally try to integrate what you observe with your prior learning to formulate hypotheses about what is happening with this person.

Supervisors often ask what you have observed in an individual patient. Your response should include such factors as the patient's language. Was the person articulate? Were the words, as well as the tone of voice, appropriate or inappropriate? If the patient was interacting with another person, did he or she allow sufficient space between them, crowd the other person, or stay far away? What did you notice about the person's hygiene? Did the person seem adequately neat and clean for the situation? These are just a few of the things you may report after only a brief interaction with a patient.

The amount of actual work you do is related to both your level of training and the type of setting where you are placed. The rules of the setting typically limit the types of activities in which you participate and the degree of independence you have. Undergraduates usually have more limitations placed on their behavior than do graduate students. A beginning graduate student, for example, may have already completed a course in cognitive assessment and thus be ready to administer some of these measures under supervision. Undergraduate students typically have only read about these measures in a tests and measurements course. The further you move through a sequence of practica, the greater will be your range of experiences and freedom to operate independently. Although you may feel you understand procedures and want to be able to do more things, you must realize that the person who is supervising you is considered responsible for any mistakes you may make. This is one of the many reasons it is important for you to be open with your supervisor about any patient interactions you have. Some beginning students are afraid of looking inadequate and do not tell their supervisors about incidents in which they believe they may not have acted appropriately. Learning to handle constructive criticism and changing your behavior based on feedback is an integral part of the practicum experience. In the long run, honest and open discussion with your supervisor will be more profitable than avoiding situations in which you may not have done your best.

Before the First Day

The type of setting in which you do your practicum also relates to the specific preplacement requirements that must be met. As soon as you have been placed, ask your professor if there are such requirements for your site so that you can arrange to complete them before the date you hope to begin your activities there. For example, many placements related to the legal system (e.g., child protective services) require fingerprinting and a criminal background check before you can start. There is a fee for this process, and it will probably involve getting a special form from the site that you take to the local police or sheriff's office. It takes time for this information to be sent back to your site. If this clearance is required, you will not be permitted to participate until your clearance has been given by law enforcement.

Hospital settings typically require that you have had a tuberculosis (TB) test within the past year. This is usually done as a skin scratch, rather than an x-ray. If you have had one through your own physician, you will need to take the results to the site for verification. Some hospitals will provide this test for you, but be aware that this testing involves going on one day for the procedure and then having the results read several days later. If you have not had a TB test and the hospital does not provide it for you, you will either have to go to your own physician for it or perhaps check to see if your university health center can do it for you. Another common requirement is a drug screen. If the hospital does not provide the screening, they will give you a list of the drugs for which you must be cleared. Although these tests may seem unnecessary to you, they are intended to protect the people with whom you will be working.

In some settings, you will be listed under their volunteer program. In such situations, you may be required to complete the training process that is required of all volunteers in that facility. Thus, you may be exposed to certain concepts that will not really be relevant to your specific setting. This procedure usually allows the facility to have you covered under the liability insurance policy they have on all of their volunteers. Because people with varied backgrounds are participating, the training must cover a broad range of situations. It is often scheduled for a day or more once they have enough new people to justify staff time to provide the training. When this type of training is required, it is typically the institution's policy that you cannot participate in the practicum activities until you have completed these training sessions. Just like the previously noted requirements, this is something that is best completed before the start of the academic term in which you take your practicum. One activity our students have learned in such training sessions is CPR (cardiopulmonary resuscitation). They were certified by the hospital and now have a highly useful life skill. Other activities they learned in the same training session are less applicable to life outside the practicum and include how to call for various emergency codes and the use of restraints. You will not, however, actually be putting restraints on the clients of the facility.

Other facilities may have online training you must complete before commencing your on-site work. In this case, they will give you log-on information, and you typically must provide some type of proof that you have completed the training. These online sessions will usually cover policies and procedures for the facility, including ethics and legal issues. Most of these programs end with a certificate of completion in your name, which you must print and bring to the appropriate agency person, such as someone in Human Resources.

Supervision at the Placement

The typical procedure for practicum placement is that a particular staff member is *responsible* for you. This person, called a *supervisor*, is responsible for both your development as a future clinician and the welfare of the patients. Many psychologists report that each of their supervisors had a distinct impact on who they became as professionals. This relationship is somewhat different from the one you have had with professors in classes. If you had an advisor with whom you developed a close relationship and discussed more than just your class selection, you may already have a foundation for this new relationship. As noted earlier, because of your supervisor's ethical and legal responsibility for you and your actions, it is important that you share whatever interactions you have had at the placement, even when you believe you may have made a mistake.

This does not necessarily mean that you will be spending time with only that one person. In facilities known as *training hospitals*, you may be assigned to work with advanced trainees, such as graduate students or predoctoral interns or postdoctoral fellows. Advanced trainees may currently be enrolled in a graduate program. This setting may be an initial or advanced practicum for that student. Other trainees may be participating in their predoctoral internship in psychology. This means they have completed all of their classroom work for the doctorate as well as initial practica. They may or may not have completed their dissertation or final project for their doctorate. If you have this type of placement, don't hesitate to ask any of these people about their educational programs. Many of these trainees will have valuable information about the daily activities of graduate school as well as suggestions about the application process. These individuals can provide information that supplements what you learn from your faculty advisor, online searches, and campus career center. Because their graduate school experience was quite recent, it is still fresh in their memory and addresses current procedures and concerns. They can also provide a unique perspective on their own program's strengths and weaknesses. These individuals will be reporting about your progress to the professional who is responsible for you. They may even participate in your final evaluation for the experience. This is part of their training in learning how to be a supervisor.

Who Will I Meet?

You may have the opportunity to work with students and professionals from other disciplines in addition to psychology. This can be a good experience given the increasing emphasis on multidisciplinary practice. It is not unusual for psychologists in private practice to be working with such professionals as psychiatrists, neurologists, social workers, music therapists, occupational and recreational therapists, dieticians, and rehabilitation counselors to name just a few. We explain about some of the other professions in more detail in a later chapter. One of my former students noted, "I was able to observe how the psychologists interact with the psychiatrists, medical psychologists [a legal term in Louisiana], and psychometrists to gain a variety of perspectives on the patient." All of the professionals she noted, as well as the disciplines, are considered among the mental health professions. These are just some examples of professional interactions that were specific to her site. Different sites will provide an opportunity to observe different professions at work. For example, in a children's hospital setting, the psychologist who is working with a diabetic child might develop a treatment plan in consultation with the dietician and the activity therapist.

You may also gain a perspective on how different subspecialties within psychology contribute to case conceptualization. As one of our students who was placed in the psychology department of a children's medical center noted, "The greatest thing I got out of the course is exposure to different fields of psychology that I previously had no knowledge about or no interest in." In her case, she worked with clinical, counseling, and applied developmental psychologists. Being in such a setting on a regular basis also gives greater insight into the day-to-day experiences of practicing psychologists. This view may be quite different from the snippets of information presented in typical undergraduate or even graduate textbooks.

What Is My Takeaway?

One of our recent students noted in her final course evaluation that "you get what you put into the course and the experience." This comment illustrates an important point about the practicum. Unlike typical psychology classes, in which the student may be able simply to put in the time and not really exert any initiative or energy, students who merely fulfill the required hours in this initial experience, without asking for extra experiences and feedback on performance, are likely to get only minimal self-knowledge as well as foundational learning. Such students will not be moving toward the development of the competencies that are needed if they intend to continue their training in psychology or have more advanced practicum experiences. The supervisor, either on site or on campus, will need to talk to this student about the impact of such behavior on potential future placements. If this initial practicum experience is on the graduate level, the insight gained may be into the type of future practicum sites that would be most beneficial for the student. The first practicum experience may provide insight into both populations and activities with which the student would like additional training or those in which the student has perhaps less interest.

Another student in that same class noted that "this course allows for better understanding of how exactly psychology is applied in practical settings. The experience is great for gaining insight into a possible career related to the practicum site." This statement illustrates the importance of this course on an undergraduate level before the student invests time in applying for graduate studies that may not be appropriate for his or her interests. Because these evaluations were provided on an anonymous basis, we cannot credit the specific students who provided these insights.

Comfort Level

Let's consider a few examples of activities that might be part of an early practicum experience and how to get the most out of them. These experiences provide only a small sample of the wide range of possibilities. Some initial experiences are placements at inpatient settings. These settings range from locked psychiatric units to various medical settings, such as rehabilitation hospitals and children's hospitals. One of the first experiences you have in these settings is evaluating your comfort level. You should be aware not only of what is expected of you but also how you feel in this environment. If you keep a personal journal of your experience, note not only what you did but also how you felt about both your surroundings and the activities there. This self-reflection is not meant as a form of evaluation of how well you felt you did that day. You are not concerned, in this case, with what you may have learned or how you responded to a particular situation. Rather, it is intended to provide you with greater self-understanding. For example, some people are just not comfortable in medical settings. Others find a level of discomfort being in a locked setting where they must find a staff member to unlock a door to leave. An undergraduate who is in her late teens or early 20s may feel uncomfortable on a locked adolescent psychiatric unit where the staff members mistake her for a new patient. We have found this to be a fairly common experience for our undergraduate students who have been placed in this type of setting.

Initial discomfort does not necessarily mean you cannot have a career in this area. It does mean, however, that you need to be aware of those feelings and compare them with your feelings later in the experience. This is one of many reasons we suggest that students keep an informal journal of their experiences. After each visit to the placement, you can make an entry. This entry is not intended to be like a chart note about the activities of the day. Although some description of the general activities may be included to provide a context for your remarks, what's more important is your feelings about the people and the placement. At the end of the term, you then have a record of those reactions. Have they changed or remained the same? Do you notice a difference in your confidence level or level of comfort? You can then relate these reactions to the competencies you hoped to develop.

Inpatient settings involve seeing patients with a range of diagnosable disorders. Placement on an adult psychiatric unit could involve interacting with someone who is physically large and verbally either incoherent or abusive. If you tend to become frightened easily, your initial response is likely to be one of discomfort. If you are the type of person who does not deal well with ambiguity, you may also find an increase in your level of discomfort in this setting.

The trainee placed on a rehabilitation unit who is working with a patient in his early 20s suffering from a traumatic brain injury resulting from a motor vehicle accident may find identification with the patient both too strong and too uncomfortable to actually learn psychological concepts. An important point of reflection for this student is whether this initial discomfort lasts or fades with added exposure to this patient.

Placement within a department of psychology at a children's medical center might find the trainee dealing with a preschool child diagnosed with cancer and undergoing chemotherapy. Such a placement requires control of your emotions both when working with this child and with the child's parents. Such placements also have the potential for you to face the death of a patient you have recently seen. This experience not only tends to be upsetting but may also lead to feelings about your own mortality. However, each of these situations may help you move toward better self-realization.

What Do All These People Do? How Can I Learn the Most From Each of Them?

Inpatient settings typically involve interaction with a range of staff members. Unlike regular campus classes where you have one professor per course, you need to learn not only names but also the roles of each of these people. As you are introduced to various staff members, keep a list of their names and roles. It may be that initially you only hear a name. Later you can add the role, such as nurse, social worker, or psychology technician. Depending on the setting, you may have the option of observing and assisting people other than the one to whom you are assigned. To take full advantage of this option, you need to know what each of these people does that might be of interest to you.

You also need to be prepared for being told that what you would like to do is not an option for you. This response is probably not personal but related to institutional policy, staff time, or training interests of the supervisor. Nonetheless, it never hurts to ask. If you are too sensitive to personal rejection, you will miss many opportunities. Unlike most of your classes where you have a syllabus with specified requirements, the practicum placement is often a more flexible experience. Although the time you are supposed to be there may be specific, the activities are usually not. The people there will not know what you would like to do unless you ask.

One Setting, Many Emotions

If you think that outpatient settings may be less intense for your first practicum experience, consider the following scenario based on experiences of some of our students. A regular placement one of us has been fortunate to have is with an interdisciplinary team from a local medical center. They work with children who have been removed from their biological parents by the courts as a result of severe neglect or abuse. These children are currently in foster care. The students have the opportunity to observe these children with both their biological parents and their foster parents. The biological parents are typically required by the courts to complete certain requirements before the court will consider returning the children to them. If they do not make an effort to make the required changes in their lives, the court may terminate their parental rights.

Most of our students come from backgrounds that are quite different from those they read about in the case histories of these families. Among the family situations have been cases in which drugs were left around infants, children saw one parent kill another, and mothers, still in their early 20s, have four or more children from multiple fathers, none of whom are currently in residence. One student noted her feelings of anger when hearing a mother say, in front of her children, that she wanted to get one of them back but was not interested in another one of them. This student was demonstrating the development of the competencies of *self-awareness* and *affective skills.* She did not express her negative emotions to the mother and so was also demonstrating her *professional development.* During class discussion about her placement, she noted that she had never appreciated the need for parent training in the schools until she had her initial practicum experience. Thus, she was also able to translate what she was observing into a community action issue. This placement did not always generate negative emotions, however. On another occasion, this same student noted with a degree of awe at how wonderful she thought a particular foster father was and that it appeared likely that the courts were going to give him permission to adopt his foster child.

In many settings, you may need to ask about extra reading material if you find that you often do not understand conversations. For example, some facilities use a large number of acronyms for local agencies or programs. Suppose a staff member says he or she needs to call DSS. Because you do not know that in that setting, those initials refer to the Department of Social Services, you will be confused about what is happening. In such a setting, they probably maintain a list of community resources and agencies. Most such agencies are known by their acronym because it is a faster way to convey information. Understanding not only the acronym but also the services provided will add to your understanding of the process. This knowledge helps you move toward another competency—*professional knowledge*.

Inpatients are frequently taking medication. Even if you are not planning to enter a medication-prescribing or medication-administering profession, it will be important for you to have some knowledge of medication names, uses and side effects. When one of us first used the phrase *medication-prescribing profession*, she found some of her students looking puzzled. They knew about physicians, and some had received medication from dentists after a dental procedure. They did not realize that there were a number of other professionals who may prescribe medication depending on the laws of a given state. In Louisiana, for example, these prescribers include specially trained and licensed psychologists, nurse practitioners, and optometrists.

There is a chapter later in this book that provides you with information about the names and purposes of various medications. This information will give you the foundation you need to understand case discussions and to ask the prescriber appropriate questions during case conferences. In specific cases, you may wish to ask either your supervisor or the prescriber for further information about whether some of the behaviors you note in the patient are related to the reason for the medication or possibly a side effect of the medication. You may also find much useful information on the Internet at sites such as http://www.webmd.com/drugs or http://www.rxlist.com/script/main/hp.asp.

Sample Activities and Learning Objectives

In some settings, you may have the option to attend the staff meetings about the patients. It is not unusual for an inpatient to be brought to the meeting and interviewed in front of everyone by a staff psychiatrist.

This will give you the opportunity to see one method of interviewing as well as to test yourself regarding the material you observe. What do you think is actually happening with this person? What important behaviors and comments did you observe during the interview?

When the staff members discuss the case and their plans for the patient, you have the opportunity to consider your skill level in addition to your interest in working in such a setting in the future. The staff meetings in outpatient settings are more likely to be discussion about what various professionals have observed and what they recommend in terms of ongoing or future treatment plans. Depending on the setting, you may be allowed to ask questions during the staff meeting. In other settings, you will need to make note of your questions and then ask your supervisor about them.

You may also have the opportunity to observe a psychologist administering psychological or neuropsychological tests. These tests may range from simple screening tests to more complicated assessment tools. Many of the tests you might see are described later in this book in the chapter on psychological testing. You may have already read about some of these tests in your psychology classes, even if you have not actually seen the test materials.

If this option is available to you, it will be important to ask the psychologist in advance if you are expected to assist or just sit quietly and observe. Depending on your course background, you may even be asked to read an objective test to a patient and record the patient's responses to the items. This may happen if a patient has reading difficulties or attention problems, for example. Although this activity may sound tedious, it provides you with exposure to the types of questions included on such tests as well as how a patient responds to the items.

If psychological testing is one of the activities available to you, be sure to discuss with your supervisor any unique behaviors you note from the patient during the testing. These observations may provide additional information that the psychologist can use in interpreting the test data. Do not worry that you may be incorrect. The psychologist will check out what your observations suggest before using them in a patient report. What you have seen may not have occurred when the psychologist was present and is thus important information. Most of the tests you might be asked to read to a patient are composed of short, simple items. Even if these appear simple, it is important for you to pronounce the words correctly and to read them precisely as they are written. Do not provide explanations or additional language in this situation.

Another possibility is that your supervisor may allow you to score one or more of the objective tests. Be careful when you do this because the totals you provide must be accurate. If they are not, the test interpretation will be inaccurate as well. This activity is also part of the competency of personal responsibility.

Community agencies are also possible placement sites. Such agencies range considerably in terms of the populations served and the types of services provided. A setting one of us has used for many years with practicum students is a community mental health center. This facility works closely with the schools. The children and adolescents sent there are already getting in trouble for misbehavior, and the concern is that this behavior could escalate to the point where they will enter the juvenile justice system. A major goal of this facility is to change the behavior before that happens.

In this setting, the practicum student observes initial interviews, called *intake interviews*. These interviews are often conducted by social workers but may also be conducted by a psychologist. Students in such a setting can observe the similarities and differences in interview style within and across disciplines.

The center also conducts groups in the evening, for children and for parents, where basic family skills are taught. The practicum student attends these groups as part of the placement experience. A recent observation by one of our students was that the parenting style of many of these parents was quite different from that used by her own when she was in her early teens. Since she was only in her early 20s during the placement, she also noted that some of the issues faced by these teens were quite similar to her own experience but that many were things she was glad she had not experienced (e.g., violence between parents).

She also attends the weekly team staff meetings. In this setting, they do not tend to have the patient present for the staff meetings. In an inpatient setting, it is easy to go get the patient. Despite the absence of the actual patient, the staff members do discuss the patient's behavior, family interactions, options for behavioral remediation, and community resources that may be helpful.

Another experience in such outpatient settings is the opportunity to observe the number of people who do not come for their appointments, the frustration experienced by the professionals who are trying to provide needed services to them, and issues of community resources (or lack thereof) and the impact of these resources on the services the agency can provide. For example, some clients may miss appointments because they do not have a car and there was a problem with the available public transportation. Facilities that are dependent on public funding may be forced to limit the number of visits per person, the type of programs the facility can offer, or even the number of staff members who are available to provide a range of services. This is especially likely to happen in state agencies in years when there are budget cuts.

State agencies typically have budgets that cover only 1 year, and so it is difficult to make long-range programmatic plans. This is true in both outpatient and inpatient settings. State budget years do not tend to follow either the academic calendar or the calendar year. Thus, funding changes may occur during a practicum. Although private agencies also have annual budgets, it is usually somewhat easier to develop multiyear programs because their funding tends to be a bit more stable.

Your Personality and Your Placement

Earlier, we noted that it is important to evaluate your feelings when you start your placement, especially if you find a level of discomfort. For some students who are preparing to take their first practicum, the *comfort zone* also relates to the population served. Because of the age issue noted previously, it is common for students to request placement with young children. These students may have had experience with younger siblings or babysitting jobs and therefore view this population as less threatening than those with which they have less familiarity. We have even had some students indicate that at least they are bigger than the child and thus less afraid.

We often challenge students to consider placement with a population with which they have little or no familiarity. A specific practicum experience in most programs typically lasts for only one term. If you really do not like working with this group, you will know that by the end of the term. On the other hand, you may find that there is some group you never considered for a career option with whom you find you have both an interest and some early interpersonal skills. It is better to learn this in your first practicum, especially if you are an undergraduate, than to invest time and money in a graduate training program only to discover that you prefer not to work with this group.

Two examples from our own students illustrate the concept of finding either a career direction or the need to change one's direction. One student had strongly believed he wanted to be a clinical psychologist and work with inpatients. Academically, there was no question that he had the ability to be admitted to an American Psychological Association–accredited clinical psychology program. He had a high grade point average, and his GRE scores made him competitive. He did an undergraduate practicum on a locked adolescent inpatient unit. After he completed the experience, he determined that, although he liked adolescents, he did not like working with those who were experiencing emotional problems. We discussed his experience, and he noted that he never really reached a feeling of comfort in that setting. The psychologist with whom he was placed noted that he had not seemed as enthusiastic as some of the former students who had been placed there. Her evaluation included the observation that he had initially indicated a strong interest in having a job like hers after he completed his PhD but later told her he was reevaluating his options. He was working on the competency of self-awareness. As he continued to explore what he had learned, he realized that it was not just adolescents but clinical psychology in general that was not for him. Although he continued to love psychology, this was just not his area of comfort. Today, he has a PhD in social psychology and is a university professor.

By contrast, another undergraduate had never even considered work with a geriatric population. After just a short period working with residents of a unit for people with dementia of the Alzheimer's type, she has now decided to apply to clinical psychology graduate programs in which she can receive specialty training in clinical geropsychology. The growing interest in, and need for, training in this specialty led to the addition of a chapter about this population in this book.

Summary

Your first practicum is the beginning of an exciting process of personal and professional development and the learning of new competencies. You will meet many people as a result of this experience. Some will be patients, some peers; others will be supervisors or professional staff. If you really open yourself to this experience, you will learn from each of them. The following chapters will give you other suggestions about how to maximize this experience, as well as helpful foundational information.

References

American Psychological Association. (2010). *Ethical standards of psychologists and code of conduct (2002, Amended June 1, 2010)*. Washington, DC: Author. Retrieved from http://www.apa.org/ethics/code/index.aspx

Baird, B. N. (2012). *The internship, practicum, and field placement handbook: A guide for the helping profession* (4th ed.). Upper Saddle River, NJ: Prentice-Hall.

Falender, C. A., & Shafranske, E. P. (2012). *Getting the most out of clinical training and supervision: A guide for practicum students and interns.* Washington, DC: American Psychological Association. http://dx.doi.org/10.1037/13487-000

Hatcher, R. L., & Lassiter, K. D. (2007). Initial training in professional psychology: The practicum competencies outline. *Training and Education in Professional Psychology, 1*, 49–63. http://dx.doi.org/10.1037/1931-3918.1.1.49

B. Max Price

Characteristics of a Helping Relationship

2

As a practicum student in psychology, you likely have many questions about this new experience: What am I expected to do in the practicum? What is my role as a practicum student? What type of clients will I be assigned? How can I be helpful to my clients? What should I do if such and such happens? What skills do I need to be an effective helper?

It is normal to have these kinds of questions and to feel anxious about what you are going to do. I can still remember my first practicum experiences. I was anxious to do well, I profited from good supervision and group discussion, and I learned a great deal from this hands-on experience.

Depending on your level of training, you may or not be expected to attempt formal therapy sessions with patients. You are not expected to be a fully trained professional therapist. Your supervisor will help you define your role(s). You will likely be asked to spend time with a patient as a friend or companion. The basic skills needed to be an effective helper in a practicum are similar to the skills needed to be effective in all helping relationships, including counseling.

http://dx.doi.org/10.1037/14672-002
Your Practicum in Psychology: A Guide for Maximizing Knowledge and Competence, Second Edition, J. R. Matthews and C. E. Walker (Editors)

In this chapter, I discuss the basic skills necessary in helping relationships and give you guidance in improving your communication skills.

Definition of Helping

Carl Rogers, the father of client-centered therapy, gave this definition of a *helping relationship:* "By this term I mean a relationship in which at least one of the parties has the intent of promoting the growth, development, maturity, improved functioning, improved coping with the life of the other" (Rogers, 1958, p. 441). Rogers stated that his definition covered a wide range of relationships that usually are intended to facilitate growth. Examples of such relationships are parent and child, physician and patient, teacher and student, and most of all counselor and client.

Robert Carkhuff, who developed the Carkhuff helping model, emphasizes interpersonal skills training as essential to becoming an effective helper. Carkhuff (2002) stated that "the purpose of helping is to engage the helpee (person receiving help) in processes leading to human growth and development" (p. 23). The work of both Carkhuff and Rogers emphasizes helping as promoting and aiding growth.

Gerald Egan has proposed a skilled helper model. In this model, he calls for a basic, practical working model of helping. He declared, "Since all approaches must eventually help clients manage problems and develop unused resources, the model of choice is a flexible, humanistic, broadly-based problem-management and opportunity-development model" (Egan, 2002, p. 25). He further stated that because problem management and opportunity development are embedded in all approaches to helping, the skilled helper model "provides an excellent foundation for any 'brand' of helping you eventually choose" (Egan, 2002, p. 25).

In *Helping Others Help Themselves: A Guide to Counseling Skills*, John Loughary and Theresa Ripley (1978) defined *helping* as "providing purposeful assistance to other people which makes their lives more pleasant, easier, less frustrating, or in some other way, more satisfying. Most every relationship you have involves the opportunity for helping" (p. 1). Using this practical definition of helping, think of the different roles you have. Are you a friend? A brother or sister? Aunt or uncle? Daughter or son? Employer? Employee? Student? Supervisor? Roommate? Club member? Teammate? Lover? Other roles?

Doesn't each of your relationships involve assisting others? You are likely to provide help in multiple relationships and have daily opportunities to help. Loughary and Ripley (1978) described *helping* as including informing people, making them feel better, listening to their problems, making suggestions, making arrangements, teaching, explaining, criticizing, and assisting them in other ways.

For you, the question is not "Do you help?" but "How effective is your helping?" You are likely to be better in particular areas of helping and with particular kinds of people. Some are better listeners. Some are better problem solvers. Some are better in practical actions.

ACCEPTANCE OF A PERSON'S BACKGROUND

Acceptance includes respecting and seeking to understand a person's background—including one's ethnicity, cultural history, religious beliefs, and sexual orientation. In your practicum you will likely be assigned to persons who have an ethnic or cultural background quite different from yours or to a person with a different sexual orientation. Your job is to accept each person. You may be uncomfortable about these differences. You will need to consult with your supervisor about how you can understand each person. If you react to a person negatively because of his or her background and lifestyle, you need to change, accept that person, or consult with your supervisor regarding whether you can help that client.

PRACTICE EXPERIENCE

Think of two people whom you consider good helpers. What specific attitudes and actions do they display? Make a list of these.

General Recommendations for Helping Behaviors

1. *Do* practice empathic listening. Empathy involves listening to another person so that you accurately understand his or her thoughts and feelings. Attentive listening is a special gift to give another human being. Example: I have found that focusing all my attention to listen and try to understand a client is the best helping behavior I can give.

2. *Do* show positive regard for the other person. This means accepting the other person and valuing that person whether you like or agree with him or her. It also means wanting the best for that person. Example: Phil had an angry, sullen adolescent named Kent for his practicum assignment. Kent did not like counselors and stated his dislike clearly. Phil demonstrated positive regard by accepting Kent as a hurting, confused, and angry young man. He did not try to straighten Kent out. He did not react in anger or let his dislike of this teen's behavior keep him from accepting and caring for Kent.

3. *Do* be optimistic. This does not mean having a naive Pollyanna attitude about everything. It does mean looking for positive outcomes. It is seeing the glass half full, not half empty. Positive thoughts and feelings will get you farther than negative thoughts and feelings. Example: Jill was struggling with a statistics course, her least favorite subject. Instead of saying, "I hate statistics; I'm not any good at it. I'm gonna fail," Jill told herself, "I'm having a difficult time in this class, but I am going to look at it as a challenge to be met." She took the positive approach of developing a plan of study that included getting help from other students.

4. *Do* be cheerful. Use humor and laughter based on the other person's responsiveness. Laughter truly is good medicine. Look for opportunities to smile and laugh with the other person during your practicum. Example: Bill took his practicum assignment seriously, but he found opportunity to laugh with Sarah while they were doing a craft project together.

5. *Do* show hope. Hope involves looking to the future and holding the belief that change can occur. Hope provides the motivation and energy to keep trying even in difficult circumstances. Example: From Example 2, practicum student Phil did not try to talk Kent out of his anger and despair. He did have hope that Kent's life could change, that it could get better. This hope helped Phil have faith that he could make a difference in Kent's life.

6. *Do* give encouragement. Point out skills, interests, and strengths that you see in the other person. He or she may not be aware of these strengths, and your encouragement can make a difference. Teachers often have a huge impact on the lives of their students by being encouragers. Example: I had a teacher in college who told me I was a good writer. I still remember his comment and his belief in me. It has given me confidence through the years to tackle numerous writing opportunities, including this chapter.

PRACTICE EXPERIENCE REVIEW

Review the list of helping behaviors. What are your strength areas in helping? What are helping behaviors you want to improve? List at least two of both your strengths and the areas you'd like to continue to work on.

The Nature of Helping Relationships

The next step is to look at the nature of helping relationships that will assist you in your role as a practicum student helper.

HELPFUL VERSUS UNHELPFUL RELATIONSHIPS

Carl Rogers (1958) asked the following question:

> What are the characteristics of those relationships which do help, which do facilitate growth? And at the other end of the scale is it possible to discern those characteristics which make a relationship unhelpful even though it was sincere in intent to promote growth and development? (p. 442)

Rogers (1958) cited a study by Heine (1950) that focused on how the person being helped perceived a relationship as being helpful or unhelpful. The subjects were clients who had received therapy from therapists with three different theoretical orientations: psychoanalytic, client centered, and Adlerian. Regardless of the type of therapy, the clients reported similar changes in themselves. Yet, when asked what accounted for the changes they had made, the clients were in agreement on the counselor attitudes that they found helpful:

- the trust they felt in the therapist,
- being understood by the therapist, and
- the feeling of independence they had in making choices and decisions.

The therapist procedure that they found most helpful was that the therapist clarified and openly stated feelings that the client had been approaching hazily and hesitantly.

The clients had a high degree of agreement as to which therapist attitudes they found unhelpful in the relationship. Unhelpful therapist attitudes reported were

- lack of interest,
- remoteness or distance, and
- too great a degree of sympathy.

Unhelpful procedures reported included giving direct, specific advice regarding decisions or emphasizing past history rather than present problems.

Research by Truax (Truax & Carkhuff, 1967) showed that therapist empathy, genuineness (congruence), and warmth (positive regard) are crucial to the success of the psychotherapeutic relationship. These qualities are important to success in other interpersonal contexts as well.

Support for these basic qualities was evident in a series of studies by Alsobrook (1962, 1967, 1969). Alsobrook constructed a scale to measure helpful versus unhelpful relationships. He labeled a person who helped his associate feel comfortable, work out problems, and do his or her best as a *health-engendering person*. Alsobrook described a contrasting kind of person who makes people feel uncomfortable or defensive or causes them to do poorly (Alsobrook, 1962, p. 6). He called this individual a *health-depressing person*.

Alsobrook's scale measured the degree to which a person possessed a conscious and deliberate concern for the welfare of others, affectional warmth and liking for others, and trust in and belief in others (Newton & Krauss, 1973). His studies found that health-engendering people had a positive impact on others in several relationships. Psychiatric patients assigned to psychiatric aides classified as health engendering improved more than patients assigned to health-depressing aides (Alsobrook, 1967). He also found that college students whose residence-hall roommates were high in health-engendering behavior made a better social and emotional adjustment to college than did students whose roommates scored low on the health-engendering scale.

Newton and Krauss (1973) found similar results in their study at the University of Georgia. They investigated the relationship between the academic and emotional adjustment of 992 freshmen women and the health-engendering behavior of their 32 resident assistants. Resident assistants were students who were in their sophomore year or above and hired to help new students adjust to their first year in college. Results were that freshmen assigned to resident assistants who rated low in health-engendering behavior manifested significantly inferior academic achievement compared with freshmen assigned to residents of high or medium health-engendering behavior.

MORE RECENT STUDIES

Dialectical behavior therapy (DBT) emphasizes compassionate treatment with a strategy of acceptance (validation). This emphasis has similarities to Rogers's, Truax's, and Carkhuff's client-centered therapy treatments, which focus on the communication skills necessary for effective helping. Marsha Linehan (1993) developed DBT as a comprehensive cognitive behavior treatment, and it has been found effective in reducing suicidal behavior, psychiatric hospitalization, treatment dropout, substance abuse, anger, and interpersonal difficulties (Linehan et al., 1999; Verheul et al., 2003).

In the 1970s, Linehan, who was trained as a behaviorist, attempted to apply cognitive behavior therapy (CBT) to the psychiatric problems of adult women. She and her research team concluded that the standard CBT format was not an effective treatment for women who met the criteria for borderline personality disorder. They made significant modifications to standard CBT. They added new strategies of acceptance-based interventions, also referred to as validation strategies. Validation means (a) finding the kernel of truth in the person's perspective or situation; (b) acknowledging the causes of emotions, thoughts, and behaviors; and (c) showing you care and understand where the person is coming from. Validation includes accurate reflection and radical genuineness. The core of DBT treatment is a balanced treatment strategy of acceptance (validation) and change (problem solving).

Behavioral Tech, founded by Linehan, trains mental health providers and treatment teams to use compassionate scientifically valid treatments and to implement and evaluate these treatments in their practice setting. The Behavior Tech website provides current DBT resources, training information, and research on DBT (http://www.behavioraltech.org).

Motivational interviewing (MI) is a client-centered, goal-directed counseling method developed by William R. Miller and Stephen Rollnick to help people change behavior. MI emphasizes two specific active components: a relational component focused on empathy and the interpersonal spirit of the method, and a technical component involving reinforcement of client change talk (Miller & Rose, 2009). Miller and Rose (2009) reported that more than 200 trials of MI have been published, and efficacy reviews and meta-analyses have begun yielding positive trials for an array of target problems, including management of chronic mental disorders, hypertension, problem drinking, and substance abuse disorders. MI emphasizes that empathy is an essential counselor skill for behavioral change to occur.

In their 2009 publication in *American Psychologist*, William Rose and Gary Rose summarized MI effectiveness:

> After three decades of research, motivational interviewing is a psychological method that is evidence based, relatively brief, specifiable, applicable across a wide variety of problem areas, complementary to other active treatment methods, and learnable by a broad range of helping professionals. A testable theory of its mechanisms of action is emerging with measurable components that are both relational and technical. This may in turn clarify more general processes that affect outcomes in other psychotherapies. (p. 12)

Miller and Rose (2009) credited Carl Rogers's hypothesis of accurate empathy, congruence and positive regard as critical therapeutic conditions that promote positive change.

EFFECTIVE HELPER CHECKLIST

Loughary and Ripley (1978, p. 24) described an effective helper as a person who is, more often than not, a reasonably objective, self-confident person who has developed purpose and direction in many areas of his or her own life. In addition, effective helpers are probably more aware of and sensitive to how people react to them. They noted that you are likely an effective helper if you can give mostly positive answers to such questions as the following:

Can you express a genuine interest in other people?
Can you listen to others express values contrary to your own without feeling defensive or resentful?
Can you empathize with other people—that is, understand their feelings without feeling sorry for them?

Can you usually refrain from giving unwanted or unasked-for advice?

Can you communicate your displeasure regarding another person's behavior without becoming unpleasant yourself?

Can you assert yourself without offending others or at least not be upset if they are offended?

BASIC HELPING SKILLS

Robert Carkhuff has been a leader in interpersonal skills models for more than 30 years. He has conducted 2 decades of research in helping skills demonstrations. Carkhuff (2002) stated that "various helpers (parents, counselors, teachers, employers) do have constructive effects upon their helpees (children, counselees, students, employees) when trained in interpersonally based helping skills" (p. 281). The Carkhuff helping model is presented in his book *The Art of Helping*, now in its eighth edition. Carkhuff (2002) said,

> We have found that all helping and human relationships may be "for better or for worse." The effects depend upon the helper's level of skills in facilitating the helpees movement through the helping process toward constructive helping outcomes. These helping skills constitute the core of all helping experiences. (p. 287)

Communication skills, facilitation skills, health-engendering skills, and helper skills all have in common an emphasis on the basic helping skills. Historically, it began with Carl Rogers's three "necessary and sufficient conditions" for change: empathy, unconditional positive regard, and genuineness (Rogers, Gendlin, Kiesler, & Truax, 1967). Carkhuff and Truax's research led them to operational definitions of "accurate empathy, respect and genuineness" (Carkhuff, 1969; Truax & Carkhuff, 1967).

The Carkhuff (1983) model defined helper skills as having two dimensions: responsive dimensions (empathy, respect, and specificity of expression) and initiative dimensions (genuineness, self-disclosure, confrontation, immediacy, and concreteness). The communication skills I recommend you emphasize in your helper roles during your practicum experiences are empathy, respect, and genuineness. These are the working definitions I use:

- *Empathy* is the accurate understanding of another person's thoughts and feelings and accurate feedback responses to that person without adding or subtracting from the helpee's expression.
- *Respect* is the helper's communicating a deep respect (positive regard) for the helpee's feelings, experiences, and potentials.
- *Genuineness* is the helper's being congruent, honest, and sincere in his or her responses to the helpee. The helper's responses are sincere as expressed in words, tone of voice, emotions, body language, and actions.

LEARNING TO DISCRIMINATE BETWEEN HELPFUL AND UNHELPFUL RESPONSES

In *Helping and Human Relations*, Carkhuff (1969) described a ratings scale that he and his colleagues used in rating helper effectiveness. This scale was also used in training helpers to discriminate between effective and ineffective helper responses. In a description of his gross ratings of facilitative interpersonal functioning, Carkhuff (1969) stated:

> The facilitator is a person who is living effectively himself and who discloses himself in a genuine and constructive fashion in response to others. He communicates an accurate empathic understanding and a respect for all of the feelings of other persons and guides discussions with those persons into specific feelings and experiences. He communicates confidence in what he is doing and is spontaneous and intense. In addition, while he is still open and flexible in his relations with others, in his commitment to the welfare of the other person he is quite capable of active, assertive and even confronting behavior when it is appropriate. (p. 115)

There are five levels of helper ratings on this 1-to-5 scale:

Level 1: The helper responses are unhelpful.
Level 2: The helper responses are somewhat helpful.
Level 3: The helper responses are more helpful than unhelpful.
Level 4: The helper responses are almost always helpful.
Level 5: The helper responses are always helpful.

Here is one of Carkhuff's (1969) examples of an excerpt from a helpee in a therapy session followed by different levels of helper responses to illustrate the system:

> I don't know if I am right or wrong feeling the way I do. But I find myself withdrawing from people. I don't seem to socialize and play their stupid games any more. I get upset and come home depressed and have headaches. It all seems so superficial. There was a time when I used to get along with everybody. Everybody said, "Isn't she wonderful. She gets along with everybody. Everybody likes her." I used to think that was something to be really proud of, but that was who I was at that time. I had no depth. I was what the crowd wanted me to be—the particular group I was with. (p. 115)

Consider how these four responses would rate on the 1-to-5 scale of helper responses described earlier:

1. Rating: Level 3 *(more helpful than unhelpful)*. You know you have changed a lot. There are a lot of things you want to do but no longer can.
2. Rating: Level 4 *(almost always helpful)*. You are damned sure who you can't be any longer but you are not sure who you are. Still hesitant as to who you are yet.

3. Rating: Level 1.5 *(unhelpful)*. Who are these people that make you so angry? Why don't you tell them where to get off? They can't control your existence. You have to be your own person.
4. Rating: Level 1.5 *(unhelpful)*. So you have a social problem involving interpersonal difficulties with others. (Carkhuff, 1969, p. 116)

PRACTICE EXERCISE

Here is another example from Carkhuff's work. Read the helpee's statement, then give your rating of each of the four helper responses as *helpful* or *unhelpful*. Compare your ratings with the experts' ratings.

> I get so frustrated and furious with my daughter. I just don't know what to do with her. She is bright and sensitive, but damn, she has some characteristics that make me so on edge. I can't handle it sometimes. She just—I feel myself getting more and more angry! She won't do what you tell her to. She tests limits like mad. I scream and yell and lose control and think there is something wrong with me—I'm not an understanding mother or something Damn! What potential! What she could do with what she has. There are times she doesn't use what she's got. She gets by too cheaply. I just don't know what to do with her. Then she can be so nice and then, boy, she can be as ornery as she can be. And then I scream and yell and I'm about ready to slam her across the room. I don't like to feel this way. I don't know what to do with it.

Rate these four helper responses as *unhelpful* or *helpful* on a 1-to-5 scale:

1. So you find yourself screaming and yelling at your daughter more frequently during the past 3 months.
2. Why don't you try giving your daughter some very precise limitations. Tell her what you expect from her and you don't expect from her. No excuses.
3. While she frustrates the hell out of you, what you are really asking is, "How can I help her? How can I help myself, particularly in relation to this kid?"
4. While she makes you very angry, you care what happens to her. (Carkhuff, 1969, pp. 118–119)

Now let's see how experts rated these responses. Response 1 was rated at 1.0—*unhelpful*. Response 2 was also rated *unhelpful* at 1.5. Response 3 was rated *very helpful* at 4.0. Response 4 was also rated *helpful* at 3.0. Think about possible reasons these responses were rated the way they were.

In my doctoral dissertation (Price, 1975), I studied how medium or low facilitation (communication) levels affect counselors' influence in getting helpees to change their opinion of themselves on a personality rating scale. I used the Carkhuff global rating scale and expert raters to sample audiotapes of 20-minute interviews between interviewers and college-student subjects. Using the expert ratings, I was able to divide the interviewers (helpers) into two groups: a low facilitation skills group that had an average rating score of 1.96 and a medium facilitation skills group with a 2.41 average rating score. The medium facilitation skills interviewers (helpers) did have more influence in changing subjects' (helpees) self-ratings. My conclusions from this doctoral dissertation and research of other facilitation skills studies are as follows:

1. Facilitation skills as defined and rated by Carkhuff and his associates are necessary characteristics of helping relationships, especially in counselor–client relationships.
2. Empathic understanding, genuineness, and respect are necessary characteristics of a helping relationship.

In his book *The Art of Helping in the 21st Century*, Robert Carkhuff (2002) stressed the great need for basic helping skills in the 21st century:

> The basic tenet of the Age of Information is interdependency. This means that we are each dependent upon the other. In this context, the basic helping skills in the Age of Information remain the interpersonal processing skills or helping skills. They enable a person to relate to the experience of others. Interpersonal processing skills include attending skills to involve the helpees in the helping process. Responding skills facilitate exploring by the helpees. (pp. 37–38)

What are the specific responding attitudes and behaviors that will make a difference in practicum students' effectiveness in their practicum roles as friend, companion, health-engendering person, and helper? *Attending* and *responding* are two basic skills that will make a difference and are the helping skills I recommend and emphasize. Both the Carkhuff model and Gerard Egan's (2002) skilled helper model provide step-by-step, systematic training in helping skills on the part of the trainee. You can improve your helping ability through practice in the basic helper skills of attending and responding. Both Egan's and Carkhuff's models are similar in their emphasis on and training procedures in these two areas. In general, most schools will have students begin to practice these skills during a practicum with their supervisor.

The first phase is called *prehelping* and involves attending. The first step is to attend physically. The next step is to attend psychologically. Attending physically means to give the other person your full and undivided attention. It is focusing on that person. Egan (1975) listed the basic elements of physical attending:

S: face the other person Squarely.
O: adopt an Open posture.
L: Lean toward the other.

E: keep good Eye contact.

R: try to be "at home" or relatively Relaxed in this position. (p. 10)

I discuss attending psychologically in the following section.

PRACTICE EXERCISE: ATTENDING

Choose a partner and take turns practicing the attending physically skill. Choose a topic such as your thoughts about a practicum. As the helper, take 4 minutes of attending to your partner. Ask that person to give you feedback as to how well you did the SOLER behavior. Reverse roles and repeat the process with you as the helpee.

Physical attending has two functions: (a) It is a sign to the other person that you are actively present and working with him or her; and (b) it helps you to be an active listener—that is, to psychologically attend.

What about attending psychologically? Carkhuff stated that observing skills are the most basic helping skills. They involve the helper's ability to see and to understand the nonverbal behavior of the helpee. The helper observes aspects of the helpee's appearance and behavior that help us to infer the helpee's physical energy level, emotional feeling state, and intellectual readiness for helping. These references are the basis for the helper's initial understanding of where the helpee is coming from—attending psychologically (Carkhuff, 2002, p. 71).

Active listening involves attending to both the verbal and nonverbal communication of the other person. Observing and listening to the other person can be quite difficult. The process requires concentration on the other person and suspending your own opinions and judgments. Your attention is one of the most helpful tools you have. Giving another person the gift of your full attentions is powerful; it is often a rare experience for another person.

A beginning active-listening behavior of attending to verbal messages is developing the ability to repeat back to the speaker what he or she has said to you. It is a beginning step in learning to communicate accurate empathy.

PRACTICE EXERCISE: RESPONDING

Choose a group of three people: a communicator (speaker), a listener, and an observer. The speaker makes a statement about himself or herself but limits it to two sentences. The listener repeats the substance of what the speaker said using the formula of "You said that. . . ." The observer gives the listener feedback as to his or her accuracy. Repeat the process until each person has practiced being a listener.

Attending is called the prehelping phase by Carkhuff and Egan. Phase 1 is *responding*: Respond to the content of what the helpee said by reflecting or communicating back to the helpee what he or she is talking about. Respond to the affect involved by reflecting how the helpee feels about what he or she is saying. Finally, the helper puts the feeling and content together in a response that reflects the meaning of the helpee's experiences. This is accurate empathy. When accurate empathy is provided, the helper responses will facilitate further exploration of experiences by the helpees (Carkhuff, 2002, p. 42).

PRACTICE EXERCISES IN COMMUNICATING ACCURATE EMPATHY

In initial training in empathic understanding, beginning helpers are trained to use the formulas "You feel _____" and "You feel _____ because _____." Later, they learn to translate these stylized formulas into more natural language.

The following exercises are excerpts from Egan's *Skilled Helper* training manual (1975). They provide you with some practical examples of training in primary-level accurate empathy:

Exercise A: The Accurate Communication of Feeling and Content (One Emotion)

Read the following statements, imagining that the person is speaking directly to you. Respond with primary-level empathy, first by using the formula "You feel _____because_____ ." Then formulate a response that includes understanding of both feeling and content, stated in your own language and style as shown in the example that follows.

Law student to school counselor:	"I learned yesterday that I've flunked out of school and that there's no recourse, I've seen everybody, but the door is shut tight. What a mess! I have no idea how I'll face my parents. They've paid for my college education and this year of law school. And now I'll have to tell them that it's all down the drain."
Formula response:	"You feel awful—helpless, because you've been dropped from school and ashamed because you've let your parents down."
Response in helper's own language:	"Your world has come crashing down. It's really painful to be dropped from school, but maybe it's even more painful to face your parents with the fact, after all they've done for you." (Egan, 1975, pp. 49–50)

Practice Example

Read the following example taken from Egan's manual. Take the role of helper and write two empathy responses, one using "You feel _____ because _____" and the second conveying accurate understanding using your natural language.

> *College student to a counselor*: "Last year I was drinking heavily and playing around with drugs. I had to drop three courses and almost ended up on probation. And today, it's practically the opposite. I woke up in my own vomit one morning and said, 'God, this can't go on—I'm killing myself.' Nobody lectured me, nobody pushed. I began making the right kind of friends. And I pulled myself out of the muck." (Egan, 1975, p. 50)

First response (using you feel _____ because_____ formula).

Second response (using your more natural style).

Two possible responses are given below. Compare these with your responses.

1. "You feel proud of yourself and your initiative because you were smart enough to get hold of yourself before it was too late."
2. "It's great to look back and see that you practically lifted yourself up by your own bootstraps—you were in the pit one year and riding high the next." (Egan, 1975, p. 104)

Egan's helping-skills training manual provides systematic training exercises that progress from primary accurate empathy to advanced accurate empathy and checklists on genuineness and respect.

Helping Applied to All Stages of Life: Childhood, Adolescence, Adulthood, and Geriatric Years

The basic helping skills apply to all ages and cultures, but the application of attending, empathic understanding, genuineness, and respect vary according to the developmental level and specific environment of the person.

If your practicum assignment is with preschool or elementary age children, your helping will likely need to include play. Play is the language of children, and toys are their words. Attending to a child involves activities that they enjoy. When you let a child choose a play activity, you are participating in the best stress management technique that children have—and that most adults have as well. Eye contact tends to be intermittent with children, but they are aware if you are noticing them and giving them your undivided attention.

Your nonverbal behavior will be an important part of your helping with children. Communicate your caring by paying attention to the child; noticing his or her moods; and taking cues from his or her responses to talk or not talk; to include you in his or her activity; or to set boundaries and want you to be an observer before he or she accepts you on his or her own timetable. Learn to be comfortable with periods of silence. Learn to listen and understand the child or teen who doesn't want to talk. Some children feel freer to talk while you walk with them than when confined to an office setting.

Responding behavior with children and adolescents may be concrete actions such as walking, playing catch, offering a snack, repairing a possession, helping with a math problem, or answering a specific question.

Helping adolescents requires flexibility. You may be assigned a very verbal adolescent who enjoys the opportunity to have you listen to him or her. You may have a sullen, angry, depressed, withdrawn young person who will not want to see you and will refuse to talk to you. You can still practice attending and responding with an unresponsive teen. He or she is most likely to respond to your showing respect and caring and to your being genuine in your talk and actions. Try to discover his or her interests. Your supervisor will likely be able to provide you some background information that will help you understand the child or adolescent to whom you are assigned. Remember to seek to understand the child's, adolescent's, or adult's background—their ethnicity, cultural history, religious and sexual background—and discuss this with your supervisor. Most adults will respond to having someone to talk with, but some adults are uncomfortable just sitting and talking. They respond better to doing something with you, such as playing a table game, participating in an art or music activity, doing a practical activity, or eating a snack.

Adults with limited intellectual ability need conversations that are at the concrete level. They may be able to talk about their feelings as being happy, sad, angry, or afraid, but they will more likely talk about an exact event regarding their feeling. They, like children, will have a hard time generalizing your help to other situations. They are not likely to apply what they have done with you to another situation, even if it is similar. No matter what adult you work with, being a friend or companion to that individual can be a helpful part of his or her care.

Seek to know adults. Try to adapt your attending to the behaviors that your helpee is comfortable with. Observe the nonverbal adult. If you attempt conversation with a nonverbal person who acts uncomfortable and rejects your well-intentioned helping efforts, wait for him or her to begin talking or responding to your presence.

With geriatric clients, you are likely to find a positive response to your one-on-one time with them. Loneliness and sadness are common experiences for elderly adults who have lost family members and some control over their lives. If an elderly adult lives in a nursing facility or other institution, he or she has lost much privacy. Seek background information from staff or supervisor to determine the person's mental state. If your geriatric clients have significant memory loss with dementia or Alzheimer's disease, they will need special care. If a client begins to talk about something in his or her past as if it were happening right now, don't argue or correct. An example is an 85-year-old woman who says to you, "I'm going to find my baby. She's lost and she needs me." I recommend an empathy response such as, "You really miss your baby." Going along with her confused state is more likely to calm her than correcting her with a statement such as, "There aren't any babies here. Your daughter is grown up and can take care of herself." Validation therapy states that going along with an individual's delusions or unrealistic statements tends to calm the person much faster than trying to get him or her "back to reality." Validating a geriatric client's delusions tends to foster cooperation with present programming faster than correcting the person.

If you are assigned to work with persons with mental illness or a mental handicap and you have had no previous experience with such clients, you are likely to be anxious and uncomfortable being around them. If you need direction and support, ask your supervisor. Above all, treat the client with respect and concern. Try to understand the world from that person's viewpoint.

Summary

Characteristics of a helping relationship consist of attitudes that you possess to some degree. Helping skills can also be learned. The basic helping skills of attending, empathic understanding, genuineness, and respect have been identified and researched for more than 30 years beginning with Rogers, Truax, Carkhuff, Egan, and other client-centered practitioners. Carkhuff and Egan have developed systematic helping-skills training models that are based on sound research. Carkhuff (1983) summarized research on helping-skills demonstrations over two decades; 164 studies were reported with 158,940 participants. Carkhuff noted that the effect of trained helpers on helpees was 96% positive (2002, pp. 281–282).

Linehan adapted CBT in developing DBT, which emphasizes the strategy of acceptance-based intervention; studies have shown DBT to be an effective treatment. CBT and DBT use helping skills that have similarities to client-centered therapy's emphasis on communication skills. MI uses the client-centered emphasis on empathic understanding (Miller & Rose, 2009).

The helping-skills models of Carkhuff and Egan have application for helpers in many situations: teacher–student, parent–child, employer–employee, and counselor–client, as well as practicum students in their various helping roles. Providing cheerfulness, optimism, encouragement, and hope are also significant helping behaviors. If you provide these helping skills in your practicum, you are likely to do good and to do no harm. Have a helping practicum.

References

Alsobrook, J. M. (1962). *A study of health-engendering-people in a campus community.* Unpublished doctoral dissertation, University of Florida, Gainesville.

Alsobrook, J. M. (1967, September). *Health-engendering aides for psychiatric patients: Implications for therapeutic milieu.* Paper presented at the 75th Annual Convention of the American Psychological Association, Washington, DC.

Alsobrook, J. M. (1969). *Effects of college student interaction upon learning and adjustment.* (USOE Project No. 5-0906). Athens: University of Georgia, Department of Psychology.

Carkhuff, R. R. (1969). *Helping and human relations* (Vol. 1). New York, NY: Holt.

Carkhuff, R. R. (1983). *The art of helping* (5th ed.). Amherst, MA: Human Resource Development Press.

Carkhuff, R. R. (2002). *The art of helping in the 21st century* (8th ed.). Amherst, MA: Human Resource Development Press.

Egan, G. (1975). *Exercises in helping skills.* Monterey, CA: Brooks/Cole.

Egan, G. (2002). *The skilled helper* (7th ed.). Monterey, CA: Brooks/Cole.

Heine, R. W. (1950). *A comparison of patients' reports on psychotherapeutic experience with psychoanalytic, nondirective, and Adlerian therapists.* Unpublished doctoral dissertation, University of Chicago, Chicago, IL.

Linehan, M. M. (1993). *Cognitive behavioral treatment of borderline personality disorder.* New York, NY: Guilford Press.

Linehan, M. M., Schmidt, H., III, Dimeff, L. A., Craft, J. C., Kanter, J., Comtois, K. A., & Recknor, K. L. (1999). Dialectical behavior therapy for patients with borderline personality disorder and drug-dependence. *The American Journal on Addictions, 8,* 279–292. http://dx.doi.org/10.1080/105504999305686

Loughary, J. W., & Ripley, T. M. (1978). *Helping others help themselves: A guide to counseling skills.* New York, NY: McGraw-Hill.

Miller, W. R., & Rose, G. S. (2009, September). Toward a theory of motivational interviewing. *American Psychologist, 64*, 527–537. http://dx.doi.org/10.1037/a0016830

Newton, M., & Krauss, H. H. (1973, July). The health-engenderingness of resident assistants as related to student achievement and adjustment. *Journal of College Student Personnel, 14*, 321–325.

Price, M. (1975). *Facilitation, expertness, and influence in counseling.* Unpublished doctoral dissertation, University of Oklahoma, Norman.

Rogers, C. R. (1958). The characteristics of a helping relationship. *Personnel & Guidance Journal, 37*, 6–16. http://dx.doi.org/10.1002/j.2164-4918.1958.tb01147.x

Rogers, C. R., Gendlin, E. T., Kiesler, D., & Truax, C. B. (1967). *The therapeutic relationship and its impact.* Madison: University of Wisconsin Press.

Truax, C. B., & Carkhuff, R. R. (1967). *Toward effective counseling and psychotherapy.* Chicago, IL: Aldine.

Verheul, R., Van Den Bosch, L. M. C., Koeter, M. W. J., De Ridder, M. A. J., Stijnen, T., & Van Den Brink, W. (2003). Dialectical behaviour therapy for women with borderline personality disorder: 12-month, randomised clinical trial in the Netherlands. *The British Journal of Psychiatry, 182*, 135–140. http://dx.doi.org/10.1192/bjp.182.2.135

Janet R. Matthews and Lee H. Matthews

Developing Rapport 3

 hen students are preparing to have their first experience in the "real world" rather than in the classroom, they often have questions about how to relate to the people they will encounter. In this chapter, we discuss issues that arise when interacting with supervisors, staff, and patients in applied settings and provide some suggestions about how to address these issues. This chapter is not intended to make you an expert in interviewing or psychotherapy. If you are an undergraduate, you will not actually be doing psychotherapy. If you are a beginning graduate student, you may be doing some psychotherapy but will have close supervision. This chapter should help you begin to enter the applied world.

First Impressions

In social settings, we are often concerned about the first impression we make. Think about how parents prepare their

http://dx.doi.org/10.1037/14672-003
Your Practicum in Psychology: A Guide for Maximizing Knowledge and Competence,
Second Edition, J. R. Matthews and C. E. Walker (Editors)

children for the first day of school. Part of that preparation involves the impression they may make on their teacher and classmates. The literature in psychology suggests that once we form an opinion about someone, we often use that information to attend selectively to future behavior by that person. We tend to remember those actions that fit our first impression and discount those that do not. This information can also be applied to your placement site. Thus, talking to other students from your program who have previously had a placement at your site before your first day there can provide useful information about what to expect. The more prepared you are, the better first impression you are likely to make.

WHAT SHOULD I WEAR?

A common question practicum students ask is, "What should I wear to the placement?" For your initial visit to the facility, it is probably best to dress as you would for a job interview. By this, we mean that you should take care in terms of both your personal hygiene and the type of clothing you select. During this initial visit, ask your site supervisor about the recommended form of dress for that particular facility. Some facilities have specific dress codes for all people on their campus, whereas others leave this decision to individual supervisors to monitor their staff. As an example, in almost all psychiatric and hospital settings, wearing of "open-toe" shoes (sandals) is not allowed. Likewise T-shirts with writing such as beer slogans, names of rock groups, and the like are generally not permitted.

Students who are placed in settings where they will be interacting with young children may find that they are asked to dress in more casual clothing than those students who are placed on an adult inpatient psychiatric ward, and those students in private practice offices or in court-related facilities may need to "dress up" more than you normally would for school. If you will be crawling on the ground with young children, for example, and you are female, wearing a dress and nylons is probably not a practical option. Likewise, wearing clothing that could encourage provocative responses from the patients, regardless of how "good" that clothing may be, is also inappropriate. To learn about the appropriate clothing for your site, it is best to schedule a brief visit before the day you will actually start your placement and discuss this issue with the site supervisor. If a short visit is not an option, try sending an e-mail inquiry.

In some cases, a supervisor may note that something about your clothing or hair is upsetting to the patients. This statement is not meant to demean you or your life choices. It is made to maximize the treatment potential of the facility. If you are unclear about why something about you is problematic, ask for additional feedback, but do so in a way that makes clear you are seeking information rather than arguing. For example, a special accessory issue we have noted in a number of facilities is body piercings. Some facilities have rules prohibiting visible attachments to the body and require that they be removed during time spent at the facility. Depending on the location and recency of the piercing, you may need to cover the area from which the object was removed with a bandage while at the placement. It is important for students who have elected to have piercings to understand that such rules are not personal but rather apply to everyone who works in that facility. Even though you are a student rather than an employee, you will probably be required to follow all such rules. Even if such removal is not a rule, think about the impression you are making if you dress quite differently from the staff.

WHO ARE ALL THESE PEOPLE?

Your experience at the placement site is likely to bring you into contact with people from a variety of disciplines, who are responsible to an organizational structure or "chain of command" in the same way that your professors are responsible to the department chair and the chair is responsible to the dean. During your initial meeting with your site supervisor, take written notes about the people with whom you will be interacting on a regular basis. In our experience, most site supervisors will give you this information at a first meeting, but if you are not prepared to take notes, it sometimes takes a while to catch on to the organizational structure. If your supervisor does not discuss the people you will be interacting with at the facility during your first meeting, ask about this topic. Lines of authority are often convoluted.

As an example of why it is important to have this information, consider a site placement on an adult inpatient unit with which the chapter authors are familiar. The student interacted with all of the following professionals. A psychiatrist was the *administrative physician* (sometimes called the *medical director*) for the unit and was responsible for the psychiatric care and overall administration of the unit. There was a *program director*, a social worker (licensed clinical social worker or LCSW), who supervised the two social workers on the unit, although these people reported on a daily basis to the unit *nurse manager*. The nurse manager (sometimes the title is *nursing director*) was a registered nurse (RN), with a bachelor's degree in nursing and was responsible for the supervision of the shift nurses. Some of the shift nurses were RNs, and others were licensed practical nurses (LPN). In addition, there were two or three unit *psychiatric technicians* (techs), who had a high school education. The three directors made up the administrative team for the unit. However, the administrative director reported to the medical director of the hospital, the charge nurse reported to the director of nursing of the hospital, and the program director was responsible to the director of social work for the hospital. Other disciplines had regular assignments on the unit but were supervised by someone at the hospital level. For example, the *creative arts therapist* (CAT) led five groups on the unit during the week (which the student attended on the days she was there) with other CAT staff on a rotating monthly schedule to cover the weekends.

Depending on the facility and the unit size, a *clinical psychologist* (PhD or PsyD) may be a part-time consultant, assigned to do only psychological assessment and behavioral interventions and attend treatment team meetings. In such cases, the psychologist will be responsible to the *chief psychologist* at the hospital level. At other sites, there may be a full-time psychologist who is involved in the same activities, in addition to doing group or individual psychotherapy. In such cases, the psychologist may have a split responsibility, with duties assigned, in part, by the program director. In our example, the site supervisor for the undergraduate student was a clinical psychologist assigned part time to the unit, and because of this schedule, the student spent some of her time working with these other professionals. Because this student might need approval to participate in specific activities from any of these staff members, it was important for her to understand not only their title but also their interrelationships.

HOW DO I BUILD RAPPORT?

Although there is no list of techniques we can give you about how to establish rapport with every patient, we can provide some general principles (Plante, 2010). Many students who elect to take a practicum course have previously been told they are good listeners or that it is easy to talk to them. If this is typical of you, you have already taken the first step toward establishing rapport. *Rapport* is a term often used by applied psychologists to describe the establishment of a positive relationship with their patients. It is the development of interactions that are trusting, accepting, respectful, and helpful. According to Pomerantz (2011), when rapport is established the patient feels the clinician has "connected with them" and "empathizes with their issues."

First, be attentive. Reduce distractions whenever possible. Allow enough time for the person to answer a question before moving to another topic, and follow up with additional comments or questions that indicate you are listening.

Second, nonverbal cues give much useful information. Attend to posture—both your own and the patient's. Are you and the patient stiff or relaxed, leaning toward or away from each other, for example? The amount of eye contact you have is important. Notice "how" statements are made. The person who says, "I am not angry" in a loud voice, with arms crossed and teeth clenched, may not be in touch with his or her own feelings. Even where you sit is important. For example, when you are talking or interviewing in a room, try to sit so that you do not block the exit from the room. It is better, and safer for you, if a person who gets upset can leave through the door, rather than through you, and then through the door. If this happens, you are then able to get help or call for help if necessary.

Third, be nonjudgmental. Show respect, acceptance, and empathy. Do not be critical. Do not be either a "know-it-all" or a "friend." Try to be warm and supportive.

Fourth, be an active listener. Ask open-ended questions, not questions requiring only a yes or no answer. Ask questions that require some detail to answer. Asking questions about what brought patients to the program, how often or how long they have had a specific difficulty or problem, what they think caused the difficulty, and what they have tried to do to cope are all ways to gain information. Ask questions to clarify or fill in gaps. Paraphrase or briefly summarize what was said to you to ensure understanding and build rapport. It is important for all parties concerned to have an understanding about such factors as confidentiality, the purpose of the student's placement, and how often the student can be expected to be available to visit the placement site. We discuss these topics more completely later in the chapter.

The interactions you have in applied settings are different from conversations you have with your friends. When talking with your friends, there may or may not be a general expectation that what is said is private and not to be repeated to anyone. In applied settings, however, this expectation of privacy is a requirement. Many facilities require students to sign a confidentiality statement. Rules of confidentiality are influenced not only by the specific facility but also by federal legislation. The Health Insurance Portability and Accountability Act of 2003, promulgated by the U.S. Department of Health and Human Services, has a privacy rule that includes the fact that people working for psychologists should only be given enough information to do their jobs. As a student in the role of assisting a mental health professional, this rule also applies to you.

Friends may tell you truly personal information. It is likely, however, that they have thought about it before talking to you. By contrast, some of what you hear at the placement may be material the person has never said out loud before. Likewise, when you talk with (or interview) a patient for the first time, there are likely to be some distortions or withheld information. This is to be expected because it is not the norm for "strangers" to openly discuss thoughts and intimate details. People in emotional crisis often display patterns of behavior that are exaggerations of their usual modes of interacting. Ask yourself questions such as the following: Does the person seem unusually dependent? Is his or her approach suspicious or surly? Is there an element of seductiveness or provocation? Is the person tearful, sarcastic, or overly happy, even when discussing extremely stressful information?

WHAT IS *INTERVIEWING?*

In basic terms, an *interview* is a conversation with a purpose or goal. Interviewing is a skill that requires practice and careful supervision so that you receive feedback and improve your technique (Sommers-Flanagan & Sommers-Flanagan, 2009).

The most common form of clinical interview is an initial assessment, when a patient comes to the clinician because of some problem in daily functioning. Patterned after the question-and-answer format used in traditional medical history taking, such psychological or psychiatric interviews are usually structured according to a sequence of important topics. Some interviews are designed to classify patient problems at that time to make a diagnosis (Morrison, 2008). Interviews focusing on describing patients and their problems in more comprehensive terms usually occur within the context of a full-scale clinical exploration that precedes treatment.

In recent years, the major developments in psychological interviewing have been on structured and semistructured interviews. The terms *structured* and *semistructured* refer to the degree to which the interviewer determines the direction of the clinical interview. The structured interview involves using a format with carefully planned questions; the semistructured interview, in contrast, has a predetermined set of topics to be covered, but the interviewer has more flexibility about how the topics are approached. This trend can be traced to several sources, including the increased reliance on procedures using operationally defined criteria for making psychiatric diagnoses. Such techniques, originally developed to gain epidemiological information, involve having the interviewer ask specific questions that can be replicated by other interviewers. Structured interviews do not eliminate open-ended questions, nor do they prevent interviewers from asking their own additional questions to clarify responses. However, they do provide detailed rules, sometimes called *decision trees*, for informing the interviewer what to do in the event of certain responses. For example, if a client answers "no" to a basic question about some class of feelings or behaviors associated with anxiety, rather than continue with that list, the examiner would move on to another problem area, such as questions on depression. Although many standardized structured interviews have good reliability and validity, some researchers have reported that structured interviews are used with only about 15% of patients (Bruchmüller, Magraf, Suppiger, & Schneider, 2011). Chapter 6 provides information about additional types of interview techniques.

BEING A PARTICIPANT-OBSERVER

In most college classes, students have a well-defined role. They are there to learn. Expectations may include taking notes, responding to questions from the professor, and participating in class discussions. The role of the student at a practicum site may not be as well defined. You are less likely to have a syllabus summarizing this activity like those you have for other courses you take. Are you just supposed to observe, or are you also expected to participate? If you participate, to what extent do you do so? These are important questions to ask both your campus professor and the site supervisor.

To illustrate these issues, we describe a couple of the sites we have used at Loyola University in New Orleans. One undergraduate placement site is a substance abuse inpatient program of a private psychiatric hospital. In this setting, the practicum student attends unit staff meetings, participates in some therapy groups, and spends time on the unit with or without the psychiatric techs when the patients are at leisure. What is the student's role in each of these activities? One goal for this specific placement is for the student to become comfortable doing the tech's duties. Most of our students find that initially they are quite uncomfortable in all of these activities. They are unsure about what to say and may not feel they have the background to contribute. Initially, their role tends to be observer in these activities. Over time, however, they begin to participate. In staff meetings, they may continue simply to observe unless one of the staff members asks them questions about a specific patient.

In various creative arts therapy activities, however, the students tend to participate equally with the therapist and patients. In this case, they may provide some personal information but should still remember that they are not there to receive treatment. They share just enough information to make the others comfortable. This is not deep, personal information. For example, students may share the size of their family or their birth order in the family, but it is not wise to discuss their own ongoing personal psychotherapy or a previous experience with substance abuse.

At this site, students also assist the therapist in some of the educational therapy groups. In this case, they may do reading about a topic or assist in a group activity. They may even be given readings by one of the staff members and subsequently lead a group discussion about that subject. As participant-observers, if they discuss some of their own background, they must be careful to maintain appropriate distance. Before providing personal information, students should learn about the policies of the facility on self-disclosure. Some facilities, for example, issue name badges to all staff and students. These badges may have the person's full name or in other cases only their first name. In the latter case, the facility may have a policy that you do not even disclose your full name to the patients. If someone asks you a personal question and you are either uncomfortable revealing the answer or are not sure about agency policy about self-disclosure, you should check with your supervisor before providing the information. In the immediate circumstance, it is best to indicate that you are uncomfortable with that question and want to think about why you are not comfortable before answering it. By saying that, you are acknowledging the person's question and explaining why you will not answer it at that specific time.

In other placements, the student's role may focus more on being an observer. At an outpatient program specializing in abused and neglected children, for example, our students have learned to use a standardized observational checklist. Along with staff members from that program, they observe children and their parents or foster parents. Some of this observation is done from behind a one-way window with the adult and child in an observation room. The student's observations are then compared with those of the regular staff members. At other times, they observe at day-care facilities and in the person's home.

Issues that arise when serving as a participant-observer may vary depending on the patient group. Practicum students, especially those who are undergraduates and who are placed with adolescents, may find it more difficult to maintain distance because they are so close in age and identify so closely with the issues being discussed. Depending on the age and physical development of the student, some adolescents may relate to them as peers rather than as representatives of the staff. Students placed with adults may find that the adults treat them like their children rather than as students or staff aides. It is important in this case for the student to let the patients know why they are participating in the program. Students may acknowledge that the adult has more life experiences than they have but add that they would like to learn.

WHAT SHOULD I SAY? FIRST SESSION

The degree of interaction students have with patients will vary considerably among facilities. In some settings, you will always be accompanied by a staff member; in others, you may have times when you are talking individually with someone, such as a patient on an inpatient psychiatric unit or a child on a playground. Although there will be a number of staff members in the vicinity, the conversation may be, to a great extent, private. It is important to approach the person with respect. Let this person know who you are and what your role is at the facility. Indicate that you are a student who will be spending time there and specify how often and for how long you will do so. For example, you might say that you are a graduate student in psychology from Local University working with Dr. Psychologist. You are taking a university course that is part of an integrated training program in clinical or counseling psychology. You will be spending 20 hours each week for the next 3 months at this facility. You plan to be there on Tuesday, Thursday, and a half day on Friday. Talk briefly about confidentiality and the limits of confidentiality. That is, explain that whatever she tells you will not be repeated outside the facility. However, you have a duty to report to your supervisor if she tells you anything indicating danger to her or to another person. You would like to talk to her and learn more about her. Then ask her if you may talk for awhile. Then begin to have a conversation. If she indicates that she does not want to talk to you, do not take it personally. Ask your supervisor whether you should pursue conversation with individuals who say no.

WHAT SHOULD I SAY?

Once you start talking with a client or patient, remember what you have learned about rapport and interviewing. It is natural to be somewhat anxious in this situation. Some people speak rapidly when they are nervous, and others just naturally speak rapidly. Pay attention to the speed of your speech. Remember local standards for speech pace as well as cultural differences that relate to rate of speech. It is easy to overwhelm the person by speaking too fast. Related to rapid speech is asking the person multiple questions without providing a chance to respond. All this is likely to do is confuse the person about what you have said. It may also cause someone who was reluctant to talk to you to decide that decision was a good one and walk away from you. Although you may be truly interested in learning about this person, do not make the conversation seem like an interrogation. Asking one question after another without any general discussion is likely to lead to a short conversation. Be aware of both verbal and nonverbal signs that the person is not comfortable. Suppose a person who was sitting quietly and talking to you begins to move around in the chair. You might say, "I notice that you are moving around a bit. Are you uncomfortable with the topic of our conversation right now?"

How you start and continue a conversation will be strongly influenced by the characteristics of the patient. When you are talking to a shy person at your placement, it is really not that different from talking to a shy person anywhere. Maintaining good eye contact and using a tone of voice and a facial expression that indicate your interest in what the person is saying to you can encourage further discussion. With some people, leaning toward them to show you are listening to what they are saying will also be helpful.

All of these suggestions, however, are influenced by the culture from which both you and this person come. For example, personal space needs vary across cultures and generations. Looking directly at a person is viewed positively in some cultures and negatively in others. A tone of voice you intend to be soft and supportive may have a different meaning to the person than it does to you. Although it is important to consider cultural factors, you should not try to be something you are not. For example, do not try to adopt slang that is not part of your regular speech. Likewise, if you are talking to a senior citizen with a sixth-grade education who is in the early stages of Alzheimer's disease, you do not want to demonstrate your ability to use five- and six-syllable words. Treat this person with respect, but also try to speak in a way that maximizes understanding. If you do not know anything about the culture from which a person comes, you may want to discuss this with your supervisor or do some independent reading before the next time you visit the facility (Sue & Sue, 2013). Knowledge of these factors will assist you in establishing rapport not only with people at the practicum site but also with new people you meet elsewhere.

When a patient asks you a question, do not assume you know why that question was asked or that your initial understanding of that question is correct. For example, suppose you are talking to a person who has a 10-year history of alcohol abuse. After you have introduced yourself to him, he says, "How can you help me when you aren't even old enough to legally buy a drink?" This comment might indicate that this man believes the only people who can help someone who is an alcoholic are people with a history of drinking. It could also indicate that his style of interacting with people is to take control of the conversation, and this comment is his attempt to show who is in charge of the interaction. It could indicate that he is sincerely interested in receiving help in the program and wants to get that help from the most qualified person. You are not expected to be a mind reader and know what he means at this point. The main concern you have is to not become defensive about your age or level of experience. Let him know that you realize it is important to him to know how you might assist his recovery. From that point, you might then let him know that you are there to learn and to listen. Perhaps over time you will find that some of your life experiences may be useful to him or that just having someone who wants to listen will help him progress through the program. How you interact with patients at your placement will also be related to the instructions you have received from your faculty sponsor and site supervisor. On some campuses, you will have been told that your role is to be a companion to the individuals and that you are only there to add to the milieu. In other cases, you will have a paraprofessional role similar to the aides in the program. If you are a graduate student, you may have a somewhat more active role. Make sure that you clarify your role before talking to the program participants.

As you can see, getting the patient to accept you can be difficult. One suggestion that may help is to try to think about this situation as a collaborative one (Falender & Shafranske, 2012). Rather than focusing on your own perspective, think about the patient's perspective. If you have access to the person's records, you may want to read them for background. For example, does this person have a history of prior treatments that were not successful? If so, it is not surprising if the person is a bit skeptical that this program will be any better than others were. If this is the first time the person has been in this type of program, he or she may be feeling uncomfortable with the loss of control or the suggestion that personal issues be discussed with strangers (Royse, Dhooper, & Rompf, 2012).

You need to be careful, however, about how much you immerse yourself in the patient's world. A challenge for practicum students is to be able to enter, but not become lost in, the world of the people with whom they interact. Part of this process is for you to be able to view the world from the perspective of the other person without feeling you must accept that worldview. If this person has had experiences that are similar to those in your own life, you may find you are reliving your own experiences and making assumptions about those feelings and experiences of the patient. In other cases, called overidentification, you become so involved in that person's feelings and reactions that you actually *need* to have the person improve. It is important to know if you have crossed this line of overidentification so that you can then develop some emotional distance from that person. This skill is useful not only at your field placement but in many other life circumstances.

Your ability to accept the people with whom you are working at your placement site is just as important as their acceptance of you. It is not unusual for beginning practicum students to experience negative reactions to patients who lie to them, manipulate them to get something, always seem to need more than the student can give, become verbally abusive or threatening, blame everyone but themselves for their problems, give only one-word answers to questions, reject all suggestions made to them, refuse to see their behavior as problematic, make it obvious they don't like the student, or refuse to work with the student. Although this list may seem like an exaggeration, you will likely face most of these problems during your training. The more of them you find in one patient, the more likely you are to be frustrated. We discuss some of these issues here and refer interested students to the suggested readings at the end of the chapter for additional information.

What about the patient who has a history of aggressive behavior? Although there is a low probability of practicum students being victims of aggressive behavior, it is important to keep this history in mind. Facilities accepting practicum students often require them to complete some form of orientation. This orientation process is likely to include information about how to deal with hostile behavior or a sense of feeling threatened if this is something often experienced there. If a person at your placement tells you, "I don't want to talk to you anymore; you are making me angry," take that person at his or her word. If you need to move away from the situation, it is always a good idea to back away, facing the person as you leave the area.

Children are less likely than adults to give you a verbal clue that it is time to stop interacting with them. With children, the first indication you may have that the child is unhappy with you is when the child attempts to hit or kick you. Fortunately, you are usually larger than the child. You may be able to use that size differential to convince the child to cease this behavior. If you cannot move away or verbally convince the child to stop, you will need to get help from the staff. There are legal liability issues if you touch the child. Even if you think you would not hurt yourself or the child, do not attempt restraint. This warning does not mean that students should only interact with a select portion of the people at their placement. Just as you would when walking through a questionable neighborhood, be aware of signs of difficulty.

Another issue that can arise when talking to people at your placement is when the person shows signs of being delusional or experiencing hallucinations. Delusional thinking may influence what this person says to you. If the information does not make sense to you, you may ask the person to repeat something, but do not keep doing this if the conversation continues in a confusing direction. Repeatedly asking the person to clarify statements is likely to lead to an end to the conversation. Remember, if the person says anything that could be interpreted as indicating something dangerous to either this person or someone else, tell your supervisor (or if your supervisor is not available, another staff person) as soon as you leave the individual. For example, suppose you are placed on an adult inpatient psychiatric unit. You are talking to a 46-year-old woman who tells you that she is planning to eat the glass in which she gets her juice because she "knows" they are planning to use her fingerprints from that glass to obtain her real identity. Although it is unlikely that she will actually eat her glass, it is important that someone in authority knows she has said she has such a plan so they can monitor her potentially self-injurious behavior.

People who are experiencing auditory or visual hallucinations may periodically respond to these internal stimuli while talking to you. It is best to ignore these responses and continue your conversation normally. A common indication that the person is having auditory hallucinations, for example, is to look upward or to the side to locate the source of the voices. You may then tell a staff member about what you observed. Another possible issue that may arise is when a patient on an inpatient psychiatric unit tells you about plans to leave without permission. Although you may have told that person that you will keep their comments confidential, you will also have said that confidentiality does not extend to conditions that are potentially dangerous. Leaving the hospital without permission falls within that exception and should be reported to your supervisor or a staff member immediately.

What about the case in which someone you meet at the placement wants to maintain contact with you away from the placement? If you are doing a good job interacting with the people at the placement, patients may ask for your phone number so they can call you when they are feeling distressed or when they have additional questions to ask you. Others, who are preparing to leave the site, may want to see you socially. Regardless of the reason the person wants your contact information, do not give it. It is important to take the time to explain to the person that although you are not part of the professional staff of the facility, you are obligated to follow the same policy regarding socializing with them as the staff members have. You do not want to give the impression that your refusal is personal to them but rather that you would give the same answer to anyone who asked for it in this setting. You may use university or agency policies as the "heavy" in this situation. Let the patient know that policies you must adhere to forbid outside contact. It is helpful to let them know that you appreciate the fact that they want to maintain contact with you but that such contact will not be possible.

Becoming too attached to a student can be expressed in ways other than asking for a phone number. A child may cling to you and beg you not to leave when it is time for you to go or refuse to talk to anyone but you. In this case, you need to talk to the child and explain that you are pleased that she enjoys your company but that you spend only a limited amount of time there. Tell the child that staff members also care about her and have much to offer and that you hope the child will gain from them, too. If the child continues to refuse to interact with anyone but you, it may be necessary for you to take the position that, even when you are there, you cannot spend one-on-one time with this child.

Another example is the adult who continues to try to touch you or invade your personal space. One of our former students, for example, reported a situation in which her supervisor had asked her to conduct a standardized interview with an adult male patient. This man continued to move his chair closer and closer to her chair as she moved through the required questionnaire. Both his chair and hers had rollers. As he moved his chair closer to hers, she moved hers away from him. She was eventually backed against a wall in the room. This incident led her to request a change of placement. Rather than honoring this request, we had a discussion of other ways she might handle this behavior in the future. How should she have handled this problem? As in the previous example, the student might acknowledge the fact that she appreciated his desire to sit closer to her but let him know that moving his chair closer to hers was not appropriate. She could tell him that she was not comfortable with his chair being that close to her. If he continued to move his chair, she would tell him if he continued to move into her personal space, the interview would have to be terminated. She would be explaining her feelings as well as setting appropriate consequences for continued inappropriate behavior. By the end of the semester, the student in our example had not only learned about the placement site but had also practiced appropriate assertiveness skills she could use elsewhere. Both of these situations should also be discussed with the site supervisor.

WHAT SHOULD I TELL MY SITE SUPERVISOR?

The way site supervision is conducted varies among programs. Usually one person is designated as being responsible for all students or for students from a specific discipline, such as psychology. Meetings with students are sometimes done in a group format when there are a number of students placed there; other sites use an individual supervision format. Chapter 4 covers issues of confidentiality, but we note a few of these issues here as well.

Students who find themselves in an individual supervision meeting with a site supervisor may wonder what they are supposed to say. As we mentioned earlier, if a student has heard something that may indicate problems, this should be reported immediately. Regular supervision meetings, however, allow for many other topics to be discussed. Asking the supervisor about the education needed for that career as well as the rewards and frustrations of the career can be useful and informative. It is also appropriate to ask about readings that may assist you in understanding things you have heard or seen at that placement. If you are participating in specific activities at the site, keep a list of questions you have about them so you can ask your supervisor during regular meetings. By having the list ready, you will make efficient use of the limited time available. If you have heard about special activities or programs at the facility, you may ask your supervisor about the possibility of observing or participating in them.

If the placement site is located in a risky neighborhood, ask your supervisor if your hours can be adjusted so that you leave before dark or at a time when many staff members are also leaving so that you are not alone in the parking lot or public transportation area. Many facilities have security available to escort you to your vehicle if requested. Students who feel fearful are likely to have difficulty establishing rapport with either patients or staff. If the student's fears are excessive, the supervisor may help alleviate them.

Just as professors vary in their teaching styles, supervisors vary in their supervision styles. Some supervisors focus on building on the strengths demonstrated by the practicum student; others seem to operate from the position that students know what they are doing well. These supervisors may use their time with the student to focus on areas needing remediation. This approach to supervision may lead to students feeling they have no skills. Under these circumstances, you may want to ask your supervisor about what strengths he or she has observed. Corey and Corey (2011) divided supervisor styles between those that are generally confrontational and those that are supportive. In this case, the term *confrontation* does not refer to an angry interaction. Rather, these supervisors will tend to spend their time with you considering ways you might do things differently from the way you are doing them. Supportive supervisors are the ones who are likely to focus on your positive interactions. Understanding the difference between these two styles can help you develop a comfortable and productive working relationship with your supervisor.

Supervision may lead to a certain degree of anxiety. In this setting, you are being asked to try new skills or apply what you have learned in a classroom setting to the real world. Part of the role of your supervisor is to give you feedback about your progress. None of us likes to hear we are not performing well. Thus, there is a tendency to avoid discussing problems you are having with individuals or activities. Other students become argumentative when receiving constructive feedback. They try to debate each point made by their supervisor. They may debate the points during supervision or remain quiet at that time but privately or with their friends debate each of these criticisms. Doing this is not productive. This is an opportunity to learn about yourself and your current skill level—use it to your advantage.

WHAT IF I SEE A PATIENT ELSEWHERE?

Although this subject was discussed in Chapter 1, we briefly cover it again here. It is quite possible that practicum students will find themselves in a situation of accidentally meeting someone from their placement away from the facility. This seems most likely in such places as the supermarket, a movie theater, or other settings where there are many other people. The first issue to consider is whether to greet this person. As a general policy, wait for the person to greet you, and let the other person's response guide your behavior. If they say hello, respond appropriately and then move on. It is especially important with children not to use their or the parent's last name. It is not advisable to engage in extended conversation. Suppose you are with some of your friends and they ask how you know that person? In this case, give a vague answer such as, "I'm not sure where we met," and then change the topic of conversation. You are still bound by confidentiality and cannot reveal how you know this person.

What about those cases in which you are still placed at the facility and you will continue to see the person? The same rules apply unless you have observed the person doing something that needs to be addressed at the facility. For example, suppose you are placed in an outpatient alcohol treatment program. You are at a parade and notice that one of the patients from the program is drinking a beer. Do not confront the person there. The next time you go to the placement, tell your supervisor what you observed so that a staff member can confront the person about this behavior.

HOW DO I LEAVE THE PLACEMENT?

Just as you may have found it somewhat difficult to establish relationships with people at your placement site, you may also find it difficult to end those relationships. Leaving the facility involves saying goodbye to both the staff and the patients. It also involves dealing with your own feelings of loss. In fact, in the first session you have with the patient, you should discuss the time limitations of the relationship. It is important to realize that although you have not been the "primary professional" for the patients at your placement site, you have been a regular part of the program for a period of time. Thus, you need to plan for the exit process.

Over the time you spend at a practicum site, it is common to develop an attachment to the facility. Some students ask if they can continue to "volunteer" there after the end of their course placement. Although some added time may be permitted at certain placements, if the practicum course is offered each term, it may be time for the next student to arrive. Most sites allow only a limited number of students because of staff and space needs. Thus, it is important to allow sufficient time to complete your placement process. If you plan to ask your supervisor for future letters of recommendation, you should discuss this request in one of your sessions near the end of the term. You should also let the patients know a few weeks and then a few days before your final day the specific time that will be your last visit. That way, any issues a person wants to address with you can be handled within your scheduled time. This also provides staff and clients an opportunity to say goodbye to you.

Some practicum programs have a formal process of feedback for both the site supervisor and the student. Regardless of whether this system is used in your program, it is a good idea to provide your supervisor with feedback about your experience. When doing this, remember what you have learned during your placement about dealing with sensitive issues. This is especially true if you have some negative feedback for your supervisor. Remember that you and your supervisor are not on an equal power level. If you have strong concerns about certain aspects of this placement, it may be best to give those to your campus faculty member rather than the placement supervisor. If your placement supervisor asks you for feedback about the experience, clarify what the supervisor is asking in much the same way you did with the residents of the program before responding. Just as you may feel close to some faculty members and not to others you have had for classes, you may have a similar range of reactions to practicum supervisors. If you do not feel especially close to your supervisor, just say thank you for your time and then leave. If you feel close to the supervisor, you may want to ask if continued contact, such as periodic e-mails, is acceptable. Whatever the case, it is important for the practicum student to be aware of personal reactions to the end of this experience. Because of the nature of the practicum experience, it has a higher probability of generating attachment feelings than the typical class.

Summary

In this chapter, we discussed the concept of rapport as it applies to students' interactions with both staff and patients in programs where they are placed. Rapport and a developing sense of professionalism begin with determining what to wear for the first visit to the site and retain their importance in interactions with staff and patients as well as during supervision sessions. We included suggestions about how to initiate and continue conversations with patients as well as how to get the maximum benefit from supervision sessions. The role of culture in understanding patients, as well as self-understanding, is part of the practicum experience. Common issues faced in these settings include learning the role of participant-observer, how to handle the circumstance of seeing someone from the placement outside that setting, and working with a range of staff members from different disciplines.

Suggested Readings

Baird, B. N. (2014). *The internship, practicum and field placement handbook* (7th ed.). Upper Saddle River, NJ: Pearson.

Chang, V. N., Scott, S. T., & Decker, C. L. (2009). *Developing helping skills: A step-by-step approach.* Belmont, CA: Cengage.

Gordon, G. R., & McBride, R. B. (2011). *Criminal justice internships: Theory into practice* (7th ed.). Cincinnati, OH: Anderson.

References

Bruchmüller, K., Margraf, J., Suppiger, A., & Schneider, S. (2011). Popular or unpopular? Therapists' use of structured interviews and their estimation of patient acceptance. *Behavior Therapy, 42,* 634 643. http://dx.doi.org/10.1016/j.beth.2011.02.003

Corey, M. S., & Corey, G. (2011). *Becoming a helper* (6th ed.). Pacific Grove, CA: Brooks/Cole.

Falender, C. A., & Shafranske, E. P. (2012). *Getting the most out of clinical training and supervision: A guide for practicum students and interns.* Washington, DC: American Psychological Association. http://dx.doi.org/10.1037/13487-000

Morrison, J. (2008). *The first interview* (3rd ed.). New York, NY: Guilford Press.

Plante, T. G. (2010). *Contemporary clinical psychology* (3rd ed.). New York, NY: Wiley.

Pomerantz, A. M. (2011). *Clinical psychology: Science, practice and culture* (2nd ed.). Thousand Oaks, CA: Sage.

Royse, D., Dhooper, S. S., & Rompf, E. L. (2012). *Field instruction: A guide for social work students* (6th ed.). Upper Saddle River, NJ: Pearson.

Sommers-Flanagan, J., & Sommers-Flanagan, R. (2009). *Clinical interviewing* (4th ed.). Hoboken, NJ: Wiley.

Sue, D. W., & Sue, D. (2013). *Counseling the culturally diverse* (6th ed.). New York, NY: Wiley.

Elizabeth Swenson

Confidentiality and Other Ethical Issues

4

A n internship or practicum is often the high point of one's undergraduate education in psychology. My students tell me that this is the time when their classroom learning really seems to come together for them. In addition, learning in the field setting helps one solidify some career decisions and rethink others. Students report not infrequently that their practicum or internship was a life-changing experience.

Among the most important things to learn and to consider carefully are the ethical issues that you come across in your fieldwork. As psychology students, you should be aware that there is a Code of Ethics for psychologists. It is officially called the "Ethical Principles of Psychologists and Code of Conduct" (American Psychological Association [APA], 2010) and can be accessed at http://www.apa.org/ethics/code/. This Code of Ethics, which took effect in June 2003, is actually the 10th revision of the Ethics Code, which has a long history. Two of its standards were amended in 2010.

You may wonder whether the ethical standards in the Code are mandatory for you to uphold. The Introduction to

http://dx.doi.org/10.1037/14672-004

Your Practicum in Psychology: A Guide for Maximizing Knowledge and Competence, Second Edition, J. R. Matthews and C. E. Walker (Editors)

the Code states that "this Ethics Code applies only to psychologists' activities that are part of their scientific, educational, or professional roles as psychologists" (Para. 2). Furthermore, it states that "membership in the APA commits members and student affiliates to comply with the standards of the APA Ethics Code" (Para. 3). If you are a student affiliate of the APA, the answer is obvious. But what if you are not a student affiliate? The best strategy is that if you are a psychology student in a practicum or internship class where you are supervised, either onsite or in your class, by a psychologist, you should follow the Ethics Code.

Psychology is not the only profession with a code of ethics. In your professional life after college, or even now, you may have an interest in the codes of related helping professions such as counseling (American Counseling Association, 2005), social work (National Association of Social Workers, 2008), marriage and family therapy (American Association for Marriage and Family Therapy, 2012), or even psychiatry (American Psychiatric Association, 2013). The websites for these codes are included in the reference list at the end of this chapter. It is interesting to see how similar they are in the ways they approach common ethical situations.

The websites of the Center for the Study of Ethics in the Professions (2013) at the Illinois Institute of Technology and Kenneth Pope (2013), a clinical psychologist and prolific writer on ethical issues in psychology, have links to a number of professional ethics codes. It might be interesting to take a controversial subject, such as sexual contact between a mental health professional and a former client, and see how the different ethics codes deal with it. For example, all codes prohibit such contact, but for varying lengths of time.

Making Ethical Decisions

When we come across a situation in which we need to make an ethical decision, we tend to rely on our own innate sense of what's right and wrong—what our parents taught us or some overarching principle such as the Golden Rule. In a professional setting, you need to go about this decision making in a more deliberate way. There are two important sources of information, both of which are contained in the "Ethical Principles of Psychologists and Code of Conduct."

Under the heading of "General Principles" are basic principles that represent the moral values of the psychology profession. These principles are as follows:

A. Beneficence and Nonmaleficence (Do good and do not do harm)
B. Fidelity and Responsibility (Be faithful to your clients and duties, and act in a responsible way)

C. Integrity (Be honest)

D. Justice (Be fair to all people)

E. Respect for Peoples' Rights and Dignity

These principles are aspirational, meaning that we strive to meet them. Their intention is to guide and inspire psychologists toward the highest ethical ideals of the profession. You may have encountered these principles before in the biomedical ethics context, where they are prominent (Beauchamp & Childress, 2009).

The second source of ethical information for psychology is the Ethical Standards of the APA Ethics Code. The Standards apply specifically to the work-related behavior of psychologists. The Standards are enforceable, meaning that they are not optional for psychologists. Although written for members of the APA, they have been incorporated into the laws and regulations of many states. As a psychology student working in an internship or practicum that is primarily psychology related, you should be familiar with the ethical standards and strive to follow them.

Often the solution to an ethical dilemma in your work is not apparent from reading the APA Ethics Code. In such a case, the following steps should be followed:

1. Identify the ethical dilemma or problem.
2. Discuss the situation with your site supervisor and university professor.
3. Generate possible alternative solutions.
4. Consult the APA Ethics Code for one or more Standards that shed some light on the solutions.
5. Consider the General Principles of the Ethics Code as they might apply to the problem.
6. Document that you have done Steps 1 through 5.
7. Make a decision in conjunction with your supervisor and document the decision.

In the following sections of this chapter, you will have opportunities to apply this decision-making model for yourself.

Confidentiality

This may be your first exposure to issues related to confidentiality. Confidentiality is a primary obligation of psychologists. This obligation means that generally all of the information about a client, including anything she or he says or anything about a client that could reveal the client's identity, must be kept confidential. There is nothing more fundamental to a therapeutic relationship than confidentiality. It is what breeds trust between the psychologist and the client and what makes the professional relationship work. As a student of psychology, you assume the obligations of confidentiality, along with your supervisor, regardless of the internship setting to which you are assigned. Read carefully all of the subsections in Standard 4 of the Ethics Code on Privacy and Confidentiality—on the protection of privacy and the instances in which it might be breached ethically.

There are some limits on confidentiality. They are listed in Standard 4.05, Disclosures, and are discussed later in this chapter. The limits of confidentiality include a risk of harm to the client or others and the need to consult a professional colleague on treatment. Both Standard 4.02, Discussing the Limits of Confidentiality, and Standard 10.01, Informed Consent to Therapy, stress that discussion of confidentiality with the client take place as early as is feasible. You should obtain instructions from your supervisor on how to go about discussing this.

CASE 1: SHOULD YOU GREET AN ACQUAINTANCE?

Olivia's internship is in a drug and alcohol outpatient treatment center. She has permission to sit in on an open Twelve Step meeting. In the meeting is her family's next-door neighbor, Martin, a young man whom she would like to date. He looks at her without apparent recognition. It seems as if he does not want to be recognized. What should she do?

In applying the decision-making model outlined earlier in this chapter, the ethical dilemma for Olivia is whether to go up and talk to Martin, perhaps reminding him of their relationship. She could do this, or she could ignore him, treating him like any other patient in the group. These are the most obvious alternatives, although there are others. This is an issue of confidentiality but also may be construed as one of a multiple relationship. (More about multiple relationships is discussed later in this chapter.) Doing anything to promote the personal relationship at any possible expense of Martin's treatment is prohibited by the Ethics Code in Standard 3.05, which is also discussed later in this chapter. Section 4 of the Ethics Code obligates psychologists to respect privacy and confidentiality. Although there are limits to confidentiality in the Code, such as for consultation or protection from harm (Standard 4.05), none of these apply here. The general ethical principles of beneficence, nonmaleficence, and respect for dignity indicate that anything that might harm Martin should be avoided. As a general practice, one should not recognize the person unless he or she recognizes the psychologist or student first. Finally, Olivia should consult her supervisor as soon as feasible about the problem.

A similar case with a slightly different twist follows.

CASE 2: DECIDING NOT TO GREET A FORMER PATIENT

Olivia has now completed her fieldwork experience and is at college finishing up the last semester of her senior year. In a nearby coffee shop, where she is working on her senior project paper, she sees Madison, a patient from the substance abuse facility where she was placed. Her natural inclination is to say hello and ask him how he is doing these days. She especially wonders, although would never ask, whether Madison is still "on the wagon." She hesitates before making contact and then decides it might not be wise.

This was a good decision. The obligation to preserve confidentiality continues after both the psychologist and the patient have gone on to other endeavors. Some people believe it lasts forever. The principle that most psychologists adhere to is to not speak to a client unless the client speaks first. The conservative approach would be to follow this advice.

CASE 3: PROTECTING A PATIENT'S PRIVACY

Tom is working with children in a teaching hospital setting. The staff members have decided that students who are doing internships for academic credit may have limited access to patients' records on a need-to-know basis. Tom has used this privilege carefully. While playing pool with a child with Apert syndrome, a congenital disorder with possible malformations of the face and extremities, the mother of another child in the playroom asks Tom, "What's the matter with her?" Tom says he does not know but feels guilty because he does in fact know the diagnosis.

Tom is correct in protecting the patient's privacy. The Health Insurance Portability and Accountability Act of 1996, better known as HIPAA, requires this. If it bothers him to deny knowledge, it might be better for him to respond that he cannot discuss patients with other people. This is a good problem for Tom to discuss with both his supervisor and the professor supervising his academic work for the course. If there is a class with several internship students in other settings, it would not be a violation of privacy for them to discuss together how to deal with this type of question.

CASE 4: DISCUSSING CONFIDENTIAL
MATTERS WITH A SUPERVISOR

On his way home from the hospital, Tom encounters his site supervisor on the elevator. Tom begins to describe the events at the hospital that were difficult for him. His supervisor says that the elevator is not a good place to discuss patients because others are present in this small space and "even the elevator walls have ears." He recommends that they stop for a coffee in the hospital cafeteria.

Tom's supervisor is wrong to think that one public place is any better than any other for discussing a patient and the problems she presents. It's a small world. The person at the next table might be an uncle of the patient and listen to every word that is said. An appropriate place to discuss problems concerning a patient would be a private office or the classroom with other internship students.

CASE 5: DISCUSSING AND REPORTING
SUSPECTED CHILD ABUSE

In her practicum at a day care center in an economically deprived part of town, one of Rane's tasks is to organize children's artwork into individual portfolios. Rane is struck by the drawings of a 4-year-old boy who depicts a child being hit by an adult with a piece of wood. In another picture, a child is shown with a gag, tied to a chair. Rane decides to investigate further by talking to the child about the pictures. The child says that he is drawing pictures from his own life at home. She notices unusual-looking bruises on his arms.

Rane should have talked with her supervisor about the drawings before setting out on her own investigation. The suspicious appearance of the bruises and the words of the child require the supervisor to report this to the child protection agency in the city. Mandated reporting is the law in all states and many other countries, to protect children, and with growing frequency, older adults and mentally challenged people, from harm. Is Rane required to report this too? This depends on the law in her area, but it may possibly require her to report her suspicions as an intern in this setting. In many cities, it is possible to call a kids' hotline anonymously. This may be the best choice for a student, after all other options have been exhausted. Is there an issue of confidentiality here? Yes. However, Standard 4.05 clearly states that disclosures can be made to protect the child. Legally, Rane may have no choice here, but it is imperative that she discuss this with her on-site supervisor and professor. What if her site supervisor thinks that no report is needed? Rane should discuss this with her professor immediately and let the professor talk to the site supervisor. If Rane still thinks that appropriate action has not been taken after that an anonymous report may be in order. The ethical issue here is that the supervisor will probably find out about this action, with some possible detriment to Rane's future career.

Duty to Warn, Protect, or Disclose

Confidentiality can be breached ethically for certain reasons. Two of these are the duty to warn and the duty to disclose. Both of these are in the list of appropriate disclosures contained in Standard 4.05(b)(3), Disclosures, protecting the client and others from harm.

CASE 6: DUTY TO WARN OR PROTECT THIRD PARTIES

Prosenjit Poddar was a student at the University of California at Berkeley. He was also a client in the university's counseling center. During the course of his counseling, Poddar told his treating psychologist that he intended to kill Tatiana Tarasoff, his former girlfriend. The psychologist, feeling that Poddar was a danger to Tarasoff, called the police, who questioned and released him. Subsequently, Poddar did kill Tarasoff. The Tarasoff family sued the University of California, including the psychologist, arguing that the psychologist had a duty to warn or to protect Tarasoff. On appeal, the Tarasoff family won the lawsuit.

This is a real case (*Tarasoff v. Board of Regents of the University of California*, 1976). The duty to protect a third party from serious harm became law in California as a result. Many states follow California law, not because they are obliged to but because California courts often set the pace for developing tort law in other states. Now most states have a law that requires psychologists to do something to warn or to protect known third parties from harm. Several questions remain including how to warn or protect in an effective way (wasn't calling the police enough to protect Tarasoff?), and what to do if the third party or parties cannot be identified. This latter case arises when a person has a sexually transmitted disease and engages in anonymous sexual activity with multiple parties. Such cases are complex and should always be discussed with a supervisor.

CASE 7: DUTY TO INFORM WHEN DEALING WITH A MINOR

Matthew, a bright 16-year-old college student, discloses to his counselor that he needs to finish school in a hurry and get on with his life. He is HIV-positive and does not expect to have a long life, particularly because he does not believe in traditional medicine. Matthew also talks about his multiple sex partners all over the region.

The psychologist needs to disclose this information, but to whom? None of the sex partners are known to the psychologist, or apparently to Matthew either. The psychologist has a duty to try to impress on Matthew how dangerous his behavior is to others, not unlike playing Russian roulette. In addition, Matthew is a minor. As such, at the beginning of the counseling, Matthew had to be informed that if he talked about being dangerous to himself or others, his parents would be told. A similar result would follow if a minor client disclosed to the psychologist that she was going to rave parties and using ecstasy on the weekends. This difficult ethical issue needs to be resolved by the site supervisor.

CASE 8: DUTY TO DISCLOSE AND PROTECT THE LIFE OF THE PATIENT

Allen, a college student, has been a client of Dr. Moore's in psychotherapy for acute depression for the past month. Recently he has been talking about how life is not worth living anymore. He has just broken up with his girlfriend of 2 years and is not going to class or taking exams. Dr. Moore asks Allen if he has thought about suicide. Allen replies that suicide is constantly on his mind. He has a plan and a time frame for implementing it. He knows it will be effective in ending his life.

Dr. Moore has a duty to disclose this information and to have Allen placed in an inpatient mental health facility, for involuntary treatment. This action is necessary to save Allen's life. The disclosure may be made to another professional, to Allen's family, or both. Depending on the state, the psychologist may actually do the involuntary commitment and may be legally obligated to do so. As with the previous case, this difficult ethical issue also needs to be resolved by the site supervisor.

CASE 9: AN OBLIGATION TO PROTECT CHILDREN

Gennaro is shadowing a child-protection case worker for part of his practicum. He knows that in the course of his duties, he will see some parts of children's lives that will shock him. He also is well versed in confidentiality issues. He knows that he is not to reveal what he sees or hears and that in this setting this will be a heavy burden at times. Today Gennaro is visiting a home where it has been reported that children are not attending school regularly. Gennaro enters the home with his supervisor and immediately smells pot. To his amazement, his supervisor does not seem to notice. She talks with the children's mother about how important it is to attend school after the mother offers multiple excuses for her children's attendance problems. They leave the home and discuss how it is that parents would not think that going to school is more important than seeing a particular television program or celebrating a birthday. Gennaro does not know what to do.

Gennaro has an obligation to tell his supervisor about the pot odor. Maybe she simply does not recognize it. Confidentiality does not preclude his talking with his supervisor about his observations. It is important for him to do so. Quite possibly the children are living in a harmful environment. Information to keep children safe is not confidential information.

Multiple Roles and Boundary Violations

While you are in your internship setting, it is important to maintain a professional relationship with the clients. When a relationship is both professional and in some way personal, then this is a multiple relationship or a violation of professional boundaries. Standard 3.05, Multiple Relationships, defines a multiple relationship as one in which the primary role is professional and at the same time there is a secondary relationship with either that person or someone closely associated or related to the person. If the secondary role is reasonably expected to "impair the psychologist's objectivity, competence or effectiveness" or where the patient could be exploited or harmed, then the psychologist is not behaving ethically. This is the test to use to determine whether a multiple relationship is unethical. This is a controversial ethical standard. There are thoughtful and principled psychologists who believe that personal relationships with clients can be helpful to the client. Others believe that the potential for harm and exploitation is always present and not easy to catch before it is too late. The question to ask is whether the secondary relationship activity is a result of your own needs or the needs of the client. As a psychology student, however, it is important to monitor your interactions with your clients to be sure that an unethical multiple relationship does not develop. Behaving conservatively means that personal relationships with clients in your practicum setting should be avoided.

CASE 10: BOUNDARY ISSUES WITH A PATIENT

Ingrid's practicum placement is in a mental health treatment facility that specializes in art therapy. She has especially enjoyed working with Rachel, a high school senior. Rachel is applying to colleges for next year. While painting, Ingrid and Rachel spend a great deal of time talking about the life of a college student. They both really like a certain actor, so Rachel asks Ingrid if she'd like to come over to her house on the weekend and they could watch his latest movie. Ingrid is not sure she should accept the invitation but does not know why she feels this way or what to say. Many institutions have a firm rule about no contact being allowed outside the facility or after the course is over. This also means no phone calls, e-mails, texts, or visits that are not strictly work related.

Once Ingrid has spent a social evening with Rachel at her house, she may lose the ability to have a professional relationship with her in the future. This is not as serious for a student as it might be for a professional psychologist, but it is still a boundary issue. Assuming that Ingrid has been therapeutically helpful to Rachel, this shift from a quasi-professional to a friend could be harmful in some subtle way. Friends are not always as accepting of each other's behavior as psychologists are of their clients' behavior. She should tell Rachel that she would like to come over but that she is not allowed to do so by agency and university policy. The student should only have contact with the patient or client in the professional setting of the practicum and under supervision—no contact outside of this or after the practicum is over.

CASE 11: FOLLOWING RULES WITH PATIENTS

Angela has been a practicum student in a children's hospital. She is supervised by a clinical child life specialist. Her role is not only to use play to normalize the environment but also to do some medical play to help the children understand and accept their illness and their medical procedures more fully. Angela is particularly fond of Eric, a 7-year-old who has been in the hospital for 2 months. Eric's parents rarely visit him, because they live in another state. It just so happens that Angela is from the same hometown as Eric. When the semester is over, Angela decides to do volunteer work on this hospital division a few hours a week so she can continue her friendship with Eric. When Eric leaves the hospital to return home, Angela gives him her cell phone number and asks him to check in once in a while.

This sounds like a difficult case because it does not seem that there is a realistic possibility of harm or exploitation here. Angela's interest in Eric is only for Eric to give her a call on occasion, if he would like to. Angela should not follow up on this by initiating the calls herself. Although not obviously unethical, some placement sites may have rules prohibiting students from giving their telephone number to the people they meet there. Students should always check on these rules before acting on this impulse. A conservative and cautious strategy would be to forgo the phone number exchange.

CASE 12: PROHIBITED SEXUAL RELATIONSHIPS

Sophia's practicum placement is on an adolescent and young adult inpatient mental health division in a teaching hospital. She is supervised by a psychologist. Her job is to visit with patients and provide them with recreational activities. As part of her training, she has been able to observe, with the patient's or the parent's permission, some psychological test feedback as well as some therapy sessions. In the course of her practicum, Sophia is smitten by Lance, one of the patients. The chemistry between them is palpable. They decide that as soon as Lance is discharged into outpatient care, they will begin dating. A sexual relationship develops immediately thereafter.

As a psychology student, Sophia should know that this activity is absolutely forbidden. Standard 10.05, Sexual Intimacies With Current Therapy Clients/Patients, makes this clear for psychologists. Students also need to follow this standard. Standard 10.08, Sexual Intimacies With Former Therapy Clients/Patients, prohibits sexual intimacy with former clients for at least 2 years, and then only under "unusual circumstances." This is also known as the "almost never" rule. Standard 10.08 (b) sets forth the factors to be considered in making this post-2-year decision. Note that Standard 10.06, Sexual Intimacies With Relatives or Significant Others of Current Therapy Clients/Patients, extends this prohibition to relatives or significant others of therapy clients. To round out this set of sexual intimacy standards, Standard 10.07, Therapy With Former Sexual Partners, prohibits psychologists from doing psychotherapy with past sexual partners.

Informed Consent

You may be familiar with informed consent to being a participant in a research project. Informed consent is just as important when dealing with psychological treatment including psychotherapy and assessment. The relevant Ethics Code Standard here is 3.10, Informed Consent.

CASE 13: OBTAINING INFORMED CONSENT

Kaja is assisting her psychology supervisor in running a group for high school students who have test anxiety. The students discuss their symptoms and relate to those of others in the group with suggestions and empathy. Kaja tells a neighbor's son to drop in one evening and join the group. He thinks it might be fun and interesting, so he decides to do so. After a few minutes in the group, he becomes afraid that he will have to participate in one way or another and runs out. Clearly, Kaja should not have done anything like this without first discussing it with her supervisor.

Even for group therapy, informed consent is necessary. For a minor, a parent's consent is needed, and the minor must give assent. According to Standard 3.10(a), consent must be obtained after explaining the therapy in reasonably understandable language. The consent is documented (Standard 3.10(d)). A minor needs to be given a careful explanation and have his or her preferences and best interests considered before obtaining parental consent and minor assent, Standard 3.10(b). Standard 10.01(a), Informed Consent to Therapy, outlines all that must be covered in the informed consent including the nature and anticipated course of therapy, the limits of confidentiality, and the opportunity to ask questions and obtain information. Informed consent is also necessary in assessment, as discussed in Standard 9.03, Informed Consent in Assessments.

Assessment

In your placement, you might have access to psychological tests. You might even be asked to assist in administering them to clients. There are often ethical issues in assessment, many of which are outlined in Standard 9, Assessment of the Ethics Code. Some of these are illustrated in the cases that follow.

CASE 14: MAINTAINING TEST SECURITY

As part of her practicum placement and in her psychological testing class, Mirada has learned a little about the Minnesota Multiphasic Personality Inventory—2 Restructured Form (MMPI–2RF) and its scoring. The results, diagnoses of emotional disorders, are interesting to her. She has access to some test forms and a manual scoring template and thinks it would be interesting to give the test to some of her neighbors in the dorm and study the results. Of course, she plans to get the permission of her supervising psychologist first.

There are several ethical issues here in this short vignette. First of all, only qualified users, with a particular level of competence, can administer psychological tests. The MMPI–2RF is a simple test to administer and score but a complicated one to interpret. With diagnosis as the end result of the interpretation, incorrectly derived results can be damaging. Therefore, this test requires the highest level of training to interpret. The psychologist should not have let the student borrow the test. Standard 9.07, Assessment by Unqualified Persons, deals with this issue. In addition, maintaining test security (Standard 9.11) is essential when dealing with psychological tests. Tests lose their reliability and validity when they are indiscriminately exposed to the public.

CASE 15: CONFIDENTIALITY OF TEST RESULTS

Andrew is in a mental health agency for his practicum. His supervisor has let him sit in on the administration of a Stanford–Binet Intelligence Test. He has also been able to watch the test being scored and informed about the results. A woman claiming to be the child's mother approaches Andrew and asks if he knows anything about tests that may have been given to the child. Andrew, feeling quite confident that this is the mother, talks about the test, the scoring, and the results.

Andrew obviously is not qualified to discuss these results with anyone other than his supervisor, even if he were positive that this was the mother, and the custodial parent, of the child. There is a privacy and confidentiality issue here as well as ones of test security and competence. Andrew's offer of information went well beyond the scope of his responsibilities and duties as a practicum student.

CASE 16: ACTING AS A TRANSLATOR

Sarah works in the same agency as Andrew. She double majors in psychology and Spanish. Geraldo, a 14-year-old Latino boy, is brought in for assessment. He does not speak English very well. The psychologist, who assumes that Sarah is fluent in Spanish from her college courses, asks her to translate when she administers the Rorschach inkblots and the Thematic Apperception Test. Sarah does her best, but the emotion-generated rapid speech of Geraldo often leaves her guessing about the meaning of his sentences. Sarah does not want to disappoint the psychologist, from whom she would like a good evaluation, so she does her best and does not qualify her translation.

Sarah means well, but by not saying she is unable to translate accurately, she is doing a disservice to Geraldo and invalidating the results of the tests. It is highly problematic to give a psychological test to someone whose native language is not English and for whom there may not be test norms that apply to the results. Standard 2.05, Delegation to Work to Others, specifically references interpreters. The psychologist is responsible for ensuring that the translation is done with competence. This would be an ethical problem for the psychologist because Sarah is not competent in the use of Spanish for this purpose and knows little about the tests.

Competence

It is mandatory for psychologists to work only in their areas of competence. Standard 2.01, Boundaries of Competence, extends the competency requirement beyond academic skills and knowledge, which are obtained by education and experience to a clear understanding of factors associated with diversity of all types. It is necessary for psychologists to either obtain the education and experience needed to work with diverse populations or to refer clients to those who have this expertise. Standard 2.03, Maintaining Competence, requires psychologists to be up to date in their fields. Most state licensing boards require psychologists to complete continuing education courses to maintain their licenses. These continuing education courses are intended to assist psychologists in maintaining their skills.

CASE 17: REMAINING WITHIN BOUNDARIES OF COMPETENCE

Adam is using his training in applied behavior analysis to work on language skills with Mary, an 8-year-old girl with autism. The child's foster mother, understanding that Adam is a psychology student, asks him for a favor. The child's biological mother needs to get counseling and parenting lessons so that she can regain custody of Mary, and she suggests that perhaps Adam could help in this capacity. Adam has no certifiable counseling skills, although his friends tell him that he a good listener. He could use the extra money.

Counseling the mother is outside Adam's area of competence. He should talk this over with his supervisor so that he knows how to handle similar requests that might arise in the future. Many people think that psychology students have special skills. Had Adam's supervisor assigned him the task of counseling the mother and teaching her about parenting, this may well have been in violation of Standard 2.05, Delegation of Work to Others. This standard requires that psychologists delegating work seek to ensure that the person to whom the work is delegated is competent to perform it and that the person does not have a multiple relationship with the client. This scenario also describes a potential multiple relationship.

An interesting aspect of competence is known as *emotional competence*. Standard 2.06 of the Code, Personal Problems and Conflicts, requires that psychologists who have personal problems that might interfere with their work get professional help and decide if they should continue on or take a break from their work. These problems include such things as illness, stress, and difficult life events.

CASE 18: APPROPRIATE PRACTICUM PLACEMENT

Angela's practicum placement is in a shelter for runaway teenage girls. One of her jobs is to monitor groups for them that deal with reasons for running away and with planning for the future. Some of the girls will return home, some will go to foster homes, and some will enter a program to help them become independent. Angela was particularly interested in this placement because she had a difficult childhood herself with emotionally abusive parents. As a teenager, she had thought many times about running away but did not have the courage or resources to do so. One of the girls in the group tells a story about her life at home that Angela relates to all too well. This story stuck a chord in Angela. Suddenly, she broke down in sobs and ran out of the group.

Angela's supervisor should have interviewed Angela carefully about her background and reasons for wanting to be with this client population before accepting her as a student here. At this time, Angela needs to explain her behavior to her supervisor and ask to be relieved of this job. Angela's reaction may also have been triggered by events in her life outside of the practicum. She should not have been placed with this vulnerable group of girls so close to her own age. Angela should explore with her academic supervisor other tasks or placements she can have to fulfill her academic requirement.

Supervision

There are many ethical issues in the supervision of internship students. One that has already been discussed is the Ethics Code Standard that relates to delegating tasks to others. Following are several more.

CASE 19: EXPLOITATION AND INAPPROPRIATE RELATIONSHIPS

Laurel loved her placement in a program for binge eating disorders. She was part of a regular meeting, assisting the group leader and her supervisor, a licensed psychologist. After each group session, Laurel and her supervisor would meet and go over the events of the group. The supervision meeting almost always began with some comment by her supervisor on Laurel's personal appearance. This made Laurel so uncomfortable that she started wearing baggy clothes and no makeup to her practicum. Yet when she did this, his comments on her appearance became an even more prominent focus of the meetings. Soon, despite Laurel's efforts to turn the conversation around, her supervisor began asking Laurel about her weekend activity and whether she had a boyfriend. The meeting setting changed as well. They went from meeting in his office, to a coffee shop, to a restaurant for dinner. Sometimes Laurel felt it was necessary to pay the dinner bill for both of them. Her supervisor did not object. Laurel felt that this was inappropriate but did not know what to do and especially did not want to run the risk of a bad evaluation.

Fortunately, Laurel had an academic supervisor and a small group of other practicum students to ask for advice. Two Code standards are particularly applicable here. Standard 3.08, Exploitative Relationships, states that psychologists may not exploit supervisees. Arguably, Laurel is being exploited when her supervisor accepts her willingness to pay the bill. Aside from this, he may be a lonely individual who enjoys Laurel's company, even though Laurel does not enjoy his but is afraid to say no. Is this behavior a slippery slope? Standard 7.07, Sexual Relationships With Students and Supervisees, prohibits this relationship from becoming sexual. This is also a good example of the abuse of power by the supervisor, a clear violation again of Standard 3.05, Multiple Relationships. In addition to the ethical issues raised here, her supervisor's behavior may qualify as sexual harassment under federal guidelines describing the hostile work environment.

Another important ethical principle is that supervisors have an obligation with respect to prompt and appropriate feedback on a supervisee's performance.

CASE 20: APPROPRIATE SUPERVISION AND FEEDBACK

Howard is in a practicum placement that deals with domestic violence. Services include a group home, classes to help victims get back on their feet, a support group, and a hotline. Howard particularly enjoys working on the hotline. He has little training for the job because his supervisor feels that Howard has an intuitive focus and understanding of his work. Howard's general orientation to these situations is that women who have been abused should fight back. He has been heard to say on the hotline, "Get the gun away from him and shoot him!" and "Cut the balls off that guy while he's asleep." Howard's supervisor knows that Howard is responding inappropriately to the women who call in, even though the comments Howard comes up with are meant to be funny.

Standard 7.06, Assessing Student and Supervisee Performance, requires Howard's supervisor to give him feedback on his work in a "timely and specific process." It also requires the supervisor to evaluate Howard on his actual performance. Howard is behaving inappropriately, and the supervisor needs to meet with him regularly and review his work. It may be necessary to remove him from the assignment. It also appears that this is a violation of Standard 2.05, Delegation of Work to Others, because without specific training, Howard is not competent to do these jobs.

What to Do If You Become Aware of an Ethical Violation

The APA Ethics Code is quite specific about what to do if you discover that a psychologist is violating the Code. Standard 1.04, Informal Resolution of Ethical Violations, requires that if one sees any possible ethical violation by another, it is brought to the attention of the alleged violator unless confidentiality rights are involved. If after this informal attempt to resolve the problem fails, then Standard 1.05, Reporting Ethical Violations requires a psychologist to report the behavior to a state licensing board or other authority. In doing so, the psychologist must balance this obligation against any harm that is done or any confidentiality rights of a client. You should discuss this with your onsite or academic supervisor and follow their lead. Do not deal with possible ethics violations on your own.

Conclusion

This chapter has covered some of the most frequently cited ethical issues and dilemmas that arise in practicum and internship settings. Other areas covered by the Code that should be of particular interest to students are the Section 7, Education and Training, and Section 8, Research and Publication. It is important to read the entire Code to put them in context.

The references include two psychology ethics textbooks (Koocher & Keith-Spiegel, 2008; Pope & Vasquez, 2011), as well as four specialized books in research ethics (Kimmel, 2007), industrial and organizational ethics (Lowman, 2006), forensic practice (Bush, Connell, & Denney, 2006), and cross-cultural counseling (Gerstein, Heppner, Aegisdottir, Leung, & Norsworthy, 2009) The book by Fisher (2013) is a thorough and critical explanation of the 2010 Amendments to the 2002 Ethics Code written by the chair of the revision task force. The Canadian Psychological Association Code of Ethics (2000) has some interesting similarities and differences from the APA Code.

References

American Association for Marriage and Family Therapy. (2012). *AAMFT code of ethics.* Washington, DC: Author. Retrieved from http://www.aamft.org/imis15/content/legal_ethics/Code_of_ethics.aspx

American Counseling Association. (2005). *ACA code of ethics*. Alexandria, VA: Author. Retrieved from http://www.counseling.org/Resources/aca-Code-of-ethics.pdf

American Psychiatric Association. (2013). *The principles of medical ethics with annotations especially applicable to psychiatry, 2013 edition*. Retrieved from http://www.psychiatry.org/practice/ethics/resources-standards

American Psychological Association. (2010). *Ethical standards of psychologists and code of conduct (2002, Amended June 1, 2010)*. Retrieved from http://www.apa.org/ethics/Code/index.aspx

Beauchamp, T. L., & Childress, J. F. (2009). *Principles of biomedical ethics* (6th ed.). New York, NY: Oxford University Press.

Bush, S. S., Connell, M. A., & Denney, R. L. (2006). *Ethical practice in forensic psychology*. Washington, DC: American Psychological Association.

Canadian Psychological Association. (2000). *Canadian code of ethics for psychologists* (3rd ed.). Retrieved from http://www.cpa.ca/docs/File/Ethics/cpa_code_2000_eng_jp_jan2014.pdf

Center for the Study of Ethics in the Professions. (2013). *Codes of ethics collections*. Illinois Institute of Technology. Retrieved from http://ethics.iit.edu/ecodes

Fisher, C. B. (2013). *Decoding the ethics code: A practical guide for psychologists* (3rd ed.). Thousand Oaks, CA: Sage.

Gerstein, L. H., Heppner, P. P., Aegisdottir, S., Leung, S. A., & Norsworthy, K. L. (2009). *International handbook of cross-cultural counseling*. Thousand Oaks, CA: Sage.

Kimmel, A. J. (2007). *Ethical issues in behavioral research* (2nd ed.). Malden, MA: Blackwell.

Koocher, G., & Keith-Spiegel, P. (2008). *Ethics in psychology and the mental health professions: Standards and cases* (3rd ed.). New York, NY: Oxford University Press.

Lowman, R. L. (Ed.). (2006). *The ethical practice of psychology in organizations* (2nd ed.). Washington, DC: American Psychological Association. http://dx.doi.org/10.1037/11386-000

National Association of Social Workers. (2008). *Code of ethics*. Washington, DC: Author. Retrieved from http://www.naswdc.org/pubs/Code/default.asp

Pope, K. S. (2013). *Ethical standards & practice guidelines for assessment, therapy, counseling, & forensic practice*. Retrieved from http://www.kspope.com/ethcodes/index.php

Pope, K. S., & Vasquez, M. T. (2011). *Ethics in psychotherapy and counseling* (4th ed.). San Francisco, CA: Jossey-Bass. http://dx.doi.org/10.1002/9781118001875

Tarasoff v. Board of Regents of the University of California, 551 P.2d 334 (Cal.Sup.Ct.1976).

Amanda S. Cherry, Noel J. Jacobs, Timothy S. Thornberry Jr., and Stephen R. Gillaspy

Psychopathology and Use of the *Diagnostic and Statistical Manual of Mental Disorders*

5

T he purpose of this chapter is to provide a brief summary and review of diagnostic terms that you may encounter in your courses and as you read patient files during your practicum experiences. We start with a brief history of diagnostic systems and then proceed to a review of the *Diagnostic and Statistical Manual of Mental Disorders* (DSM), which is intended to provide a quick reference to general diagnostic criteria so that you will be able to better understand the diagnosed disorders of the patients with whom you come into contact. Additionally, this overview will assist you in understanding the criteria patients meet to reach a diagnosis for various disorders. Finally, the conclusion of the chapter allows you to test your clinical judgment with two case vignettes.

http://dx.doi.org/10.1037/14672-005
Your Practicum in Psychology: A Guide for Maximizing Knowledge and Competence, Second Edition, J. R. Matthews and C. E. Walker (Editors)

Diagnostic Systems—
A History

Appropriate classifications and diagnoses are imperative for understanding patients, stimulating research, providing guidelines for empirically supported treatments, and obtaining reimbursement for services. One of the first documented attempts in classification of mental disorders was the 1840 census, which included one single category of "idiocy/insanity." This was then expanded to seven categories for the 1880 census: mania, melancholia, monomania, paresis, dementia, dipsomania, and epilepsy (American Psychiatric Association, 2014a). However, one of the earliest guides for diagnoses, *Statistical Manual for the Use of Institutions for the Insane*, was developed in 1917 by the "Committee on Statistics," which was formed from the National Commission on Mental Hygiene and a group now known as the American Psychiatric Association (Grob, 1991). During World War II, there was a major shift in the role of psychiatrist from mental institutions to assessing and treating soldiers. During this period of war, the Medical 203 was developed as a classification system issued as a "War Department Technical Bulletin" under the Auspices of the Surgeon General (Houts, 2000). The committee involved in the development of the Medical 203 was chaired by a brigadier general and psychiatrist, William C. Menninger. In addition to chairing this committee, Menninger led a group of his colleagues in forming the Group for Advancement of Psychiatry (Houts, 2000). The means to classify mental health disorders further evolved in 1949 when the World Health Organization (WHO) published the sixth edition of the *International Statistical Classification of Diseases* (*ICD–6;* 2010), which included for the first time a section on mental disorders (American Psychiatric Association, 2014a). However, the *ICD–6* was designed for international application, and therefore after this event an American Psychiatric Association committee was empowered to develop a version specific to the United States as well as to standardize a system for classification. Thus, in 1950, the committee undertook the process of reviewing and consulting to compile the *DSM*. The initial version of the *DSM* (*DSM–I*) was approved in 1951 and published in 1952. Since that time, the *DSM* has undergone a process of evolution with each edition.

DSM–I contained 106 diagnostic categories. This initial edition was not well received because of its subjective nature. Therefore, the *DSM–II*, released in 1968, had the aim of diagnostic accuracy and shifted to a more distinct disease model. The major criticism of the second edition was the *DSM*'s dehumanization of patients because it was viewed as treating conditions and not individuals. Then the *DSM–III*, released in 1980, was geared toward improving epidemiological accuracy and diagnostic validity, which became a guideline for insurance and reimbursement for services. With the revised third edition, classifications of disorders were given to correspond with diagnostic coding of the WHO's *ICD*, which is the official medical coding system used within the United States. The *DSM–IV* (American Psychiatric Association, 1994) and *DSM–IV–Text Revision* (American Psychiatric Association, 2000) continued to evolve with responses to epidemiology and cultural diversity, as well as continue to correspond with the *ICD* codes.

As the authors of the *DSM–IV* attempted previously, the authors of the *DSM–5* have designed the book to give the clinician a conceptual guide and a tool book for greater understanding and practical application. Their goal in this new edition is to synthesize the latest medical and behavioral research with the existing understanding of mental disorders as it has been applied to clinical, pharmaceutical, legal, and social work with individuals. As research and clinical practice have evolved over t ne, new understandings (and new questions) have led to successive editions of this manual seen by many as the "bible" of mental health. However, the authors of each new edition try to make changes that improve not just the utility of the manual itself but also the understanding of mental illness as a whole. This edition was organized as a parallel diagnostic code manual to the medical diagnostic manual titled the *International Classification of Diseases, 10th Revision* (*ICD–10*). Additionally, the authors of the *DSM–5* have reorganized the groupings of disorders and redefined and renamed other disorders in new ways to "stimulate new clinical perspectives" (American Psychiatric Association, 2013, p. xli). You will find, if you are somewhat versed in the categories and disorder descriptions of the *DSM–IV* already, that the new manual attempts to give more explicit consideration, even when brief, to developmental experience, cultural influence, and risk factors in the development and expression of emotional and behavioral difficulties. One of the most obvious differences you will notice between the previous and current editions is the elimination of the "axes" (used to differentiate primary psychological disorders from mental retardation, personality disorders, and primary health diagnoses) into a combined, nonaxial list followed by a designation of important contextual or interpersonal aspects of the difficulties that the patient is facing.

The *DSM* has undergone revisions into four editions since World War II and has become a standard classification system used by psychiatrists, other physicians, and mental health providers. It describes the essential features and full range of mental health disorders. The most current version, the *DSM–5*, was released in May 2013. The current version, like its predecessors, has been challenged to appropriately define and classify mental disorders.

Although this chapter focuses on *DSM–5* definitions of mental health disorders, one should be aware that other classification systems exist that will likely have a growing impact on psychological practice, conceptualization, and research. Along with *DSM–5*, there exists the previously mentioned *ICD*, now in its 10th revision (*ICD–10*) with the 11th revision due in 2017. The American Psychological Association (2009) offers a comparison of the *DSM* and *ICD*. *ICD* is a product of the WHO and was the culmination of an international effort from its inception. In contrast, *DSM–III* was initially characterized by minimal international participation and was notably different from its then-companion *ICD–8*. However, these different coding systems have become more similar with subsequent iterations and increasing collaboration between the two organizations.

Although it has been suggested that the *DSM* will eventually be unjustifiable to maintain as a separate diagnostic system from *ICD*, it is also suggested that *DSM* will continue to be useful because of its inclusion of details of mental health disorders that will never be incorporated in the *ICD* (American Psychological Association, 2009). The most recent edition of the *DSM* attempts to maintain its utility in a health care system that uses *ICD* codes for billing and reimbursement purposes. According to the *DSM–5*'s website (American Psychiatric Association, 2014b), *DSM–5* provides a dual code system, including *ICD–9* and *ICD–10* codes with *DSM–5* diagnoses, in an effort to provide sufficient information needed to assign *ICD–10* diagnoses to patients. It is also noteworthy that *ICD* and *DSM* are intended for different audiences, with *ICD* focusing on maximizing clinical utility for nonspecialist medical providers (Stein, Lund, & Nesse, 2013). Thus, both systems will likely maintain some utility in their respective professional groups. Psychologists are considered to be included in this nonspecialist medical providers group and therefore are required to use *ICD* codes under the Affordable Care Act for insurance reimbursement purposes.

In addition to *DSM* and *ICD*, the National Institute of Mental Health (NIMH) developed the Research Domain Criteria (RDoC) system in an attempt to find the basic, universal components of disordered thought and behavior and bolster research connecting clinical symptoms with underlying neurobiological mechanisms (Doherty & Owen, 2014; Stein et al., 2013). The RDoC system conceptualizes mental disorders as disorders of neurocircuitry with a biopsychosocial influence. It is hoped that the RDoC system will stimulate research that can help bridge the gap in our understanding between what we observe in the clinic and the biological and physiological substrates from which these symptoms emerge (Stein et al., 2013). At present, NIMH is encouraging RDoC research to remain independent of *ICD* and *DSM* work to minimize restrictions in research direction (Doherty & Owen, 2014).

Stein et al. (2013) pointed out that all three of these classification systems have their benefits and drawbacks and that a true understanding of mental health concerns, an understanding that considers the contexts of global and public mental health, heterogeneous presentations, and multicausality, will require an understanding of all three of these systems. They posited that for one to gain a better understanding of psychopathology and its treatment, one must analyze the complex, multilevel mechanisms of mental disorders emphasized by all of these classification systems.

Neurodevelopmental Disorders

The group of conditions with an onset during childhood is qualified as neurodevelopmental disorders. This qualification is primarily due to the nature of the disorders' manifestations early in development and may include developmental deficits involving personal, social, academic, and occupational functioning. Within this group, the range of developmental deficits can vary from global impairments in social skills or intellectual functioning to very specific limitations in learning or control of executive functioning. Included within this category are disorders characterized by deficits in intellectual, communication, relational, motor, and learning abilities.

For example, Intellectual Disability is one disorder within this group that is characterized by generalized deficits in mental abilities, including reasoning, problem solving, planning, abstract thinking, judgment, academic learning, and experiential learning. The resulting impairment in adaptive functioning of this disorder limits the individual in attaining standards of personal independence and social responsibility in one or more areas of daily living (e.g., communication, social, academic, occupational functioning).

Another disorder in this group, Global Developmental Delay, which can result in similar impairments, is diagnosed when expected developmental milestones are not met in several areas of functioning. This diagnosis is often appropriate for individuals who are unable to undergo standardized assessments of functioning, including young children who are not old enough for such tests. Although intellectual disability occurs in all races and cultures, it is important to consider the individual's cultural, ethnic, and linguistic background when assessing for such a disability.

Disorders defined by communication difficulties also fall under the umbrella of neurodevelopmental disorders due to onset early in life and possible lifelong functional impairments. These include language disorder (deficits in the development and use of language), speech-sound disorder (deficits in the development and use of speech), and social (pragmatic) communication disorder (deficits in the development and use of social communication). Childhood-Onset Fluency Disorder is also clustered with these communication disorders and is characterized by disturbances in the motor production and normal fluency of speech.

Persistent deficits in social communication and interaction across multiple settings characterize autistic spectrum disorder. These deficits can include problems in social reciprocity, nonverbal communication, and skills in developing and maintaining relationships. In addition to these deficits in social communication, restricted, repetitive patterns of behavior, interests, or activities are required to meet criteria for this disorder. It is important to consider cultural differences in norms for social interactions, nonverbal communication, and relationships. However, individuals with autism spectrum disorder are diagnosed due to being markedly impaired against the norms of their individual culture. Various specifiers are used to individualize and clearly communicate individuals with this disorder.

Another neurodevelopmental disorder, Attention-Deficit/Hyperactivity Disorder (ADHD), is characterized by impairments in attention, disorganization, hyperactivity–impulsivity, or a combination of these. Examples of problems in inattention and disorganization include difficulty staying on task, losing things, and seeming not to listen, whereas examples of hyperactivity–impulsivity include being overly active, fidgeting, difficulty staying seated, interrupting others, and difficulty waiting turns. It is also expected that these symptoms are to be present at levels excessive of age and developmental level. This disorder, although typically first appearing in childhood, can persist into adulthood with resulting impairments in social, academic, and occupational functioning.

Neurodevelopmental disorders involving deficits in motor abilities include developmental coordination disorder, which is defined by deficits in acquiring and executing coordinated motor skills. Individuals with this disorder demonstrate clumsiness and slowness or inaccuracy of motor skills, which result in interference in activities of daily living. Individuals with repetitive, purposeless, and seemingly driven motor behaviors that result in impairment in functioning are diagnosed with Stereotypic Movement Disorder. Examples of such behavior include body rocking, hand flapping, head banging, and self-biting. In contrast, individuals with motor or vocal tics (sudden, rapid, recurrent, nonrhythmic, stereotyped motor movements or vocalizations) are diagnosed within tic disorder diagnoses. Tourette disorder is diagnosed when both motor and vocal tics are present for at least a year. Persistent Motor or Vocal Tic Disorder is given when only motor tics or vocal tics are present. Race, ethnicity, and culture may affect how tic disorders are perceived and managed by a family and community, which can then influence patterns of help seeking or acceptance of treatment choices.

Finally, among the neurodevelopmental disorders that entail deficits in learning abilities is Specific Learning Disability. This diagnosis is given when an individual experiences deficits in the ability to perceive or process information efficiently and accurately in a specific area. As a result, the individual's performance in the affected academic area is below average for age, level of education, or what is expected given the individual's intellectual abilities. This diagnosis typically manifests early in the years of formal schooling and continues to cause impairment in learning skills in reading, writing, or math (or a combination of these) throughout schooling. Assessment for specific learning disabilities should take into account the linguistic and cultural context of the individual in addition to the individual's educational and learning history in the original culture and language.

Schizophrenia Spectrum and Other Psychotic Disorders

Key features of diagnoses within the schizophrenia spectrum include positive symptoms (delusions, hallucinations, disorganized thinking, grossly disorganized or abnormal motor behavior) and negative symptoms. The *positive symptoms* of schizophrenia are referred to as positive because their presentation is an excess in or distortion of the individual's normal functioning; *negative symptoms* refer to a decrease in or loss of normal functions. Positive symptoms of schizophrenia are characterized by disturbances in thinking, perceptions of reality, and disorganized or abnormal behaviors. *Delusions* are defined as fixed beliefs that are both false and unresponsive to change despite evidence against these thoughts. Common content themes of delusions include persecutory, referential (i.e., thinking certain environmental cues, such as a song or a passage from a book, are directed at the individual), grandiose, erotomanic, nihilistic, and somatic delusions. *Hallucinations* are perceived experiences that occur with the absence of an external stimulus. These experiences are vivid, clear, and lack voluntary control. However, within some cultural contexts, hallucinations may be seen as a normal part of a religious experience. The presence of disorganized thinking is most commonly assumed from the individual's speech as evidenced by switching topics rapidly (derailment or loose associations), responding in a tangential manner, or so disorganized that the person can hardly be comprehended (e.g., word salad). Grossly disorganized or abnormal behavior can include catatonia (i.e., unresponsiveness or stupor) and can be manifest in a variety of ways and intensities. Finally, negative symptoms within the schizophrenia spectrum are characterized by mental abilities that the patient has lost or abilities that the patient can no longer perform. Negative symptoms include diminished emotional expression, including flattened affect, lack of eye contact, and intonation in speech or nonverbal actions that give emphasis to speech; avolition, which is a decrease in motivation to complete self-initiated purposeful activities; alogia, which is a diminished speech output; anhedonia, or decreased ability to perceive pleasure from positive stimuli; and asociality with a lack of interest in social interactions.

Delusional Disorder and Catatonia are two conditions defined by abnormalities limited to one domain of psychosis (e.g., delusions and grossly disorganized or abnormal behavior). Brief Psychotic Disorder, Schizophreniform Disorder, and Schizophrenia are primarily differentiated by duration in the abnormalities. Brief Psychotic Disorder has a duration of more than 1 day but remits by 1 month; Schizophreniform Disorder has a duration of less than 6 months; and schizophrenia lasts for at least 6 months, and generally much longer, with at least 1 month of having active symptoms.

Mood-Related Disorders

In regard to the following two sections of the *DSM–5*, Bipolar and Related Disorders and Depressive Disorders, it is imperative to understand the criteria required for meeting Manic, Hypomanic, and Major Depressive Episodes.

A manic episode is characterized by a distinct period of abnormally and persistently elevated, overly expansive mood, as well as abnormally persistent and increased goal-directed activity or energy with a duration of 1 week or longer. Three or more of the following symptoms must also be present: inflated self-esteem or grandiosity, decreased need for sleep, more talkative or pressured speech, racing thoughts, distractibility, psychomotor agitation, and high-risk behaviors. A Manic episode causes significant impairment in social or occupational functioning and often requires hospitalization.

A Hypomanic Episode differs from a manic episode in duration and severity. A Hypomanic Episode must last for at least 4 consecutive days and does not cause marked impairment in social or occupational functioning sufficient to require hospitalization.

A Major Depressive Episode has a minimum duration of 2 weeks and includes five or more of the following symptoms: depressed mood, marked or diminished interests or pleasure in activities, appetite disturbance, sleep disturbance, fatigue or loss of energy, diminished ability to think or concentrate, and recurrent thoughts of death or suicide. These symptoms also must be severe enough to cause significant impairment in social and occupational functioning.

Bipolar and Related Disorders

To meet criteria for Bipolar I disorder, full criteria for at least one manic episode must be met. Although it is not necessary to meet criteria for a major depressive episode for a diagnosis of Bipolar I disorder, most individuals with this disorder experience major depressive episodes. In contrast, the diagnosis of Bipolar II disorder requires the experience of at least one episode of hypomania and at least one episode of major depression during the person's lifetime. Because of their significant mood instability, individuals with this disorder often experience significant impairment in academic, work, and social functioning. For adults experiencing at least 2 years' duration of hypomanic and depressive symptoms (1 full year for children) without meeting full criteria for a mania, hypomania, or major depressive episode, a diagnosis of cyclothymic disorder can be given.

Depressive Disorders

The presence of sad, empty, or irritable mood is the common feature of the depressive disorders, which differ in terms of their duration, timing, and presumed etiology. The mood disturbance component of depressive disorders is accompanied by somatic and cognitive changes that significantly interfere with tasks of daily functioning. Major depressive disorder is diagnosed with change in affect, cognition, and neurovegetative functions occurring during a discrete episode of 2 weeks or longer. Dysthymia, in contrast, is an appropriate diagnosis for a more chronic and persistent form of depressive disorder that has mood disturbance with a duration of at least 2 years in adults and 1 year for children.

Although Bereavement is not included in the Depressive Disorders Category, it is often necessary to distinguish it from Major Depressive Disorder. It is helpful to remember that with bereavement, the predominant feelings are of loss and emptiness, whereas in Major Depressive Disorder, depressed mood and inability to anticipate happiness or pleasure are predominant. In addition, grief is often experienced in waves, whereas depression is more likely persistent and not tied to any specific thoughts or reminders.

Within the depressive disorders category, two new diagnoses were added to the *DSM–5*. One is the Disruptive Mood Dysregulation Disorder which is characterized by severe and recurrent temper outbursts as well as chronic and severe irritability. The recurrent temper tantrums must be inconsistent with the developmental level of the individual and have a frequency of three or more times per week. The other, Premenstrual Dysphoric Disorder, is characterized by mood disturbance present in the week before menses that weaken or diminish the week after menses.

Anxiety Disorders

This group of disorders is characterized by excessive fear, anxiety, and related behavioral problems. The anxious person has an emotional response to a real or perceived threat, either present or expected to occur. Many of these disorders can overlap; however, they also can differ in the objects or situations that elicit fear, anxiety, avoidance behavior, and associated cognitions. Anxiety disorders are different from developmentally normative fears in that they are excessive or persist beyond what is deemed appropriate and cause significant distress or impairment in social, academic, occupational, or other functioning. The patient may not recognize that the fear is disproportional to the stressor, so it may be up to the clinician to decide if the patient's fear is excessive given the patient's thoughts, behaviors, and cultural context.

A few disorders previously categorized under disorders of infancy and childhood have been moved to the anxiety disorders classification because it has been recognized that these disorders can occur across the life span. For example, separation anxiety disorder includes excessive fear related to separation from home or major attachment figures. The patient may fear that his or her attachment figure will be harmed or lost or that some event will occur with the patient (e.g., getting lost or kidnapped) that will prevent contact with the attachment figure. Actual or anticipated separation from the attachment figure may also lead to somatic complaints, including headaches, stomachaches, and other physical symptoms. Separation anxiety disorder is the most prevalent anxiety disorder in children under 12 years of age, with prevalence decreasing with age. The onset of the disorder can occur in adulthood as long as the fear is not transient.

Selective mutism is characterized by consistent failure to speak in social situations during which one is expected to speak. The patient is able to speak in other situations (i.e., the disturbance is not the result of a communication disorder) and has sufficient knowledge of and comfort with the required spoken language. Selective mutism is often associated with social anxiety disorder or other anxiety disorders.

Specific phobia consists of fear or anxiety related to or avoidance of certain objects or situations. In children, this fear may manifest itself as crying, tantrums, freezing, or clinging behaviors. The phobic stimulus must consistently produce fear, anxiety, or avoidance; be persistent (i.e., occur for at least 6 months); and cause significant distress or impairment. Possible phobic situations and objects vary and can include animals; the natural environment (e.g., storms, heights, water); blood, injection, and injury (e.g., needles, medical procedures); situational contexts (e.g., planes, elevators, enclosed spaces); and other stimuli (e.g., loud noises, costumes, choking or vomiting). Many patients have multiple phobias.

Individuals with social anxiety disorder exhibit fear or anxiety in one or more social situations varying from daily activities (e.g., conversing, meeting new people, eating or drinking in public) to particular events (e.g., giving a speech). In children, this fear must interfere with interactions with peer as well as with adults. The fear relates to the patient's thinking she or he will behave in a way that others will evaluate negatively, leading to humiliation, embarrassment, or rejection. Because of this fear, patients may avoid situations or endure them with intense discomfort. People from Asian cultures (e.g., Japan, Korea) may develop a fear that they will make other people feel uncomfortable rather than fear of personal discomfort.

Panic Disorder consists of recurrent, unexpected panic attacks followed by either fear of additional attacks or significant behavioral change related to attacks. A panic attack is an abrupt surge of fear or discomfort that peaks in minutes. These attacks can follow calm or anxious emotional states and can include increased heart rate, palpitations, sweating, shaking, difficulty breathing, chest pain, abdominal upset, dizziness, numbness or tingling, derealization, depersonalization, and fear of losing control or dying. Patients can interpret these symptoms as significant health concerns, leading to unnecessary hospitalizations, emergency room visits, absences from work or school, and, ultimately, unemployment or attrition. Panic attacks can be added as a specifier to any *DSM–5* disorder. Rates of panic disorder are significantly higher in American Indian populations, followed by non-Latino whites. Females are twice as likely to be affected.

Agoraphobia includes excessive fear or anxiety about situations in which the individual perceives it may be difficult to escape or get help should paniclike or other incapacitating or embarrassing symptoms arise. This fear leads to avoidance of such situations (e.g., public transportation, open or enclosed spaces, crowds, other places outside of the home). At its most extreme, agoraphobia may render people completely homebound and dependent on others.

When individuals experience excessive, difficult-to-control anxiety and worry about multiple events or activities, they may meet diagnostic criteria for generalized anxiety disorder. The subject of worry can vary (e.g., work-related responsibilities, health, finances, family members, school). Affected individuals may experience restlessness, fatigue, difficulty concentrating, irritability, muscle tension, or sleep difficulties. People with generalized anxiety may also display headaches, muscle soreness, sweating, nausea, and diarrhea. Culturally, generalized anxiety disorder tends to occur more in individuals of European descent and individuals from developed countries.

Obsessive–Compulsive and Related Disorders

This group of diagnoses is characterized by obsessions (i.e., recurrent and persistent thoughts, urges, or images that are intrusive and unwanted) and compulsions (e.g., repetitive behaviors or mental acts that the individual feels driven to perform). Obsessive–Compulsive Disorder (OCD) is characterized by the presence of both obsessions and compulsions, which are time-consuming and/or cause distress or impairment in social, occupational, or other types of functioning. OCD occurs worldwide; however, cultural context may shape the content of the obsessions and compulsions. Other presentations of OCD are characterized by either cognitive factors or recurrent body-focused repetitive behaviors. Of those characterized by cognitive symptoms, Body Dysmorphic Disorder includes perceived defects or flaws in physical appearance, whereas Hoarding Disorder includes the perceived need to save possessions. Trichotillomania (hair pulling) and excoriation (skin picking) are characterized by recurrent, body-focused behaviors.

Trauma- and Stressor-Related Disorders

This category of disorders includes those in which exposure to a traumatic or stressful event is part of the diagnostic criteria. The five primary disorders in this category represent a broad range of symptoms and are reflective of the variable psychological distress response individuals can experience following exposure to a traumatic or stressful event. These symptoms include anxiety- or fear-based symptoms, anhedonic and dysphoric symptoms, externalizing angry and aggressive symptoms, and dissociative symptoms. Reactive Attachment Disorder and Disinhibited Social Engagement Disorder require social neglect or the absence of adequate caregiving during childhood as a diagnostic requirement. Although these two disorders share a common etiology, the expression of symptoms is quite different and distinct, with attachment disorder characterized by internalizing symptoms such as depressive symptoms and withdrawn behavior and disinhibited social engagement disorder characterized by disinhibition and externalizing behavior.

Specifically, Reactive Attachment Disorder occurs in infancy or early childhood and is characterized by an absent or grossly under-developed attachment between the child and caregiving adults. When distressed, these children make no significant attempts to obtain comfort or support from caregivers and do not respond to comforting efforts of caregivers. Because of their compromised emotion regulation capacity, these children will display unexplained episodes of negative emotions of fear, sadness, or irritability.

Disinhibited Social Engagement Disorder is characterized by a pattern of behavior that involves culturally inappropriate, overly familiar behavior with relative strangers, such as approaching and interacting with unfamiliar adults or willingness to go off with an unfamiliar adult. This disorder may co-occur with developmental delays, especially cognitive and language delays, and other signs of severe neglect, such as malnutrition.

Posttraumatic stress disorder (PTSD) is characterized by exposure to actual or threatened death, serious injury, or sexual violence and the presence of the following: intense and intrusive memories of the traumatic event; persistent avoidance of stimuli associated with the traumatic event; negative alterations in cognitions and mood associated with the traumatic event; and increased arousal and reactivity associated with the traumatic event. The duration of these symptoms is more than 1 month and results in clinically significant distress or impairment in social, occupational, or other important areas of functioning. There is an increased suicide risk for individuals who have experienced traumatic events such as childhood abuse. Also, PTSD is associated with suicidal ideation and suicide attempts.

The diagnostic features of Acute Stress Disorder are similar to those of PTSD, but the duration of symptoms is 3 days to 1 month after exposure to one or more traumatic events. It is estimated that half of individuals who develop PTSD initially experienced an acute stress disorder.

Adjustment Disorders are characterized by emotional or behavioral symptoms in response to an identifiable stressor(s) occurring within 3 months of the onset of the stressor(s). Symptoms result in marked distress beyond what is expected and cause impairment in social, occupational, or other important areas of functioning.

Dissociative Disorders

Dissociative disorders include disruptive symptoms related to one's consciousness, memory, identity, emotion, perception, body representation, motor control, and behavior. These symptoms may be experienced as losses of continuity in subjective experience, such as a loss of identity, depersonalization (i.e., subjective experience of detachment or observing one's own speech and actions; an "out of body experience"), and derealization. They can also occur as an inability to access information, such as amnesia. Dissociative disorders often occur after a trauma. Before diagnosing these disorders, it is important that the clinician determine whether symptoms occur as part of culturally acceptable practices (e.g., religious experience, childhood pretend play) or due to substance use or a co-occurring medical condition (e.g., complex partial seizures).

Dissociative Identity Disorder includes a disruption of identity in which an individual has at least two distinct personality states. This disruption can affect a person's sense of self, sense of agency or control, affect, behavior, consciousness, memory, perception, cognition, and sensorimotor functioning. In children, it is important to ensure that symptoms are not better accounted for by fantasy play. People with dissociative identity disorder may also experience dissociative fugues in which they "come to" in a location without knowing how they arrived there. Symptoms can be influenced by cultural factors and may present as unexplained neurological symptoms or perceived demonic or spiritual possession.

Dissociative Amnesia is characterized by forgetting of important personal information, usually related to traumatic or stressful events. These symptoms are more severe than ordinary forgetfulness and can relate to isolated incidents or generalize to one's entire identity or life history. Dissociative amnesia can also occur with fugue. Onset for generalized amnesia is usually sudden, but it may be more difficult to assess for selective amnesias because the patient does not realize or report forgotten events. Dissociated memories may be regained with time and removal from the traumatic situation. However, recovered memories may lead to further distress, suicidality, or posttraumatic symptoms.

Depersonalization includes the experience of unreality, detachment, or outwardly observing one's own thoughts, feelings, sensations, body, or actions (e.g., "out-of-body experience"). Derealization relates to the experience of unreality or detachment from one's surroundings (e.g., individuals or objects appear distorted). In depersonalization-derealization disorder, the affected individual may experience either or both of these symptoms. During these dissociative experiences, the individual can still differentiate between perception and reality but may feel "in a fog" or emotionally numb. Although approximately half of adults have experienced transient depersonalization or derealization symptoms, relatively few meet full criteria for this disorder.

Somatic Symptoms and Related Disorders

This grouping of disorders reflects another new category in *DSM–V*, with all disorders sharing a common feature: the prominence of somatic symptoms associated with significant distress and impairment. Individuals with these disorders may or may not have an actual medical diagnosis and are typically encountered in primary care and other medical settings.

Somatic Symptom Disorder is characterized by one or more somatic complaints that are distressing and result in significant disruption to daily life. Additionally, individuals must display abnormal thoughts, feelings, and behaviors in response to these symptoms, such as disproportionate and persistent thoughts about the seriousness of their symptoms, persistently high level of anxiety about their health or symptoms, or engage in excessive time and energy devoted to their symptoms or health concerns. In individuals with this disorder, it is less about the specific symptoms and more about how the individual presents and interprets his or her symptoms.

Another newly described disorder, Illness Anxiety Disorder, has preoccupation with having or acquiring a serious illness for at least 6 months as a central feature. Individuals with this disorder also have a high level of anxiety about health and either perform excessive health-related behaviors or display maladaptive avoidance.

Conversion Disorder (Functional Neurological Symptom Disorder) includes one or more symptoms of altered voluntary motor or sensory functioning for which there is an inconsistency between the symptom(s) and recognized neurological or medical conditions. In individuals with a disorder of Psychological Factors Affecting Other Medical Conditions, there is the presence of one or more psychological or behavioral factors (e.g., symptoms of depression or anxiety, stressful life events, coping styles) that adversely affect a medical condition by increasing the risk for suffering, death, or disability.

Factitious Disorder is characterized by the falsification of symptoms (medical or psychological) in oneself or others. Additionally, the individual may do this in the absence of obvious external rewards but seeks to appear more ill or impaired, which can lead to excessive clinical intervention and attention.

Feeding and Eating Disorders

This category includes six disorders in which disturbance of eating or eating-related behavior has an impact on consumption or absorption of food and there is significant impairment in psychosocial functioning or physical health. All but one disorder (Pica) in this category have diagnostic criteria that are mutually exclusive, so individuals can receive only one diagnosis during a single episode. Pica can be diagnosed simultaneously with any of the other feeding or eating disorders. This disorder is characterized by eating of nonnutritive, nonfood substances, which is developmentally inappropriate and not part of a culturally supported behavior. In contrast, Rumination Disorder involves the repeated regurgitation of food over a period of 1 month, which is not due to a medical condition. Individuals meeting criteria for Avoidant/Restrictive Food Intake Disorder avoid or restrict food intake, which results in failure to meet nutritional requirements. Anorexia Nervosa is characterized by the following three primary features: persistent food restriction, which leads to significantly low body weight; an intense fear of gaining weight or becoming fat, despite being at a significantly low weight; and disturbed perception of the individual's body weight or shape. An individual with Bulimia Nervosa engages in recurrent binge eating and inappropriate compensatory behaviors (self-induced vomiting; misuse of laxatives, diuretics, or other medications; fasting; or excessive exercise) to prevent weight gain. Last, Binge-Eating Disorder is characterized by recurrent episodes of binge eating that occur at least once a week for 3 months, and distress over the binge-eating episodes. The individual engaging in excessive food intake must experience a lack of control over the eating for the episode to be considered binge eating. Individuals with binge-eating disorder do not engage in inappropriate compensatory behaviors as in bulimia nervosa.

Elimination Disorders

Elimination disorders involve elimination of urine (enuresis) or feces (encopresis) into inappropriate places (e.g., in one's clothing, in bed, on the floor). These behaviors can occur during the day, night, or both and are considered inappropriate according to developmental age (defined as 5 years for enuresis and 4 years for encopresis). Inappropriate voiding of urine or passage of feces can be either voluntary or involuntary. Enuresis and encopresis typically occur separately but can co-occur. To meet diagnostic criteria, duration of soiling for both enuresis and encopresis must be 3 months, although required frequency differs (at least twice weekly for enuresis and once monthly for encopresis). Specifiers for encopresis include with or without constipation and overflow incontinence. Elimination disorders have two courses: the primary type describes individuals who have never achieved urinary or fecal continence, and the secondary type describes those who develop symptoms after establishing continence.

Sleep–Wake Disorders

This collection of disorders involves sleep–wake complaints related to the quality, quantity, and timing of sleep. As a result of insufficient sleep, individuals with a sleep disorder may have functional difficulties or distress during the day (e.g., fatigue, daytime sleepiness). Sleep difficulties may present with comorbid depression, anxiety, and cognitive deficits (e.g., difficulties concentrating, attending, remembering) and may increase the risk of a patient developing other mental health concerns. Furthermore, sleep difficulties may be a clinical feature of additional mental health problems (e.g., major depression).

The broad category of sleep–wake disorders include insomnia, hypersomnolence disorder, and narcolepsy. Insomnia is characterized by difficulties initiating or maintaining sleep. Children with insomnia may be able to initiate or return to sleep only with caregiver assistance. The disturbance must occur at least 3 nights per week, persist for at least 3 months, and occur despite adequate opportunity to sleep. Insomnia is the most common sleep disorder, with approximately a third of adults reporting symptoms.

Hypersomnolence disorder consists of excessive sleepiness and difficulty staying awake during the day despite at least 7 hours of sleep at night. Like insomnia, symptoms must occur at least 3 times per week for at least 3 months before diagnosing.

A similar disorder, narcolepsy consists of recurring periods of irrepressible sleep multiple times per day. Diagnosis requires at least one of the following: cataplexy (brief episodes of sudden loss in muscle tone or spontaneous grimaces, jaw opening, or tongue thrusting behaviors), documented hypocretin deficiency, or nocturnal sleep polysomnography documenting rapid-onset REM sleep or mean sleep latency less than or equal to 8 minutes and at least two sleep-onset REM periods. Individuals with narcolepsy may display automatic behaviors ("autopilot"), vivid hypnagogic hallucinations, sleep paralysis, nocturnal eating, or nightmares. Individuals with true narcolepsy, as opposed to conversion disorder, will not have reflexes during cataplexy.

The second category of sleep disorders, Breathing-Related Sleep Disorders, includes obstructive sleep apnea hypopnea, central sleep apnea, and sleep-related hypoventilation. The most common breathing-related sleep disorder, obstructive sleep apnea hypopnea, consists of multiple episodes of upper airway obstruction during sleep (with *apnea* being total blockage of airflow and *hypopnea* being partial reduction in airflow) as documented by polysomnography. Furthermore, these patients exhibit daytime sleepiness, nighttime snoring or gasping, fatigue, or unrestorative sleep despite sufficient opportunity. Central sleep apnea disorders are characterized by periodic breathing, that is, hyperventilation alternating with hypoventilation, or variations in respiratory effort without evidence of obstruction. This form of apnea may co-occur with obstructive sleep apnea hypopnea syndrome, a condition known as complex sleep apnea. Although they can also be asymptomatic, individuals with central sleep apnea may present with sleepiness, insomnia, and frequent awakenings due to shortness of breath. Sleep-related hypoventilation can be observed during polysomnography as episodes of decreased respiration leading to increased CO_2 levels or decreases in hemoglobin oxygen saturation. These conditions may also be associated with daytime sleepiness, nighttime awakenings, morning headaches, and insomnia. They may also co-occur with obstructive sleep apnea hypopnea or central sleep apnea.

Circadian Rhythm Sleep-Wake Disorders relate to persistent or recurrent sleep disruption due to an altered circadian system or a mismatch between the patient's circadian rhythm and the sleep–wake schedule demanded by the patient's environment. There are six subtypes of circadian rhythm sleep–wake disorders: delayed sleep phase type (onset and awakening too late), advanced sleep phase type (onset and awakening too early), irregular sleep–wake type, non–24-hour sleep–wake type (consistent daily drift, usually later and later), shift work type, and unspecified type. This group of disorders is often diagnosed with the assistance of a detailed sleep diary or actigraphy, which is the objective measuring of gross motor activity during sleep. These sleep disturbances cause excessive sleepiness and/or insomnia. In delayed and advanced sleep phase types, the individual would have normal sleep quality and duration if allowed to set his or her own sleep schedule independent of social, occupational, or environmental constraints. However, these two types go beyond normative "early birds" and "night owls," and sleep phase is generally shifted 2 to 4 hours earlier or later than desired or deemed conventional.

The group of disorders describing the abnormal behavioral, experiential, or physiological events related to sleep are known as Parasomnias. Sleepwalking and sleep terrors are manifestations of incomplete awakening from sleep. These are typically brief (i.e., 1–10 minutes, but can be longer) phenomena that usually occur during the first third of one's sleep cycle during slow-wave, deep sleep. It is extremely difficult to awaken someone during episodes of sleepwalking or sleep terrors. Following sleepwalking or terror events, individuals will typically not recall the event or any dreams associated with the event. Subtypes of sleepwalking behavior include sleep-related eating behavior and sleep-related sexual behavior.

Unlike sleep terrors, the dreams of nightmare disorder are well remembered and upsetting, usually involving themes of threats to survival, security, or physical integrity. These dreams typically occur during the second half of sleep (i.e., REM sleep), and the affected individual usually becomes quickly oriented and alert upon awakening.

REM sleep behavior disorder includes "dream-enacting behaviors" (e.g., vocalization and/or complex motor behaviors) occurring during REM sleep, typically 90 minutes after sleep onset and more frequently during the later portions of sleep. Behaviors related to this disorder can be disruptive and alarming and can include running, punching, and screaming, for example. REM sleep behavior disorder can be associated with an underlying neurodegenerative disorder (e.g., Parkinsonism) and tends to occur in men aged 50 years or older.

Restless legs syndrome is a sensorimotor, neurological sleep disorder that involves an urge to move legs or arms to relieve uncomfortable tingling, burning, or other sensations. This urge worsens during inactivity and at night. This disorder disrupts sleep by delaying onset or causing nighttime awakenings. This can negatively affect mood and energy and can lead to depressive, generalized anxiety, panic, and post-traumatic stress disorders. During a sleep study, individuals with restless legs syndrome likely exhibit periodic leg movements during sleep and wakefulness.

Sexual Dysfunctions

The rather diverse group of disorders classified within Sexual Dysfunctions all have one or two traits in common, and perhaps not much else, but they may coexist in the same patient. Their commonalities include an objective realization of significant distress due to impairment in either sexual responsiveness or sexual pleasure that is not a result of a lack of adequate sexual stimulation and a period of 6 months or more of the associated symptoms. These disorders can be considered *generalized*, which means global, or unrelated to partner, situation, type of contact stimulation, or *situational*, in which they only happen under specific circumstances or with certain individuals. Disorders in this classification assume that the patient has adequate neurological and biological capacity and, with the exception of one disorder, Substance/Medication-Induced Sexual Dysfunction, are assumed to be related to developmental or experiential barriers to response or pleasure. An additional designation, *lifelong* (implying since sexual maturity), differentiates these individuals from those who had a period of healthy sexual functioning before the onset of symptoms. Other significant factors that these disorders share include difficulties the current sexual partner may be facing; nonsexual interpersonal behavior in the relationship; comorbid psychiatric problems of the patient or vulnerability factors, which are subclinical but may affect functioning; cultural and religious issues; and any medical factors that may not have caused but may exacerbate the problem or make it more difficult to treat.

Some sexual dysfunctions are necessarily tied to sexual anatomy, making them specific to male and female patients. In the group of disorders affecting males, Delayed Ejaculation is marked by a male's distress in having significant unwanted delay in ejaculation most of the time, even when stimulated and experiencing pleasure. By contrast, Premature Ejaculation is marked by distress at ejaculating within 1 minute of beginning vaginal intercourse. It does not account for time to ejaculation outside of vaginal intercourse because there are no clinical criteria established for this. Erectile Disorder is diagnosed in men who are having difficulty obtaining, maintaining, or keeping sufficiently rigid the penile erection during sexual activity in a majority of encounters that is not caused by medical problems. Male Hypoactive Sexual Desire Disorder is marked by a significant drop in or absence of interest in sexual activity and erotic thoughts and fantasies in the individual.

For females, a separate group of disorders with some significant similarities may be diagnosed. Female Orgasmic Disorder is characterized by dysfunction in the experience of orgasm, either by decreased frequency or total absence, or significantly reduced intensity, which causes disruption of pleasure in most sexual activities. By contrast, Female Sexual Interest/Arousal Disorder, similar to Male Hypoactive Sexual Desire Disorder, describes elimination of or significant decrease in overall sexual function. Genito-Pelvic Pain/Penetration Disorder is a disorder in females characterized by a pattern of sensory pain before or during sexual activity.

Last, some issues may cause significant impairment or distress in either sex. A diagnosis of Substance/Medication-Induced Sexual Dysfunction describes difficulties in either arousal or experience of pleasure that appear to be related to the use of certain substances, which may be illegal drugs or prescribed medications. Other Specified Sexual Dysfunction describes conditions that cause significant distress and impairment of sexual function or experience but do not meet all necessary criteria for another sexual function disorder. Unspecified Sexual Dysfunction describes conditions that rise to the level of disorder related to sexual function or experience but for which the clinician chooses not to specify named symptoms or does not have enough information to be more specific.

Gender Dysphoria

Gender Dysphoria is marked by significant distress or functional impairment regarding the difference between an individual's assigned (phenotypic/physical) gender and his or her expressed or desired gender. This distress must last at least 6 continuous months and must include a minimum of six related symptoms, including desiring, discussing, or manifesting physical, dress, and social and play attributes opposite to their assigned gender. The individual with this disorder can also manifest symptoms of dislike for her or his own sexual anatomy and desire for the anatomy and sex characteristics of the desired gender. The disorder has age designations (childhood, adolescence, and adulthood) based on the age at diagnosis, not the age at which the symptoms began, and can co-occur with biologically based disorders of sex development. If the criteria for this disorder are not fully met but several symptoms related to gender dysphoria cause significant distress or functional impairment, a diagnosis of Other Specified Gender Dysphoria or Unspecified Gender Dysphoria can be made.

Disruptive, Impulse Control, and Conduct Disorders

Broadly, these disorders involve problems in self-control of behavior and emotion that violate the rights of others or defy societal norms or authorities. Individuals with oppositional defiant disorder exhibit a pattern of disruptive behavior related to angry/irritable mood, argumentative/defiant behavior, or vindictiveness toward at least one nonsibling individual. These behaviors must be more severe than expected given one's developmental level (i.e., occurring most days for children under age 5 and at least weekly for children 5 years and older). Oppositional defiant disorder may present with other disruptive behavior disorders (e.g., ADHD) as well as depression, anxiety, substance abuse, and suicidality.

Intermittent explosive disorder includes physical or verbal (e.g., temper tantrums, arguing) and nondestructive aggressive outbursts.

These impulsive outbursts occur without warning and are grossly disproportionate to the provocative stressor(s). Furthermore, these behaviors are anger-driven, impulsive, and not instrumental in nature. Left untreated, aggressive behavior associated with this disorder can lead to negative social consequences, employment issues, and legal concerns.

Conduct disorder is characterized by a pattern of behavior that violates the rights of others or societal norms and can include aggression towards people or animals, destruction of property, deceitfulness or theft, or chronic violations of rules. Childhood onset (before age 10) of conduct disorder is likely to persist into adulthood; it typically occurs in males and includes physical aggression, peer relational problems, a history of oppositional behavior, and concurrent ADHD symptoms. In contrast, adolescent-onset (after age 10) conduct problems tend to occur equally in boys and girls, are less persistent, tend to be less aggressive in nature, and are less related to peer relationship problems. *DSM–5* includes a conduct disorder specifier that allows the clinician to indicate limited prosocial emotions, including lack of guilt or empathy, apathy about performance, and shallow or superficial affect. Known as "callous and unemotional" traits in the research literature, this presentation tends to occur with childhood onset and more severe symptoms.

A pattern of purposeful and deliberate fire-setting behavior preceded by tension or affective arousal characterizes pyromania. An individual with pyromania experiences pleasure or relief when setting fires or participating in the aftermath of a fire and may be apathetic of the consequences of his or her behavior. Pyromania does not include fire-setting behavior associated with anticipated monetary gain, expression of anger, sociopolitical ideology, or delusional or hallucinatory behavior. Similar to pyromania, kleptomania is characterized by a pattern of behavior (theft) that is preceded by tension and associated with pleasure or relief during the act. In addition, items stolen are not needed for personal use or for monetary value, and the behavior is not an expression of anger or a result of delusional or hallucinatory behavior.

Substance-Related and Addictive Disorders

This category of disorders includes disorders associated with the use of 10 separate classes of drugs: alcohol, caffeine, cannabis, hallucinogens, inhalants, opioids, sedatives, stimulants, tobacco, and other substances. A feature of all substances taken in excess is that the substance use results in direct activation of the brain reward system. This system is involved in the reinforcement of behaviors and memory production. Because of the significant activation of the reward system by substances, normal activities or adaptive behaviors may be neglected, and substances are used to directly activate the reward system. For each of the 10 classes of drugs, an individual can be diagnosed with substance use disorder, substance intoxication, or substance withdrawal. A substance use disorder is characterized by cognitive, behavioral, and physiological symptoms demonstrating that an individual continues to use the substance despite significant problems resulting from the substance use. An individual can be diagnosed with a substance use disorder for all of the substances listed earlier except caffeine. Although some individuals who consume caffeine have symptoms consistent with problematic use, like tolerance and withdrawal, current data are not available to determine the clinical significance of a caffeine use disorder or its prevalence. The primary feature for Substance Intoxication is the development of a reversible substance-specific syndrome due to recent ingestion of the substance. Tobacco is the only substance listed that does not apply to this category, because nicotine intoxication is rare. Substance Withdrawal is characterized by the development of a substance-specific problematic behavioral change, with physiological and cognitive symptoms, which is due to the cessation or reduction in heavy and prolonged substance use. Gambling Disorder is also included in this category of disorders due to the evidence that gambling behaviors activate reward systems similar to drugs of abuse. Individuals who meet criteria for this disorder engage in persistent and recurrent maladaptive gambling behavior that disrupts personal, family, or vocational pursuits.

Neurocognitive Disorders

Neurocognitive disorders share one feature that sets them apart. Each of the syndromes described involves disordered functioning for which the cause and type of current problems may be investigated and identified medically. In fact, after the description of Delirium, which must have evidence of a direct relationship with causative factors such as substance ingestion or withdrawal, all other diagnoses in this category are made with designations of level of dysfunction (mild or major) and the suspected or known origin (e.g., Lewy bodies, which are irregularly shaped clumps of protein inside brain cells and other nerve cells that can cause functional change). What the diagnoses also share is acquired (separate from any developmental difficulties) functional and cognitive impairments, including problems of complex attention, executive function, learning and memory, language, perceptual–motor abilities, and social cognition. For each named disorder, a thorough history and assessment is necessary to satisfy both the origin and the type and level of each functioning area, and there must be no better explanation for the symptoms related to physiological or mental disorders.

Delirium is identified and diagnosed on the basis of self-report or informant-report. The disorder entails significant problems with volitional attention, awareness (described as *reduced orientation to the environment*) and at least one other area of cognition. Patients may not remember details from earlier in the day, although they remember everything else (memory); they may not be able to "find" words easily when they are speaking (language production), or they have trouble walking without hitting objects or walls because of change in depth perception (visuospatial functioning). The symptoms appear in a relatively short period of time, fluctuate throughout the hours the patient is conscious, and show evidence of being caused by a diagnosable medical condition (known or unknown), a substance (drug or toxin ingestion or withdrawal), or multiple knowable causes. The designation of Neurocognitive Disorder Unspecified may only be used when the patient clearly meets all necessary criteria for a neurocognitive disorder but for which there is insufficient medical certainty of the cause or the clinician decides not to list it.

Major Neurocognitive Disorders (the clinician must identify the known cause or causes, or identify it as "unspecified") are characterized by a major decline in cognitive function from a previously higher level in at least one cognitive functioning area as noticed by the individual or a reliable informant and documented by an acceptable level of assessment. In addition, the functioning difficulties must be known to cause impairment in ability to function independent of assistance; must not occur solely during a period of delirium; and cannot be explained by a different mental disorder known to cause cognitive impairment, such as schizophrenia. They typically demonstrate a quiet and sometimes unnoticeable onset with progression over time. By contrast, Mild Neurocognitive Disorder shows similar causal pathways and functional deficits but noticeably less disability of function. With this designation, the patient shows somewhat hampered cognitive function (e.g., attention, awareness, memory) and known functional impairment in behaviors of independence but can still function with some personal compensation strategies.

When possible, neurocognitive disorder must be given a classification related to the suspected cause. Known causes and specifiers for major and mild neurocognitive disorders such as Alzheimer's disease, frontotemporal disorder (classified as the behavior and personality changes that accompany physical changes in brain tissue in the affected regions), Lewy bodies development, vascular changes (changes in circulation in the brain), traumatic brain injury, substance or medication,

HIV infection, prion disease (damage to or infection in brain tissue by malformed proteins), Parkinson's disease, or Huntington's disease.

Personality Disorders

Personality Disorders comprise a group of diagnoses focusing on interpersonal and inwardly focused behaviors that are significantly different from social norms or expectations of others within the individual's culture. Areas of disruption include the person's thoughts and perceptions, emotional behavior, relational behavior, and impulse control. The behaviors represented within these disorders can cause significant occupational, romantic, and other relational difficulties for the individual regardless of the individual's perceived experience of difficulties or insight. The disordered behavior must be stable and pervasive; resistant to change; cannot be better explained as a result of a physiological cause, medical condition, or a different mental disorder; and must have some behavioral evidence from childhood or adolescence. These disorders, on the basis of research and areas of cognitive and relational disturbance, are grouped into clusters according to common characteristics. Because the behaviors consistent with personality disorders often overlap with other mental disorders, they may not be diagnosed when they have occurred only during the course of a separate disorder.

Cluster A Personality Disorders are disorders that tend to disrupt the individual's ability or desire to connect or develop relationships with others as a result of fearful or delusional thoughts, or a desire to withdraw. Paranoid Personality Disorder is characterized by the belief that others in the person's life may desire or be planning harm, leading to behaviors of suspicion and reluctance to trust others, including romantic and close relationships. Schizoid Personality Disorder, on the other hand, is characterized by aloof interpersonal behaviors and apparent lack of emotional expression. Individuals with this disorder often have few social interests, a lack of close friends, and do not seek close relationships or sexual experiences. Schizotypal Personality Disorder is different from Schizoid Personality Disorder in that the deficits in relationships are more related to thought difficulties such as misperceptions during social interactions, odd beliefs and unusual experiences, as well as excessive and externally focused social anxiety or paranoia.

Cluster B Personality Disorders tend to disrupt the individual's ability to establish or maintain relationships because of an intrusive and self-centered pattern of behaviors within relational contexts or across social areas. Antisocial Personality Disorder is characterized by a generalized willingness to harm others and a pattern of lack of concern for the well-being of others. Behaviors within this disorder can include a pattern of legal infractions, putting others or self at risk of harm, interpersonal violence or theft, lying or consistently failing to follow fair expectations of work or financial duties, and apparent lack of guilt or shame in these behaviors. Individuals with Antisocial Personality Disorder must be at least 18 but must have shown signs of meeting the criteria of conduct disorder prior to age 15. Borderline Personality Disorder is distinguished by a pattern of unstable interpersonal relationship behaviors that are related to instability in the individual's self-image and emotions. These may be extreme, often occur in the context of close relationships, and seem focused on polar (very positive and very negative) views of others. These individuals vacillate between extremely oversolicitous behavior and anger outbursts in relationships. Impulsivity, self-harmful behavior, and threats may be involved in eliciting relational help. Histrionic Personality Disorder is marked by strong behaviors of attention-seeking and extreme emotional displays, including sexually or emotionally provocative displays toward others. Narcissistic Personality Disorder denotes a significant and sustained difficulty in interpersonal behavior in which the person is self-centered and focuses on his or her importance at the expense of concern or compassion for others. Individuals with this disorder are often unrealistic in their positive self-beliefs and ways they think others see them.

Cluster C Personality Disorders differ widely in terms of interpersonal behavior but seem to all have a goal of anxiety reduction related to negative beliefs about self. Individuals with Avoidant Personality Disorder have strong feelings of inadequacy and fear criticism or negative assessment from others. As a result, they tend not to engage in relationships, activities, or social behavior that could potentially expose them to ridicule or negative feelings. Dependent Personality Disorder, by contrast, is representative of individuals who consistently engage in attempts to get others to take care of them and may even demonstrate self-deprecating behaviors to maintain this help. They may feel incapable of self-managing or being safe without the constant support and approval in most or all areas of their lives. Obsessive–Compulsive Personality Disorder is marked by thoughts and behaviors that are disruptive to the individual's daily functioning but seem focused on rigid and uncompromising control of the self, others, and the environment. This apparent rigidity and need for control appear in behavior in many forms, such as moral and behavioral perfectionism and fixation on environmental and personal issues, such as cleanliness, orderliness, and complete consistency in daily behaviors and interactions with others. Individuals with Obsessive-Compulsive Disorder may also demonstrate a rigid attachment to objects, money, self-managing tasks, and ideas.

Paraphilic Disorders

Paraphilia is defined as an intense and persistent sexual interest other than interest in preparatory fondling or genital stimulation with phenotypically normal, physically mature, consenting humans. Paraphilias primarily concern an individual's erotic activities or the erotic targets. In all of the following paraphilic disorders, two criteria must be met. The first (Criterion A) specifies the qualitative nature of the paraphilia, and the second (Criterion B) specifies the negative consequences of the paraphilia. The diagnosis should be used only when an individual meets both criteria.

Common classification themes group the disorders within the paraphilic disorders. The first group is based on anomalous activity preferences and has subdivisions of courtship disorders (those resembling distorted components of human courtship behaviors) and algolagnic disorders (those that involve pain and suffering). Within the courtship subdivision, Voyeuristic Disorder (spying on others in private activities), Exhibitionistic Disorder (exposing the genitals), and Frotteuristic Disorder (touching or rubbing against a non-consenting individual) are included. The algolagnic disorders include Sexual Masochism (undergoing humiliation, bondage, or suffering) and sexual sadism (inflicting humiliation, bondage, or suffering). The second group of disorders is based on anomalous target preferences, which include those directed at other humans and elsewhere. Pedophilic Disorder consists of 6 months or longer of recurrent intense sexually arousing fantasies, sexual urges, or behaviors involving sexual activity with a prepubescent child. Fetishistic Disorder consists of recurrent and intense sexual arousal from either the use of nonliving objects or a highly specific focus on non-genital body parts. Transvestic Disorder is described as a recurrent and intense sexual arousal from cross-dressing that is manifested by fantasies, urges, or behaviors. Finally, Other Specified Paraphilic Disorder and Unspecified Paraphilic Disorder can be used when a presentation of symptoms characteristic of a paraphilic disorder cause distress or impairment in social, occupational, or other areas of functioning, but full criteria for a paraphilic disorder are not met. More specifically Other Specified Paraphilic Disorder is used when the clinician chooses to communicate the reason for the presentation not meeting full criteria for a paraphilic disorder, whereas, Unspecified Paraphilic Disorder is used when the clinician chooses not to specify the reason that full criteria are not met.

Cultural Formulation

Although the authors of the *DMS–5* make explicit the need to consider cultural explanations and issues in diagnosis and treatment of mental disorders, Section III: Emerging Measures and Models, gives consideration to specific ways of assessing and understanding the influence of culture. The term *culture* is seen as the full context, environment, and history of the individual, with an attempt to understand the influences on how he or she thinks, self-reflects, behaves, and relates to others over time, as well as the way this is transmitted to generations over time within a group. Culture can include the individual's economic background and resources, religion, ethnicity, race, language, worldview, educational milieu, and family structure, among other things. Psychologists have a special need to carefully consider the influence of experience and context on the whole person when diagnosing or trying to treat patients. The authors have provided an interview for clinical practice use titled "Cultural Formulation Interview," with forms for conducting it with both patients and informants. This interview assesses several components of the individual being diagnosed and treated and the factors of culture that may affect treatment focus and structure. The Cultural Formulation section continues and provides the outline recommended by the authors for formulating the diagnosis and treatment plan based on a more full cultural understanding, including consideration for the patient's self-understood cultural identity, the relationship between the patient and his or her cultural experience and support, and the relationship between the patient and the provider. One of the strengths of this section is the authors' goal to affect every patient–provider encounter. The provider of assessment and treatment should consider the importance of culture for every patient, regardless of whether the provider believes he or she shares the culture of the patient because assumptions within a group may be as detrimental to accurate diagnosis and treatment formulation as when the apparent cultures differ. An example would be Sam, a 24-year-old White male middle manager with a business degree, raised within a deeply racist community, coming to you dealing with anxiety, poor relations with employees under his supervision, and work-related stress because he is in a highly racially heterogeneous factory. A cultural formulation could significantly help in understanding the origins of his feelings, provide a framework for therapy goals, and minimize the chance that the therapist would create barriers to engagement and support.

Application and Practice

The following exercises are intended to assist in the application of diagnostic decision making and material from this chapter. Throughout the two exercises, as well as when you apply the material from this chapter and *DSM–5* to clinical practice, we encourage you to keep in mind and discuss with your supervisor the following questions and considerations.

Consider the cultural context related to the patient's presenting issues—is this a problem within his or her culture? Is the problem related to difficulties acculturating to the dominant culture? Is the patient reacting expectedly to his or her environment? Are there problems in the family system to which we can attribute the development, maintenance, or exacerbation of problematic thoughts or behaviors? Are there recent stressors involved, such as a death in the family, change in or loss of job, or change in schools?

Use a developmental perspective in conceptualizing your case. Is the target behavior appropriate for the patient's given age (chronological or mental)? Given the patient's age, what factors do we consider to be important in diagnosing or conceptualizing the case? Is the problem related to aging? How might the presenting problem have started? Where is it likely to progress if we do not do anything?

Use an assessment-driven or clinical hypothesis–driven treatment approach. Keep in mind possible etiological or other factors that may contribute to or maintain target cognitions or behaviors. What factors do we believe contribute to the given problem? How do we assess those factors in a meaningful way? Are there any evidence-based assessments that can serve these purposes with this given patient in this particular context? Who could we ask to provide more information about the presenting concern? A spouse? Teacher? Grandparent? More perspectives can help you form a complete picture of the situation (but don't get carried away and expect varying opinions and conflicting data to arise). What assessment modalities might we use to gather clinical data? Standardized pencil-and-paper measures? Observations? Projective tests? Structured diagnostic interviews?

Are there operating interpersonal factors at play? Has the client mentioned recent peer or coworker relational problems? Has there been a recent breakup or divorce with a significant other? What was the client's early childhood like? How might those early patterns of interactions influence present interpersonal functioning? Did a friend move away? Is the patient grieving the loss of someone?

Vignette 1: "Mikey"

Mikey is a 6-year-old boy who was brought to the psychology clinic by his mother due to behavior problems. Mikey's mother wants to know whether his behavior problems are worse than those of other kids or whether she is overreacting. Her husband, Mikey's stepfather, thinks Mikey is "just being a boy" and that all he needs is "a good whoopin'." Mikey's mother doesn't know what else to do, and she wants help getting Mikey's behavior under control before he gets kicked out of school. After prompting for more specific information related to Mikey's reported behavior problems, his mother reported Mikey will say "No!" when she asks him to "clean up" or "get ready."

QUESTIONS TO CONSIDER

Disruptive behavior is one of the most common referral problems in clinical work with children. A multitude of factors can lead to child behavior problems, including impulsivity caused by ADHD, moodiness caused by depression, or anxiety related to social situations or trauma. The following information will be helpful in determining an appropriate diagnosis and treatment plan:

- What additional information do we need to determine a diagnosis?
- When did these behavioral problems start? Did they begin after a major stressor, trauma, life event, or change in the family environment or structure? Or has he always had a "difficult" temperament?
- Do these behaviors present throughout the day or at specific times (before school, at dinner, at bedtime)?
- Are there any concerns related to physical abuse in this situation? What do you do if you suspect abuse?
- What is Mikey's behavior like at school and with other adults? Is he defiant with his teacher as well as his mother? How is his behavior with his stepfather?
- How is Mikey behaving in the clinic? How does he respond to attention from you? Does he appear nervous or angry?
- What is Mikey's home life like? Who lives at home with him? Does he have siblings with similar behavioral concerns?
- What's Mikey's typical mood like? Is he often irritable or sad?
- What happens after Mikey says "No!" or is defiant? Does he get out of any unwanted situations, like cleaning up?

Vignette 2: "Leon"

Leon is a 60-year-old veteran who served in the U.S. Army during the Vietnam War. He was referred to the psychology clinic by his VA primary care provider, who reports presenting concerns including irritability, medical nonadherence, and chronic back pain that the primary care provider believes is not fully explained by medical problems. Leon and his provider (the fifth provider he has had in 5 years) disagree about whether he should be prescribed opioid painkillers to help him cope with his back pain. Leon says his medications work best when he has "a few" alcoholic drinks to "wash them down." The veteran says he cannot work and has limited mobility because of his back pain and demands that you help him get more service-connection pay from the VA. When you ask about Leon's sleep, he laughs and says, "haven't slept since 'Nam." He then becomes quiet and distracted.

QUESTIONS TO CONSIDER

Often, medical professionals will refer patients to psychology professionals with specific concerns and proposed plans of action in mind. Clinicians can be placed in a precarious position in which they are balancing the needs and perceived goals of the patient with the perceived goals of the physician (who may decide not to refer to them in the future). Clinicians can be placed in a precarious position where they are balancing the needs and perceived goals of the patient with the perceived goals of the physician (who may decide not to refer to you anymore). On the one hand, the physician is focused on the threat of prescription painkiller abuse. On the other hand, the veteran believes he is being ignored and is tired of being abused by "the system."

- What possible factors are contributing to Leon's irritability? Sleep? Medication or substance withdrawal? Trauma-related symptoms of hyperarousal? Chronic pain?
- What impact has the veteran's military service had on his perceptions of himself and others? Does he trust his doctor or you? Does he trust his own judgment?
- What effect can alcohol have on Leon's sleep, trauma symptoms, medications, and interpersonal and occupational functioning?
- How might stress and negative emotions influence Leon's perception of pain?
- What should your target of treatment be? What forms of treatment would be most acceptable to the patient? Would he do well in a group setting or an individual setting? How should you present possible treatment options to Leon to gain buy-in?

Diagnostic decision making and treatment planning are complex processes. The case vignettes and application questions provided here are opportunities to practice applying diagnostic decision making, including use of the diagnostic criteria listed in the *DSM–5*, as well as considering the cultural context, developmental stage, assessment-driven or clinical hypothesis–driven treatment approaches, and interpersonal factors relevant to each individual. These case vignettes and application questions should also provide opportunities for discussions with your supervisor(s) to assist in making the information provided in this chapter meaningful in your growth as a future professional in the field of psychology.

References

American Psychiatric Association. (1994). *Diagnostic and statistical manual of mental disorders* (4th ed.). Washington, DC: Author.

American Psychiatric Association. (2000). *Diagnostic and statistical manual of mental disorders* (4th ed., text rev.). Washington, DC: Author.

American Psychiatric Association. (2013). *Diagnostic and statistical manual of mental disorders* (5th ed.). Washington, DC: Author.

American Psychiatric Association. (2014a). *DSM: History of the manual*. Retrieved from http://www.psychiatry.org/practice/dsm/DSM-history-of-the-manual

American Psychiatric Association. (2014b). *Understanding ICD–10–CM and DSM–5: A quick guide for psychiatrists and other mental health clinicians*. Retrieved from http://www.dsm5.org/Documents/Understanding%20ICD%2002-21-14%20FINAL.pdf

American Psychological Association. (2009). *ICD* vs. *DSM*. *Monitor on Psychology, 40*, 63. Retrieved from http://www.apa.org/monitor/2009/10/ICD-dsm.aspx

Doherty, J. L., & Owen, M. J. (2014). The Research Domain Criteria: Moving the goal posts to change the game. *The British Journal of Psychiatry 204*, 171–173.

Grob, G. N. (1991). Origins of *DSM–I:* A study in appearance and reality. *The American Journal of Psychiatry, 148*, 421–431.

Houts, A. C. (2000). Fifty years of psychiatric nomenclature: Reflections on the 1943 War Department Technical Bulletin, Medical 203. *Journal of Clinical Psychology, 56*, 935–967.

Stein, D., Lund, C., & Nesse, R. (2013). Classification systems in psychiatry: Diagnosis and global mental health in the era of *DSM–5* and *ICD–11*. *Current Opinions in Psychiatry, 26*, 493–497.

World Health Organization (2010). *International classification of diseases* (10th revision). Geneva, Switzerland: Author. Retrieved from http://www.who.int/classifications/icd/en

Lee H. Matthews

Psychological Assessment

6

D uring the course of your practicum or field placement experience, you may be exposed to psychological testing. Psychological assessment may include a wide range of observational and testing procedures. It is not possible within one chapter to cover all the material that is usually covered in a course in tests and measurements. The examples listed here and in Appendices 6.1 and 6.2 are some of the most common measures you may encounter during your placement. This chapter provides basic information about reliability and validity, interviewing, mental status assessments, screening instruments, and full battery assessments primarily related to adult testing, although some of the more common child tests are mentioned. It should be noted that the distinction between a screening and complete assessment might be somewhat arbitrary, especially when discussing visuomotor, attention, and mood or personality assessments.

Psychological testing has a long and consistent history. In a review of the psychological tests most commonly used in

http://dx.doi.org/10.1037/14672-006
Your Practicum in Psychology: A Guide for Maximizing Knowledge and Competence, Second Edition, J. R. Matthews and C. E. Walker (Editors)

clinical practice, Camara, Nathan, and Puente (2000) noted that many of the tests were just newer versions of tests that had been on similar lists from the 1960s, indicating continuity in the development of the most common measures. Exhibit 6.1 lists the websites of the largest publishers of psychological assessments, as well as additional resources on testing and assessment.

Many types of psychological assessments exist, and the following is only a brief overview of some of the various areas in which testing may occur. *Interviewing* is used to obtain historical information and determine the individual's capacity to handle other testing. An interview is a conversation with a purpose or goal. Interviewing is a skill that requires practice and careful supervision to learn. In recent years, the major developments in psychological interviewing have been on structured and semistructured interviews because of the emphasis on making a specific diagnosis for payment reimbursement, especially in mental health facilities. There are several excellent sources available on the elements of an interview (Sommers-Flanagan & Sommers-Flanagan, 2008; Zuckerman, 2010).

A *mental status examination* such as the Mini-Mental Status Examination—2 (Folstein, Folstein, White, & Messer, 2010) may be given to obtain organized behavioral observations and basic orientation for individuals presenting with a variety of symptoms and diagnoses, including cognitive disorganization, confusional states, and dementia. *Attention and concentration* tasks may be used; examples of these include immediate recall of longer strings of numbers (digit span) to assess atten-

EXHIBIT 6.1

Selected Websites

The following are some of the largest publishers of psychological assessments:

- http://www.psychcorp.com
- http://www.pearsonassessments.com
- http://www.wpspublish.com
- http://www.parinc.com
- http://www.proedinc.com
- http://www.mhs.com
- http://www.riverpub.com

The following are sources for testing information and textbooks on assessment:

- http://www.apa.org/science/programs/testing/find-tests.aspx
- http://www.buros.org
- http://www.wiley.com
- http://global.oup.com/academic

tion; more complex tasks, such as recall of numbers in reverse order (digits backward); or concentration tasks, such as attending to verbal material in a visual presentation and identifying a predetermined target. Many of these tasks are computer based and are called *continuous performance tasks* (Conners, 2004). These tests are used to assess distractibility, and impaired ability to maintain purposeful focus. Deficits in these areas may represent a global disability, or involve one or more expressive or receptive modality, such as reaction time, vigilance, visual search, and matching tasks. *Intelligence* or *cognitive* tests, such as the Wechsler series covering preschool through adults or the Woodcock cognitive tests (Schrank, McGrew, Mather, & Woodcock, 2014; Wechsler, 2012), are generally reported on the basis of IQ. Although no one definition of intelligence is likely to satisfy all psychologists, many experts say it is the overall ability to excel at a variety of tasks, usually involving both verbal and performance tasks and related to success in schoolwork or life. The concept of IQ provides a method of comparing a person's score to the performance of the average individual of the same age. An IQ or Standard Score (a newer term is *Index*) with a mean of 100 indicates that the person performed similarly to the average performance of other people the same age.

Achievement tests, such as the Woodcock–Johnson Test of Achievement—IV (Schrank et al., 2014) and the Wide Range Achievement Test—4 (Wilkinson & Robertson, 2006), are used to assess past training, usually academic in nature, and evaluate general areas such as reading, spelling, and arithmetic or more specific areas, such as knowledge of psychology, history, or social studies. Tests of *mood* or *personality* status may involve either *self-report* (objective) or *free response* (projective) testing. *Objective* tests are self-report instruments, such as the Beck Depression Inventory—II (BDI–II; Beck, Steer, & Brown, 1996) or the Minnesota Multiphasic Personality Inventory—2 (MMPI–2; Butcher et al., 2001; Ben-Porath & Tellegen, 2008). *Projective* measures, such as the Rorschach Inkblot Technique (Exner, 2005; e.g., "What does the inkblot look like?") and the Thematic Apperception Test ("Tell me a story that goes with this picture"), use ambiguous stimuli to obtain a dynamic view of the personality. *Visual-spatial* testing, such as the Bender Visual-Motor Gestalt Test—II (BGT–II; Brannigan & Deckert, 2003), may assess skills such as copying or construction of drawings, reproduction of block designs, or integration of visual information. *Language* assessment measures, such as the Peabody Picture Vocabulary Test—4 (PPVT–4; Dunn & Dunn, 2007), may involve receptive, expressive, or comprehension of language. *Memory* tests, such as the Wechsler Memory Scale—IV (WMS–IV; Wechsler, 2009b), assess immediate, delayed, and working memory. Many memory screenings assess only one area, such as learning a list of words, recalling sentences, or repeating stories. More comprehensive memory assessment may involve auditory, visual, tactile, or other types of input.

Neuropsychological tests, such as the Repeatable Battery for the Assessment of Neuropsychological Status (RBANS; Randolph, 2012), assess brain–behavior relationships and are used to determine the effects of head trauma, strokes, brain tumors, and toxic or degenerative disorders on daily functioning. Two approaches to testing are used, *fixed batteries* (the same group of tests is administered in a standardized way to every person) and *flexible batteries* (results of one test are used to determine if another test is to be administered, so the number of tests given varies across people or problems). *Behavioral* measures may assess developmental levels in areas such as communication, daily living skills, socialization, and motor skills (Vineland Adaptive Behavior Scales—II; Sparrow, Balla, & Cicchetti, 2005), or behavior, emotions, academic problems, or behavioral excesses or deficits (Conners' Comprehensive Rating Scales; Conners, 2008).

When considering the use of any test, at least two psychometric properties are important in the interpretation of results: reliability and validity. *Reliability* refers to the consistency and stability of test scores across situations (Urbina, 2011). When making important decisions about a person on the basis of the results of the testing, you want to have confidence that if two psychologists had given the test, on a different day or in a different place, the results would have been essentially the same. This is an example of *test–retest reliability* and is only one type of reliability. Psychological tests, like many forms of measurement, do not have perfect reliability. It should be noted that psychologists use several methods for evaluating the reliability of test scores.

The *validity* of a test is the degree to which the test measures what it purports to measure (Urbina, 2011). There are at least three important types of validity: face validity, predictive validity, and construct validity. *Face validity* is based on the surface content and relates to whether, "on the face of it," the questions deal with the concept in which the designer is interested. Thus, questions such as "How sad do you feel?" and "How often do you feel sad?" simply ask what the test designer wants to know. Unfortunately, face validity does not guarantee that the test is valid in other more important ways. There are numerous reasons for this, but one is that individuals may not always see themselves accurately or describe accurately how they are feeling. *Predictive validity* (also known as *criterion validity*) is based on comparing scores from one test with the same person's score on another test or a real-world measure of performance that is related to what the test is intended to measure. For example, if a test is designed to predict levels of success in undergraduate school, then grades in undergraduate school might be an accurate criterion. *Construct validity* is the degree to which a test correlates positively with other valid measures of the construct. For example, a new test for depression has construct validity if it is highly correlated with other valid measures that define the construct of depression. For more details on this topic, consult a tests and measurements textbook, such as *Essentials of Psychological Testing* by Urbina (2011).

Related to both reliability and validity is the concept of *normative sample*. Normative groups are statistical tables of how various types of people have performed when they took the test. The examiner can compare a person he or she has tested with the performance of others who have taken the test in the past. For example, comparisons may be made between a person's performance and a large sample of a specific age, such as comparing the vocabulary skills of a 6-year-old girl with local as well as national norms for 6-year-olds. Norms are important primarily to the extent that they are based on large, carefully selected samples that are relevant to the individual you are testing.

Psychological Screening

Screenings can aid in the referral, diagnosis, treatment, or termination of therapy for a client (outpatient) or patient (inpatient). Screenings, in contrast to more comprehensive evaluations, have a more limited point of focus. In the mood and personality section, many are single scales with the emphasis on either anxiety disorders or depression, both often described as "the common colds of mental health" because they are among the most frequent disorders seen in general clinical practice. Appendix 6.1 lists some examples of the more commonly used screening procedures. These are arranged by type of assessment and include age ranges as well as a brief description of the instrument.

FULL BATTERY ASSESSMENTS

A *full battery*, or comprehensive, assessment may be limited to a certain area, such as personality assessment, but more often involves evaluation of an individual's level of functioning across a variety of cognitive, achievement, personality, and other areas of assessment. The aim is to sample behavior across situations that vary from structured, to semi-structured, to unstructured. Appendix 6.2 lists some adult and child examples of the most commonly used full battery assessments. It provides age ranges and a brief description of these instruments, which are arranged by type of assessment.

CURRENT TRENDS

In recent years, some significant trends have developed within the area of psychological assessment. The major developments in psychological interviewing have been on structured and semistructured interviews. This trend can be traced to several sources, including the increased reliance on diagnostic procedures that use carefully defined criteria to make psychiatric diagnoses; these are required for statistical purposes and for the practitioner to be paid for her or his services.

Although mental status examinations were developed primarily to assess confusional states and dementia in older populations, they have been increasingly used for individuals presenting with a variety of symptoms and diagnoses, including cognitive disorganization, patients with a physical disorder showing acute mental disturbances, and psychiatric patients.

Screenings have grown in popularity in concert with changes in the mental health care delivery system in this country, driven primarily by efforts to keep costs of care down. Some risks are inherent in using screening instruments, such as reliability errors due to a small number of test items being administered; however, these may be partially overcome by focusing on highly specific referral questions. With cognitive screening measures, questions of validity must also be considered. For example, there is a tendency for some of these instruments to overestimate or underestimate the actual level of intellectual functioning of the person being examined. In a similar manner, too brief a personality or neuropsychological screening may underestimate the degree of pathology. Careful selection of tests, with an eye toward reliability and validity, can greatly decrease these types of errors.

Since 2000, managed care has had a profound impact on psychological assessment. For example, the markedly shorter length of psychiatric inpatient hospital stays (down from an average of 21 to 5 days), combined with decreased funds available for psychological assessments and the need to obtain approval from a third-party payer (insurance company) before an assessment may be performed, has shortened the length of time in which a psychological evaluation can be accomplished. This, of necessity, has led to a shift in the delivery of inpatient assessment services from complete evaluations that may take several hours spread over a couple of days, to screening measures that can be accomplished in one brief session.

Another trend in the past 5 years has been the privatization of state facilities such as hospitals, group homes for patients with coexisting intellectual disability and mental illness, and changes in community mental health centers. Provision of these services by outside contractors who are attempting to make a profit have resulted in increased patient loads, along with decreasing numbers of staff members. Again, all of these changes have called for more rapid assessment and the shift to screenings.

At the same time, as noted earlier, many of the comprehensive instruments in most common use in clinical practice are newer editions of the tests used for the past 50 years. Several trends have emerged in full battery assessment. One is the development of different types of tests that are conormed on the same sample and have the same structure for scoring, such as the same type of index scores across the Wechsler series of achievement, intellectual, and memory tests. Thus, comparisons among scores can be made with greater accuracy and validity than would be possible by comparing scores from separately normed instruments. The advantages are in making interpretations and the detection of deficits and strengths across testing areas much easier.

The emphasis on shorter, more focused outpatient treatment is another trend that has influenced psychological assessment. Often a person's insurance company will only pay for a predetermined and limited number of sessions. The use of screening tests to assess severity and to evaluate progress is gaining more attention.

As to the future of psychological assessment, there is increased interest in outcome studies on the effectiveness of various treatment modalities and techniques. Thus, there is likely to be a greater demand for short, repeatable instruments (perhaps in multiple parallel forms) to assess therapeutic progress. The use of screening and comprehensive psychological evaluation has always had a place in clinical psychology, and, while faced with multiple difficult issues, it will have a vital future in the field.

Appendix 6.1: Psychological Screening Instruments

MENTAL STATUS EXAMS

1. *Mini-Mental Status Examination* (2nd ed.; MMSE–2; Folstein, Folstein, White, & Messer, 2010). Application: A brief questionnaire that is used to screen for cognitive impairment or dementia or to follow cognitive changes over time. Ages: 18 to 100 years. The MMSE–2 comes in several versions. The Standard Version has 30 items, is administered in 10 minutes, and assesses orientation, registration, attention, calculation, serial subtractions, recall, short-term memory, naming, and language repetition. Shorter and expander versions are also available. A Cognitive Impairment Screener mobile application is also available. Separate norms for clients who are illiterate, older than age 80 years, or have less than ninth-grade education are provided.

2. *The Mental Status Examination* (4th ed.; Strub & Black, 2000). Application: A systematic mental status exam to accurately

differentiate patients with organic brain disease from normal persons and those with functional disorders. Ages: 16 to adult. Areas assessed include language skills, identification of clothing and objects that are commonly found in clinic or hospital rooms, reading, writing, and spelling. Memory functions, simple and complex copying of drawings and higher cortical functions are assessed, as well as, geographic orientation and visual neglect and frontal lobe dysfunction.

3. *The COGNISTAT* (Kiernan et al., 2013). Application: To assess cognitive/intellectual functioning in five basic areas: Language (Spontaneous Speech, Comprehension, Repetition, and Naming subtests); Construction; Memory; Calculations; and Reasoning (Similarities and Judgment subtests). Measures of Attention, Level of Consciousness, and Orientation are assessed independently. Ages: 20 to 94 years. Norms are based on two standardization age groups (20–39 years and 40–66 years), a geriatric group (70–92 years), and a neurosurgical group (25–88 years) with documented mixed brain lesions (e.g., stroke, brain tumor). There is a shorter version to assess for mild cognitive impairment and dementia based on three of the subtests.

4. *The Dementia Rating Scale—2* (DRS–2; Jurica, Leitten, & Mattis, 2001). Application: Measures cognitive status in adults with possible cognitive impairment. Ages: 55 to 105 years. Items are similar to a neurologist's bedside mental status exam. Subtests include Attention, Initiation/Perseveration, Construction, Conceptualization, and Memory. There is a DRS–2 Alternative Form for retest. Age and education-corrected norms and percentile comparisons are available.

ATTENTION AND CONCENTRATION TESTS

1. *Digit Span subtest of the Wechsler Adult Intelligence Scale—IV* (Wechsler, 2008). Application: Digit Span is perhaps the most widely used method for the assessment of immediate auditory attention and working memory. Includes both Digits Forward and Digits Backward, (reversing longer sequences of numbers), so it assesses mental control. Ages: 16 to 89 years. A subtest scale score, based on age, with a mean of 10 can be calculated.

2. *Stroop Color and Word Test—Revised* (Golden & Freshwater, 2002). Application: The Stroop measures cognitive processing, flexibility, and resistance to interference. It consists of three tasks, reading a list of repeating printed words (Word), verbalizing the color of ink (Color), and an interference task (Word–Color). The latter requires naming the color in which words are printed and disregarding the verbal content (the word *red* printed in

blue ink with the correct response naming the blue color of the ink. Ages: 15 to adult. Norms based on *t* scores. Clinical interpretations are provided.

INTELLECTUAL AND COGNITIVE TESTS

1. *Wechsler Abbreviated Scale of Intelligence—II* (WASI–II; Wechsler, 2011). Application: The WASI–II provides estimates of general cognitive ability as Index scores. It can be administered in a two-subtest (15 minutes) or four-subtest (30 minutes) format. All test items parallel the WAIS–IV and WISC–IV. Ages: 6 to 90 years. The raw scores for each subtest are converted to *t* scores. The four-subtest format also gives estimates of crystallized abilities (based on Vocabulary and Similarities) and nonverbal fluid abilities and visuomotor-coordination skills (Block Design and Matrix Reasoning) as Index scores.

2. *Kaufman Brief Intelligence Test—2* (Kaufman & Kaufman, 2004a). Application: An estimate of intellectual/cognitive functioning. Ages: 4 to 90 years. Administration time is 20 minutes. Crystallized (Verbal), Fluid (Nonverbal), and IQ Composite scores can be calculated. Verbal includes both receptive and expressive vocabulary items. Fluid intelligence uses a Matrices subtest.

3. *Shipley Institute of Living Scale—2* (Shipley, Gruber, Martin, & Klein, 2009). Application: The Shipley–2 is a measure of intellectual functioning and cognitive impairment. Ages: 7 to 89 years. Administration time is 20 to 25 minutes. It is possible to calculate both Crystallized Knowledge and Fluid Reasoning. To assess fluid ability, the test offers two options: the original Abstraction scale or a new Block Patterns scale. Vocabulary, Abstraction, and Total Scores are calculated. It is also possible for adults to calculate an Impairment Index.

ACHIEVEMENT TESTS

1. *Wide Range Achievement Test—4* (WRAT–4; Wilkinson & Robertson, 2006). Application: The WRAT–4 assesses word reading, sentence comprehension, spelling, and arithmetic skills in about 35 minutes. Ages: 5 to 94 years. It has two alternative test forms to provide test–retest capacity. Age-corrected norms provide Standard Scores, grade equivalents, and percentiles.

2. *Kaufman Test of Educational Achievement, Brief Form* (KTEA; Kaufman & Kaufman, 2004b). Application: The KTEA—Brief is a short achievement test ideal for screening. Ages: 4.5 years to 90 years. It has three subtests: Reading, comprising word recognition and reading comprehension; Math, comprising

calculation and application; and Written Expression, using spelling and written language. It is conormed with the Kaufman Brief Intelligence Test—II. Scoring is based on norm-referenced subtest scores and a battery Composite score

MOOD AND SYMPTOM TESTS

1. *Beck Depression Inventory—II* (BDI–II; Beck, Steer, & Brown, 1996). Application: The BDI–II is the most widely used test for depression. It has 21 items that measure intensity of depression based on multiple symptoms and requires about 5 minutes to complete. Ages: 13 to 80 years. Cut scores based on the fourth edition of the *Diagnostic and Statistical Manual of Mental Disorders* range from minimal to severe depression.
2. *Beck Anxiety Inventory* (BAI; Beck & Steer, 1993). Application: The BAI consists of 21 items (4-point scale), each descriptive of some anxiety symptom. Ages: 17 to 80 years. Time to complete is 10 minutes. The BAI total score provides cut score interpretations from minimal to severe ratings.
3. *Symptom Checklist—90—Revised* (SCL–90–R; Derogatis, 1994). Application: The SCL–90–R is a 90-item self-report inventory that measures nine primary symptom dimensions and provides three global indices of distress. Ages: 13 and older. Norms are available for adult nonpatients, adult psychiatric outpatients, adult psychiatric inpatients, and adolescent nonpatients. It takes approximately 15 minutes to complete.

VISUOSPATIAL TESTS

1. *Bender Visual-Motor Gestalt Test* (2nd ed.; Brannigan & Deckert, 2003). Application: A test of visuoperceptual and visuomotor functioning. Ages: 5 to 85+ years. This test consists of a series of cards, each displaying a unique figure. The revised test has seven new figures. A new visuomotor memory recall procedure is also used. New norms for both Copy and Recall procedures are available.
2. *Test of Visual-Motor Skills* (3rd ed.; Martin, 2010). Application: The test consists of copying 39 geometric designs of increasing complexity. Ages: 3 to 90 years. Standard scores, percentile ranks, and age equivalents can be calculated.

LANGUAGE TESTS

1. *Peabody Picture Vocabulary Test—Version 4* (PPVT–4; Dunn & Dunn, 2007). Application: Ages: 2.5 to 90 years. The PPVT–4 is a test of

receptive one-word picture vocabulary. It uses a multiple-choice design and correlates significantly with more comprehensive measures of reading, language, and general achievement. Age- and grade-based Standard Scores, percentiles, and age equivalent scores can be calculated.

2. *Expressive One-Word Picture Vocabulary Test—4* (Martin & Brownell, 2010a). Application: The EOWPVT-4 is a test of speaking vocabulary based on the ability to name, with one word, objects, actions, and concepts when presented with color illustrations. Ages: 2 to 80 years plus. Norms are based on 2010 sample and co-normed with the ROWPVT.

3. *Receptive One-Word Picture Vocabulary Test—4* (ROWPVT–4; Martin & Brownell, 2010b). Application: The ROWPVT–4 assesses receptive vocabulary skills based on matching a word (object, action, or concept) spoken by the examiner with one of four pictures. Ages: 2 to 80+ years. Based on a 2010 normative group and co-normed with the Expressive One-Word Picture Vocabulary Test—4 (Martin & Brownell, 2010a).

MEMORY TESTS

1. *California Verbal Learning Test* (2nd ed.; CVLT–2; Delis, Kramer, Kaplan, & Ober, 2000). Application: Ages: 16 to 89 years. The CVLT–2 is a list-learning task that measures immediate memory span, learning curve, and effects of retroactive and proactive interference. There is also a Short Form and an alternative form for retesting. At least 19 scores can be obtained.

2. *Wechsler Memory Scale—IV Flexible Approach* (WMS–IV; Wechsler, 2009b). Application: Various combinations of the 10 standard WMS–IV subtests (ranging from four to seven subtests) can be used to calculate three batteries (Older Adult/Abbreviated, Logical Memory/Visual Reproduction, Logical Memory/Designs). The use of supplemental subtests permits the calculation of two other batteries (Visual Reproduction/Logos and Logos/Names). Ages: 16 to 90 years. Administered in 30 to 45 minutes. All of the short batteries using the standard 10 subtests yield Immediate, Delayed, Visual, and Auditory Memory Indexes.

NEUROPSYCHOLOGICAL TESTS

1. *The Kaufman Short Neuropsychological Assessment Procedure* (K-SNAP; Kaufman & Kaufman, 1994). Application: A brief measure of cognitive functioning. The K-SNAP has four subtests; Mental Status, Number Recall (Digit Span), Gestalt Closure, and Four-Letter Words. Ages: 11 to 85 years. Administered in 25 minutes.

Norms include a variety of neurological deficits, Alzheimer's disease, reading disabilities, clinical depression, and mental retardation. Scale scores, percentile ranks, descriptive categories, as well as an overall Composite (Standard) score and an Impairment Index can be calculated.

BEHAVIORAL TESTS

1. *Eating Disorders Inventory—3* (EDI–3; Garner, 2004). Application: The EDI–3 is organized into 12 primary scales and yields six composites. One that is eating disorder specific (i.e., Eating Disorder Risk) and five that are general integrative psychological constructs such as Ineffectiveness, Interpersonal Problems, Affective Problems, Overcontrol, and General Psychological Maladjustment. Ages: 13 to 53 years. The EDI–3 has clinical norms based on percentile and *t* scores for adolescents in addition to U.S. and international adult clinical norms.
2. *Independent Living Scales* (ILS; Loeb, 1996). Application: The ILS assesses the ability to handle daily tasks in those with cognitive decline. It has five scales: Memory/Orientation; Managing Money, Managing Home and Transportation; Health and Safety; and Social Adjustment. Ages: 17 to 65 years. Norms are provided for impaired patients older than 17 years and older than 65 years for those in varied levels of independent living.

Appendix 6.2: Instruments for Extended Psychological Assessments

ATTENTION AND CONCENTRATION TESTS

1. *Trailmaking Test, Part A and Part B* (Reitan, 1992). Application: Measures attention, visual search, mental flexibility, and motor skills. Part A, a visual search task, requires connecting numbers in order, which are randomly scattered over a page. Part B includes circled numbers and letters randomly placed on a page, and the task involves alternating sequentially between numbers and letters in a serial order ("connect 1 to A, A to 2, 2 to B"). It has two versions of different lengths, each consisting of two parts. Ages: 9 to 14 (Older Child) and above 15 years (Adult). Norms are available based on age and level of education.

2. *Continuous Performance Test—II, Version Five* (Conners, 2004). Application: This is a computer-based test to investigate the neurological performance of individuals with attention, impulsivity, or activity control problems. Ages: 6 to adult. Norms are based on age and gender. Commission and omission errors, percent of target hits and reaction times are scored.

INTELLECTUAL AND COGNITIVE TESTS

1. *Wechsler Adult Intelligence Scale* (4th ed.; WAIS–IV; Wechsler, 2008). Application: The WAIS–IV is the most widely used adult measure of general intellectual functioning and the most commonly used test by clinicians. Ages: 16 to 90 years. Administration time is 6 to 90 minutes. Conorms with WISC–IV and Wechsler Memory Scale—IV. Index scores are calculated for Full Scale IQ, Verbal Comprehension, Perceptual Reasoning, Working Memory, and Processing Speed.
2. *Wechsler Intelligence Scale for Children* (4th ed.; WISC–IV; Wechsler, 2003). Application: The WISC–IV measures children's cognitive functioning. Test results can be linked to other tests in the Wechsler series. Ages: 6 to 16 years, 11 months and 30 days. Calculations of Full Scale IQ and Index scores are the same as WAIS–IV.
3. *Wechsler Preschool and Primary Scales of Intelligence* (4th ed.; Wechsler, 2012). Application: Measurement of cognitive development for preschoolers and young children, including working memory tasks. Age groups are 2 years, 6 months to 3 years, 11 months; and 4 years to 7 years, 7 months. Within each age group, specific (but different) core subtests are used to calculate Full Scale IQ and Index scores similar to the WAIS–IV, as well as Fluid Reasoning and Ancillary Index scores for Vocabulary Acquisition, Nonverbal, General Ability, and Cognitive Proficiency.
4. *Stanford–Binet Intelligence Scale* (5th ed.; SB–5; Roid, 2003). Applications: Ages: 2 to 85 years. The SB–5 assesses five factors of Fluid Reasoning, Knowledge, Quantitative, Visual-Spatial Processing and Working Memory. A Full Scale IQ, Verbal and Nonverbal IQ, and composite indices for the five domains as well as subtest scale scores can be calculated.
5. *Woodcock–Johnson IV* (WJ–IV; Schrank, McGrew, Mather, & Woodcock, 2014). Consists of three separate batteries. Application: The WJ–IV *Tests of Cognitive Abilities* measures multiple specific cognitive abilities and provides a general intellectual ability score. Ages: 2 to 90+ years. The Standard Battery consists of 10 tests and the Extended Battery another 8 tests.

Standard Scores, *t* scores, percentiles, age and grade equivalents, and developmental levels can be computed.

6. *Leiter International Performance Scale* (3rd ed.; Roid, Miller, Pomplun, & Koch, 2013). Application: The Leiter–3 is a non-verbal measure of general cognitive ability that requires no verbal instructions. Ages: 3 to 75+ years. It measures domains of Visualization, Reasoning, Attention, and Memory. IQ scores, subtest scores, and composite scores, as well as an examiner rating scale and percentile and age-equivalent scores, can be obtained.

ACHIEVEMENT TESTS

1. *Woodcock–Johnson IV* (Schrank et al., 2014). Application: Tests of Achievement measures academic achievement and helps to assess students for learning disabilities. Ages: 2 to 90 years. The Standard Battery consists of 11 tests and has three parallel forms. There is a single form of the Extended Battery with an additional nine tests. Standard Scores, *t* scores, percentiles, and age and grade equivalents can be calculated.

2. *Wechsler Individual Achievement Test—III* (WIAT–III; Wechsler, 2009a). Application: With 16 subtests, the WIAT–II measures all eight areas of achievement important for identifying and classifying learning disabilities. Ages: 4 to 85 years. The WIAT–III also includes college student norms across four areas: Reading, Mathematics, Language, and Writing. Standard Scores, age and grade-based Composite scores, percentile ranks, and age and grade equivalents can be obtained.

3. *Peabody Individual Achievement Test—Revised/Normative Update* (PPVT–R/NU; Markwardt, 1997). Application: The PPVT–R/NU measures academic achievement and specific learning disabilities in the areas of Mathematics, Reading Recognition, Reading Comprehension, Spelling, Written Expression, and General Information. Ages: 5 to 22 years. Standard scores, Composite scores for Written Language and Total Reading, and grade equivalents and percentiles can be calculated.

OBJECTIVE PERSONALITY TESTS

1. *Minnesota Multiphasic Personality Inventory—2* (MMPI–2; Butcher et al., 2001). Application: The MMPI–2 is the most widely used, comprehensive self-report measure of psychopathology. Ages: 18 to 80 years. It has 567 questions, 10 primary clinical scales, multiple validity scales, and specialized content scales. Interpretations across a range of diagnostic categories and problem areas are based on *t* score comparisons. The MMPI–2–RF (Ben-Porath &

Tellegen, 2008) has only 338 items, contains nine validity and 42 substantive scales.

2. *Minnesota Multiphasic Personality Inventory—Adolescent* (MMPI–A; Butcher et al., 1992). Application: The MMPI–A is a 487-item, self-report measure of adolescent psychopathology. Ages: 14 to 18 years. It includes the same primary clinical and validity scales as the MMPI–2, as well as adolescent-specific scales. A manual supplement was published in 2006.

3. *Clinical Multiaxial Inventory—III* (MCMI–III; Millon, 1994). Application: The MCMI–III is especially useful to assess personality disorders. Ages: 18 and older with eighth-grade reading level. Norms were updated in 2009. It has 11 Clinical Personality Pattern scales, three Severe Personality Pathology scales, seven Clinical Syndrome scales, three Severe Syndrome scales, three Modifying Indices (for response style), and one Validity Index. Norms are based on inpatient and outpatient clinical, forensic, residential treatment, and inmate correctional samples.

4. *Personality Assessment Inventory* (PAI; Morey, 2007). The PAI assesses adult psychopathological syndromes. It has 22 scales comprising validity, clinical diagnostic, treatment, and interpersonal scales. Ages: 18 to 89 years. It has 344 items, requires only a fourth-grade reading level, and usually takes less than an hour to complete. *t* scores are calculated and "cut levels" are provided that facilitates comparison of the patient's responses on each scale to clinical samples.

PROJECTIVE PERSONALITY TESTS

1. *Rorschach Inkblot Technique* (Exner, 2005). Application: In this classic projective technique, the task is to respond to 10 unique inkblot designs; the responses reflect aspects of personality. Ages: 5 to adult. Scoring is based on many aspects of the responses, such as form, color, and movement, with the most widely used scoring system that of Exner.

2. *Thematic Apperception Test* (TAT; Murray & Bellak, 1973). Application: The TAT consists of 31 pictures to which the individual must make up stories. Ages: Children and adults. Although formal scoring systems exist, most clinical interpretation is based on primary themes, basic needs, social or interpersonal problems, conflicts, or emotions expressed.

3. *House–Tree–Person Projective Drawing Technique—Revised* (HTP; Buck, 1981). Application: The HTP task is to produce three drawings—of a house, a tree, and a person. Ages: 3 to adult. Interpretations are based on inferences of personality traits and past experiences.

VISUAL-SPATIAL TESTS

1. *Beery-Buktenica Developmental Test of Visual Motor Integration* (6th ed.; Beery–VMI; Beery, Buktenica, & Beery, 2010). Application: The Beery–VMI detects visuomotor deficits. It requires the reproduction of 27 geometric designs within a structured format. There are also two supplemental tests: a Visual Perception task, requiring selection of one form from among others that exactly matches a standard, and Motor Coordination, requiring tracing a design within a double-lined path. Ages: 2 to 100 years. The Short Format is often used with children ages 2 to 8 years. Standard Scores, percentiles, and age equivalents can be obtained.

2. *Rey Complex Figure Test and Recognition Trial* (RCFT; Meyers & Meyers, 1996). Application: The RCFT is a complex visual figure, composed of 18 scoring elements, that assesses visual spatial construction and visual memory. There are four separate administration tasks. Ages: 6 to 17 (children) and 18 to 89 (adults). Includes Copying, Immediate Recall, a 30-minute Delayed Recall, and a Recognition task. An Accuracy score can be computed for each task. Normative information is available on a large cross-section of populations including geriatric ages.

LANGUAGE TESTS

1. *Test of Adolescent and Adult Language—Fourth Edition* (TOAL–4; Hammill, Brown, Larsen, & Wiederbolt, 2007). Application: The TOAL–4 has six subtests and measures receptive and expressive language skills. Ages: 12 to 24 years. Scale scores, an Overall Language Ability score, and Composite quotients can be calculated.

2. *Clinical Evaluation of Language Fundamentals—Fifth Edition* (Semel, Wiig, & Secord, 2013). Application: Measures of receptive, expressive, language structure, and language content. Ages: 5 to 21 years. Standard scores, percentile ranks, growth scale values, and age equivalents can be calculated.

MEMORY TESTS

1. *Wechsler Memory Scale* (4th ed.; Wechsler, 2009b). Application: A comprehensive memory battery, including a brief older adult battery. Ages: 16 to 90 years. It has eight Primary Index scores in the areas of auditory and visual memory (both immediate and delayed), working memory, and a General Memory Index. It is conormed with the WAIS–IV, allowing comparisons between memory and intellectual functioning. Percentile ranks as well as age-corrected Index scores can be obtained.

2. *Wide Range Assessment of Memory and Learning* (2nd ed.; Adams & Sheslow, 2003). Application: An integrated set of memory tests across the life span. Ages: 5 to 90 years. The battery has Verbal Memory, Visual Memory, Attention-Concentration, Working Memory, and General Index scores. Index and subtest scores can be converted to standard scores and percentiles for age-based performance comparisons.

NEUROPSYCHOLOGICAL TESTS

1. *Short Category Test, Booklet Format* (Wetzel & Boll, 1987). Application: Assessment of complex concept formation, abstract reasoning, and ability to learn. Ages: 20 to 79. Normative and standardization samples included a wide range of socioeconomic and educational levels that encompass individuals with both psychiatric and neurological diagnoses in the clinical sample. *t* scores and percentile ranks are calculated.

2. *Halstead–Reitan Neuropsychological Test Composite Battery* (Reitan & Wolfson, 1993). Application: The composite is three separate batteries of individual tests. Testing time for each is 5 to 8 hours. Ages: Children (5–8), Older Children (9–), and Adults (15 and older). Norms tables by Reitan and other authors permit calculations of Level of Performance and an Impairment Index.

3. *Repeatable Battery for the Assessment of Neuropsychological Status—Update* (RBANS; Randolph, 2012). Application: The RBANS is a brief neurocognitive battery with four alternate forms. Ages: 12 to 89 years. It has four parallel forms, permitting retesting. There are 12 subtests measuring the five domains of Immediate Memory, Visuospatial/Constructional, Attention, Language, and Delayed Memory. Subscale scores and Standard Index scores can be obtained. Normative data cover Alzheimer's Disease, Vascular Dementia, HIV Dementia, Huntington's Disease, Parkinson's Disease, Depression, Schizophrenia, and Closed Head Injury.

BEHAVIORAL TESTS

1. *Vineland Adaptive Behavior Scales II* (Sparrow, Balla, & Cicchetti, 2005). Applications: This is the leading instrument for supporting the diagnosis of intellectual and developmental disabilities. Includes these forms: Survey Interview, Parent/Caregiver Rating, Expanded Interview. Ages: Birth to 90 years old for all forms except the Teacher Rating, which is for ages 3 years, 0 months to 21 years, 11, months. It has semistructured interview and questionnaire formats that assess domains such as Communication, Daily Living Skills, Socialization, and Motor Skills. Standard

Scores, percentile ranks, stanines, adaptive levels, and age equivalents can be calculated.

2. *Conners Comprehensive Rating Scales* (3rd ed.; Conners, 2008). Applications: Multidimensional scales that assess attention deficit/ hyperactivity disorder (ADHD) and comorbid disorders. Ages: 6 to 18 years. Also short forms for Parent, Teacher, and Adolescent ratings. Normative sample based on 2000 census. *Diagnostic and Statistical Manual of Mental Disorders* (4th ed., text revision; *DSM–IV–TR*) symptom–based. New *t* score cutoff categories and category descriptions.

3. *College ADHD Response Evaluation* (Glutting, Sheslow, & Adams, 2002). Application: Measures ADHD symptoms in older teenagers and young adults. Ages: 17 to 23 years. It has two scales, a Student Response Inventory and a Parent Response Inventory. Test items that relate to anxiety disorders, mood disorders, somatic disorders, disruptive behavior disorders, and substance abuse form the comorbidity screener. Norms include average college students and *DSM–IV* adults with ADHD. Cut scores are provided.

References

Adams, W., & Sheslow, D. (2003). *Wide Range Assessment of Memory and Learning* (2nd ed.). Wilmington, DE: Wide Range.

Beck, A. T., & Steer, R. A. (1993). *Beck Anxiety Inventory*. San Antonio, TX: The Psychological Corporation.

Beck, A. T., Steer, R. A., & Brown, G. K. (1996). *Beck Depression Inventory—2 Manual*. San Antonio, TX: The Psychological Corporation.

Beery, K. E., Buktenica, N. A., & Beery, N. A. (2010). *The Beery-Buktenica Developmental Test of Visual-Motor Integration* (6th ed.). San Antonio, TX: Pearson.

Ben-Porath, Y. S., & Tellegen, A. (2008). *Minnesota Multiphasic Personality Inventory—2 Restructured Form: Manual for administration, scoring, and interpretation*. Minneapolis: University of Minnesota Press.

Brannigan, G., & Deckert, S. L. (2003). *Bender Visual-Motor Gestalt Test* (2nd ed.). San Antonio, TX: The Psychological Corporation.

Buck, J. N. (1981). *The House–Tree–Person technique: A revised manual*. Los Angeles, CA: Western Psychological Services.

Butcher, J. N., Graham, J. R., Ben-Porath, Y. S., Tellegen, Y. S., Dahlstrom, W. G., & Kaemmer, B. (2001). *Minnesota Multiphasic Personality Inventory—2: Manual for administration and scoring* (Rev. ed.). Minneapolis: University of Minnesota Press.

Butcher, J. N., Williams, C. L., Graham, J. R., Archer, R., Tellegen, A., Ben-Porath, Y. S., & Kaemmer, B. (1992). *Minnesota Multiphasic Personality Inventory—Adolescent: A manual for administration, scoring, and interpretation*. Minneapolis: University of Minnesota Press.

Camara, W. J., Nathan, J. S., & Puente, A. E. (2000). Psychological test usage: Implications in professional psychology. *Professional Psychology: Research and Practice, 31*, 141–154. http://dx.doi.org/10.1037/0735-7028.31.2.141

Conners, C. K. (2004). *Continuous Performance Test* (2nd ed., Version 5). North Tonawanda, NY: Multi-Health Systems.

Conners, C. K. (2008). *Conners Comprehensive Rating Scales*. San Antonio, TX: Pearson.

Delis, D. C., Kramer, J. H., Kaplan, E., & Ober, B. A. (2000). *California Verbal Learning Test* (2nd ed.). San Antonio, TX: The Psychological Corporation.

Derogatis, L. R. (1994). *Symptom Checklist—90—Revised manual*. Minneapolis, MN: Pearson Assessments.

Dunn, L. M., & Dunn, D. M. (2007). *Peabody Picture Vocabulary Test* (4th ed.). San Antonio, TX: The Psychological Corporation.

Exner, J. (2005). *A Rorschach workbook for the comprehensive system* (5th ed.). Asheville, NC: Rorschach Workshops.

Folstein, M. F., Folstein, S. E., White, T., & Messer, M. A. (2010). *Mini-Mental State Examination* (2nd ed.). Lutz, FL: Psychological Assessment Resources.

Garner, D. M. (2004). *Eating Disorders Inventory* (3rd ed.). Lutz, FL: Psychological Assessment Resources.

Glutting, J., Sheslow, D., & Adams, W. (2002). *College ADHD Response Evaluation*. Wilmington, DE: Wide Range.

Golden, C. J., & Freshwater, S. M. (2002). *Stroop Color and Word Test (Revised)*. Chicago, IL: Stoelting.

Hammill, D. A., Brown, V. L., Larsen, S. C., & Wiederbolt, J. L. (2007). *Test of Adolescent and Adult Language* (4th ed.). San Antonio, TX: Pearson.

Jurica, P. J., Leitten, C., & Mattis, S. (2001). *Dementia Rating Scale–2: Professional manual*. Lutz, FL: Psychological Assessment Resources.

Kaufman, A. S., & Kaufman, N. L. (1994). *Kaufman Short Neuropsychological Assessment Procedure*. San Antonio, TX: Pearson.

Kaufman, A. S., & Kaufman, N. L. (2004a). *Kaufman Brief Intelligence Test—2*. San Antonio, TX: Pearson.

Kaufman, A. S., & Kaufman, N. L. (2004b). *Kaufman Test of Educational Achievement, Brief Form*. Circle Pines, MN: AGS.

Kiernan, R. J., Mueller, J., & Langston, J. W. (2013). *COGNISTAT Paper Test*. San Francisco, CA: Cognistat.

Loeb, P. A. (1996). *Independent Living Scales*. San Antonio, TX: Pearson.

Markwardt, F. C. (1997). *Manual for the Peabody Individual Achievement Test—Revised: Normative Update.* Circle Pines, MN: American Guidance Service.

Martin, N. A. (2010). *Test of Visual-Motor Skills* (3rd ed.). Novato, CA: Academic Therapy.

Martin, N. A., & Brownell, R. (2010a). *Expressive One-Word Picture Vocabulary Test* (4th ed.). Novato, CA: Academic Therapy.

Martin, N. A., & Brownell, R. (2010b). *Receptive One-Word Picture Vocabulary Test* (4th ed.). Novato, CA: Academic Therapy.

Meyers, J. E., & Meyers, K. R. (1996). *Rey Complex Figure Test and Recognition Trial.* Lutz, FL: Psychological Assessment Resources.

Millon, T. (1994). *Millon Clinical Multiaxial Inventory—III.* Minneapolis, MN: Pearson Assessments.

Morey, L. C. (2007). *The Personality Assessment Inventory professional manual.* Lutz, FL: Psychological Assessment Resources.

Murray, H. A., & Bellak, L. (1973). *Thematic Apperception Test.* Cambridge, MA: Harvard University Press.

Randolph, C. (2012). *Repeatable Battery for the Assessment of Neuropsychological Status: Update.* San Antonio, TX: The Psychological Corporation. http://dx.doi.org/10.1037/t15149-000

Reitan, R. M. (1992). *Trail Making Test.* Tucson, AZ: Reitan Neuropsychology Laboratory.

Reitan, R. M., & Wolfson, D. (1993). *Halstead–Reitan Neuropsychological Test Composite Battery.* Tucson, AZ: Reitan Neuropsychology Laboratory.

Roid, G. H. (2003). *Stanford–Binet Intelligence Scales* (5th ed.). Itasca, IL: Riverside.

Roid, G. H., Miller, L. J., Pomplun, M., & Koch, C. (2013). *Leiter International Performance Scale* (3rd ed.). Chicago, IL: Stoelting.

Schrank, F. A., McGrew, K. S., Mather, N., & Woodcock, R. W. (2014). *Woodcock–Johnson IV: Tests of Achievement and Tests of Cognitive Ability.* Rolling Meadows, IL: Riverside.

Semel, E., Wiig, E. H., & Secord, W. A. (2013). *Clinical evaluation of language fundamentals* (5th ed.). San Antonio, TX: Pearson.

Shipley, W. C., Gruber, C. P., Martin, T. A., & Klein, A. M. (2009). *Shipley Institute of Living Scale–2.* Los Angeles, CA: Western Psychological Services.

Sommers-Flanagan, J., & Sommers-Flanagan, R. (2008). *Clinical interviewing* (4th ed.). Hoboken, NJ: Wiley.

Sparrow, S. S., Balla, D. A., & Cicchetti, D. V. (2005). *Vineland Adaptive Behavior Scales* (2nd ed.). San Antonio, TX: Psychological Corporation.

Strub, R. L., & Black, F. W. (2000). *The mental status exam in neurology* (4th ed.). Philadelphia, PA: F. A. Davis.

Urbina, S. (2011). *Essentials of psychological testing* (4th ed.). Hoboken, NJ: Wiley.

Wechsler, D. A. (2003). *Wechsler Intelligence Scale for Children* (4th ed.). San Antonio, TX: The Psychological Corporation.

Wechsler, D. A. (2008). *Wechsler Adult Intelligence Scale* (4th ed.). San Antonio, TX: The Psychological Corporation.

Wechsler, D. (2009a). *Wechsler Individual Achievement Test—III.* San Antonio, TX: The Psychological Corporation.

Wechsler, D. (2009b). *Wechsler Memory Scale* (4th ed.). San Antonio, TX: The Psychological Corporation.

Wechsler, D. (2011). *Wechsler Abbreviated Scale of Intelligence* (2nd ed.). San Antonio, TX: The Psychological Corporation.

Wechsler, D. (2012). *Wechsler Preschool and Primary Scale of Intelligence* (4th ed.). San Antonio, TX: The Psychological Corporation.

Wetzel, L., & Boll, T. J. (1987). *Short Category Test, Booklet format manual.* Los Angeles, CA: Western Psychological Services.

Wilkinson, G. S., & Robertson, G. J. (2006). *Wide Range Achievement Test* (4th ed.). Lutz, FL: Psychological Assessment Resources.

Zuckerman, E. (2010). *Clinician's thesaurus: The guide to conducting interviews and writing psychological reports* (7th ed.). New York, NY: Guilford Press

Peter E. Nathan and Morgan T. Sammons

Interventions
Evidence-Based Treatments

7

What Treatments for What Disorders?

Determining which psychological and somatic treatments are most strongly supported by research—and most likely to assist an individual patient—is, of course, one of the most important tasks for mental health professionals. We have attempted to distill the voluminous literature on both these subjects into a form that is accessible to practicum students. We have chosen treatments that are (a) widely used and (b) have the greatest empirical support to provide practicum students with source material about these treatments that we believe will be of value during the practicum and after it has concluded. We hope that undergraduate practicum students will go beyond the confines of this chapter and seek out suggested references that will help them decide whether a career as a mental health professional makes sense for them. For graduate practicum students, this

http://dx.doi.org/10.1037/14672-007
*Your Practicum in Psychology: A Guide for Maximizing Knowledge and Competence,
Second Edition*, J. R. Matthews and C. E. Walker (Editors)

chapter and these references should help guide them as they begin the process of learning how to provide these interventions under supervision.

We have limited our coverage of treatments for psychological disorders to treatments for four of the most common of these disorders: mood disorders, anxiety disorders, alcohol use disorders, and schizophrenia. We chose to review treatments for these conditions because the disorders are highly prevalent: Students will almost certainly encounter patients with these diagnoses in their practicum setting.

Reviews published during the past few years, including those in Nathan and Gorman (2007) and Barlow (2011), emphasize advances in the methodology and quality of research examining outcomes of both psychological and somatic treatments. This research has also documented the increased effectiveness of a number of these evidence-based treatments.

Psychologists and psychiatrists do not always agree that evidence-based treatments should consistently be the treatments of choice. To this end, a number of psychologists (e.g., Nathan, 2004; Spring & Neville, 2011) have raised questions that pose challenges to fully accepting the usefulness of evidence-based treatments. These include the inaccessibility to date of certain treatments, most notably psychoanalytic methods; a lack of empirical study; and questions about the adequacy of the methodology of some studies and the reliability of treatment outcomes. This does not mean the practicum student should not pay attention to new treatments that their supervisors have begun to explore, but students should be prepared to weigh the adequacy of research on the treatments and, if possible, discuss this with their supervisor.

We refer here to both the quality and quantity of research on evidence-based psychological treatments that support effectiveness claims. *Research quality* refers to generally agreed-on standards attesting to superior research methodology, including adequate sample size, random assignment of subjects to experimental and control groups, and use of appropriate statistical methods to analyze outcome data. The effectiveness of the psychological treatments highlighted in this chapter has been supported by a substantial number of studies that meet these quality standards.

Evidence-Based Psychological Treatments for Mood Disorders

BIPOLAR DISORDER

Bipolar disorder is characterized by at least one manic episode and at least one episode of major depression. Pharmacotherapy has been the primary treatment option for bipolar disorder for several decades.

Frontline maintenance medication treatment has typically included one of the mood stabilizers, most often lithium; anticonvulsant drugs, including valproic acid (Depakote) and carbamazepine (Tegretol), which may be substituted for lithium; and one or more of several antipsychotic drugs. Mood stabilizers and antipsychotic medications have repeatedly shown effectiveness in moderating both manic and depressive episodes in bipolar disorder (Keck & McElroy, 2007).

More recently, pharmacotherapy for bipolar disorder has been coupled with psychological treatments, prominently including cognitive–behavioral therapy (CBT) and marital and family therapy. Research suggests that drug and psychological treatments in tandem often yield better results, including reduced risk of relapse and rehospitalization, than either alone (Muralidharan, Miklowitz, & Craighead, in press; Otto & Applebaum, 2011).

CBT for bipolar disorder generally includes sessions designed to teach relapse prevention (Hsu & Marlatt, 2012) in anticipation that patients with bipolar disorder will probably experience relapses during their recovery. Relapse prevention incorporates several behavioral techniques designed to help prepare the patient for mood lapses to depression or mania by reassuring them that relapses can be contained and teaching them concrete steps they can take to contain the mood lapse. Sessions employing Beck's classic CBT for depression (Beck, Rush, Shaw, & Emery, 1979) are also typically incorporated into CBT for bipolar disorder. CBT for depression, still a treatment of choice despite its early appearance in the development of behavioral therapy (BT) and CBT, is described in some detail in the following section of this chapter.

One of the most significant studies of CBT for bipolar disorder to date took place in the United Kingdom (Scott et al., 2006). It was a well-designed clinical trial that recruited patients from five sites and randomly assigned them to CBT plus medication (22 sessions) or treatment as usual, which consisted of brief counseling and medication. CBT was associated with longer periods free from mood disorder for patients with fewer than 12 previous episodes, whereas treatment as usual led to longer periods free from mood disorder in patients with more than 12 previous episodes. These findings suggest that CBT may be more effective for patients with bipolar disorder early in the course of their disorder.

Marital and family therapy, almost always offered in conjunction with pharmacotherapy, has also been shown to reduce relapse risk and improve interpersonal, social, and occupational functioning in patients with bipolar disorder. Marital and family therapists believe that a wide range of disorders reflect family problems, including marital discord, substance abuse affecting one or both partners, and a range of other social and occupational problems. Accordingly, marital and family therapy generally focuses on these family and marital symptoms, often with cognitive behavioral methods. If your practicum has given you the opportunity to observe marital and family therapy for bipolar disorder, you have probably come to appreciate the usefulness of working with the bipolar patient as well as providing the patient's partner and family information about the disorder, its treatment, and its likely course. Outcomes of research on marital and family therapy, often including a specific therapeutic focus on substance abuse as a contributor to family problems, have generally been quite positive (e.g., Miklowitz, George, Richards, Simoneau, & Suddath, 2003).

Psychoeducation, designed to educate patients with bipolar disorder and their families about the disorder and its pharmacological management and treatment, is now widely used to deal with the troublesome issue of nonadherence to medication treatment. Maintenance dosages of the mood stabilizer drugs, especially lithium, are difficult to achieve, in part because of troubling side effects, which often cause patients to discontinue use of these drugs despite their effectiveness in treating symptoms of bipolar disorder (Otto & Applebaum, 2011). Psychoeducation is designed to help patients recognize the usefulness of the mood stabilizers in helping them control their bipolar disorder despite their side effects.

MAJOR DEPRESSIVE DISORDER

A growing number of randomized clinical trials and several meta-analyses have established the efficacy of CBT and interpersonal therapy for major depressive disorder (MDD), most often in conjunction with antidepressant medication. Most MDD treatment studies that directly compared the outcomes of psychosocial and pharmacological treatments for MDD have concluded that the two are comparable in efficacy, although at least one major study suggested that combined psychosocial and pharmacological treatment for MDD is more effective than either treatment alone (Craighead, Sheets, & Brosse, 2007).

Because CBT has been studied more extensively and has generated more encouraging outcome data than any other psychological treatment for depression, we go into some detail here describing its most important components. CBT for depression typically involves 16 to 20 sessions over 12 to 16 weeks. Its principal focus is on helping patients change their negative worldview. Cognitive behavioral clinicians consider a negative worldview to be both a result and cause of depression. Beck's classic treatise on CBT for depression (Beck, Rush, Shaw, & Emery, 1979) first proposed this view of the reciprocal nature of depression symptoms. It has since been widely accepted by the field. That is why clinicians typically believe that depressive thoughts precipitate depressive feelings, which explains CBT's emphasis on disputing depressive thoughts to reduce the intensity and longevity of depressive feelings.

Early in the course of CBT for depression, patients are encouraged to increase their level of activity (behavioral activation) so that they can begin to self-monitor their behavior, along with associated thoughts and feelings. In turn, the self-monitoring may help depressed patients to gradually identify logical errors in their thinking as well as in the principal schemas that underlie and strongly influence their negative thoughts and logical errors. Beck and his colleagues (Beck, Emery, & Greenberg, 2005; Beck et al., 1979) defined *schemas* as basic beliefs about oneself and the world that filter, color, and organize experiences; they suggested that the negative schemas of depressed patients are largely responsible for their depression. Accordingly, clinicians trained to use Beck's CBT for depression aim to identify and then successfully challenge these negative schemas and the logical errors that typically accompany them. As the therapy moves toward its conclusion, patient and therapist also work to identify cognitive strategies (e.g., thought stopping, mindfulness exercises) that could prevent a relapse to depression by a return of negative schemas. Observing an experienced clinician using Beck's cognitive therapy for depression would be a high point of a student's practicum experience.

Evidence-Based Psychological Treatments for Anxiety Disorders

Outcomes of behavioral and cognitive behavioral treatment for the anxiety disorders have been explored in a substantial number of high-quality studies over the past 30 years (Leyfer & Brown, 2011). Findings from these studies strongly support the view that panic disorder (with or without agoraphobia), specific and social phobias, and social and generalized anxiety disorder (GAD) respond positively to these treatments (Barlow, Allen, & Basden, 2007). Although the distinguishing symptoms of these disorders differ, all appear to respond favorably to the behavioral interventions described here.

THE ANXIETY–DEPRESSION SYNDROME

Leyfer and Brown (2011) included a chapter in *The Oxford Handbook of Clinical Psychology* titled "The Anxiety-Depression Syndrome." The chapter's take-home message was the striking similarity in symptoms of anxiety and depression, the high frequency with which anxiety and depression co-occur, the similarity in theories of their etiology, and the growing recognition that treatments for anxiety disorder and treatments for depressive disorder have become less distinctive. They certainly are in psychopharmacology, where antidepressants and antianxiety agents are often combined for one or the other condition. Similarly, Leyfer and Brown predicted that psychological treatments for the anxiety and depressive disorders are in the process of converging, so that at some point an anxiety–depression spectrum disorder will ultimately be addressed by essentially interchangeable treatments. Barlow, with whom Leyfer and Brown work at Boston University, has also written and spoken widely on these issues (e.g., Barlow, Allen, & Choate, 2004).

PANIC DISORDER

A great many studies have established the efficacy of situational in vivo exposure for persons with panic disorder with or without agoraphobia. Situational in vivo exposure (Craske & Barlow, 2007) requires patient and therapist to construct a hierarchy of fear situations based on their capacity to cause fearfulness or panic. Behavioral coping strategies may then be taught to the patient in the effort to modify or eliminate irrational or otherwise unjustified fearful thoughts so that the patient can visualize fear-inducing situations without experiencing disabling fear and panic. Once this intervention is successful, patients are then accompanied by the therapist or a family member during an in vivo desensitization phase of treatment, when they actually expose themselves to the fear-inducing situation. Through these means, most patients achieve significant and lasting clinical gains (Barlow, Allen, & Basden, 2007).

SPECIFIC AND SOCIAL PHOBIAS

In vivo exposure has also been shown to be effective in treating specific and social phobias (Barlow et al., 2007). Several CBT packages have been developed to treat social phobias, the most common of all anxiety disorders. They typically include social skills training, relaxation training, exposure-based procedures, and multicomponent behavioral treatment. However, Barlow and his colleagues (2007) observed that only the procedures that actually expose patients to feared social situations in the real world seem to produce meaningful changes in social phobia.

GENERALIZED ANXIETY DISORDER

GAD, among the most common of the anxiety disorders, has been treated with psychological treatments alone (usually CBT) and in combination with antianxiety or antidepressant medication. CBT for GAD is designed to help the patient recognize his or her selective attention to negative events and/or the maladaptive nature of persistent worrying. Several meta-analyses support the usefulness of CBT in managing GAD (Barlow et al., 2007). Despite these efforts, GAD remains among the most difficult of the anxiety disorders to treat successfully, in part because situational in vivo exposure, generally helpful in treating the panic and phobic disorders, is more difficult to use with GAD because the anxiety is not tied to a specific object or situation. GAD is even harder to treat when the GAD patient, as is often the case, also experiences serious depression.

Evidence-Based Psychological Treatments for Alcohol Use Disorder

Finney, Wilbourne, and Moos (2007) reported findings from a number of well-designed reviews of treatments with documented effectiveness for alcohol use disorders. All five of the most effective treatments are cognitive–behavioral interventions designed to help patients adapt to their challenging and stressful life circumstances.

- *Cognitive–behavioral treatments* include *social skills training, self-control training,* and *stress management training* (Winters et al., 2012). All are designed to enhance patients' self-efficacy and ability to cope with everyday life challenges (including situations that threaten to induce relapse), and all have the capacity to improve the match between patients' abilities and the demands of the environment.
- *Community reinforcement* (Azrin, Sisson, Meyers, & Godley, 1982; Carr, 2009) is a comprehensive behavioral treatment package that offers patients access to a wide array of interpersonal, vocational, and financial reinforcers in a community setting contingent on continued sobriety and retention in treatment. Patients who meet these contingencies might be able to use the facilities of a social club and have access to food from a food pantry, housing, and recreational opportunities.
- *Contingency management* (Carroll et al., 2006; Litt, Kadden, Kabela-Cormier, & Petry, 2009) includes three key elements: monitoring of patient substance use, provision of positive reinforcers for desired reductions in substance use, and withholding of reinforcers for substance-using behaviors that are unwanted. Thus, in a contingency management program designed to encourage patients gradually to reduce their alcohol consumption, monitoring of blood alcohol level on a regular basis permits the clinician to provide tangible reinforcement (most often, money) for gradually decreasing blood alcohol level readings and to withhold reinforcement when those readings remain at high levels.

A large-scale clinical trial of alcoholism treatment, Project MATCH, has provided important data on treatments that have now become standard interventions for alcohol problems. Project MATCH (1993, 1998) was a randomized, multisite, national clinical trial of more than 1,700 patients that compared the following three individual, manualized psychosocial treatments.

- *Cognitive–behavioral coping-skills therapy (CBCST)* was a 12-session treatment developed in the belief that out-of-control drinking is related functionally to inability to cope adequately with major problems in life. CBCST, accordingly, offered patients training designed to correct skills deficits (e.g., assertive behavior, anger management, social skills, marital functioning) so they would be better able to cope with stressful situations in their environments that might lead to relapse.

- *Motivational enhancement therapy (MET)* was a brief intervention lasting only four sessions that focused on helping patients recognize the extent of their alcohol problems and increase their motivation to work actively to deal with them. Detailed feedback on the likely negative consequences of abusive drinking was provided. MET therapists were thoroughly trained in providing feedback in an empathetic and supportive fashion so they did not cause defensiveness in their patients. The stages of change model (Prochaska & DiClemente, 1986) was an important source of information on patients' initial and continuing motivation to change their drinking behavior.

- *Twelve-step facilitation therapy (TSF)* was a 12-session treatment heavily influenced by the tenets of Alcoholics Anonymous (AA). Central to AA philosophy is the belief that alcoholism is a spiritual and medical disease. As a consequence, among TSF's primary goals were to promote patient acceptance of the disease model of alcoholism, stress the importance of spirituality, and enhance the value of AA's 12-step program. By means of role-playing and behavioral rehearsal, TSF patients learned to anticipate the challenging interpersonal situations to which they would be exposed when attending AA meetings as newly recovering alcoholics.

Two independent, parallel matching studies were conducted in Project MATCH. The first included 952 outpatients (of whom 72% were men), and the second enrolled 774 aftercare patients (of whom 80% were men). Follow-up began 3 months after treatment ended and continued every 3 months for a year, then at 2- and 3-year marks. At the end of the first year, more than 90% of patients were located; they demonstrated "significant and sustained improvements in drinking outcomes from baseline to 1-year posttreatment. . . . There was little difference in outcomes by type of treatment" (Project MATCH Research Group, 1998, p. 1302). The 24- and 39-month follow-ups revealed, overall, that patients maintained the gains in drinking behavior they had demonstrated immediately after the cessation of treatment.

Practicum students will surely encounter many patients with the diagnosis of alcohol use disorder. These conditions are most commonly seen in outpatient clinical settings, the sites of most practicums. Although practicum students are unlikely to have the responsibility for treating these patients, most of whom will also suffer from co-occurring disorders such as depression and anxiety, they will likely learn to identify the signs and symptoms of the disorder, under supervision. They may also observe treatment sessions conducted by a supervisor.

Empirically Supported Psychological Treatments for Schizophrenia

The treatment of choice for schizophrenia remains antipsychotic medication, including the so-called atypical or second-generation drugs that many clinicians believe retain the effectiveness of the earlier phenothiazine drugs without some of their more serious side effects (e.g., Abbas & Lieberman, in press; Mueser & Duva, 2011). However, these drugs do not consistently improve negative symptoms or cognitive impairment in schizophrenia and have their own set of troubling side effects (Meyer et al., 2008). One of the most challenging problems with medication for schizophrenia is nonadherence: Because of side effects or limited behavioral effectiveness (or both), patients often decide to discontinue taking their medication (Yamada et al., 2006). A number of the psychosocial treatments for schizophrenia focus on efforts to increase patients' adherence to medication, along with a focus on symptom change.

One of the first and most successful psychosocial treatments for chronic schizophrenia is the *token economy* (Ayllon, 1968; Paul & Lentz, 1977). Patients in a token economy, often longtime residents on a custodial ward, receive tokens or other tangible reinforcers (candy, cigarettes, other food items) when they emit desired behaviors (e.g., engaging in social interaction with other patients or staff) and reduce unwanted behaviors (e.g., behaving bizarrely or aggressively). Although token economies do not cure schizophrenia, they often allow chronic patients and their caregivers in institutional settings to lead lives of higher quality.

Other psychosocial treatments for schizophrenia include supported employment (which helps persons with schizophrenia return to work, either part or full time, often in a sheltered environment); *social skills training* (which focuses on one of the most prominent symptoms of schizophrenia, impairment in social relationships); *family psychoeducation* (which provides support and training to families with the responsibility for looking after a parent or child suffering from schizophrenia; a focus of this training is often on efforts to maintain adherence to anti-psychotic medication); and *assertive community treatment* (which targets those chronic schizophrenic patients in the community, often homeless, who have failed to access supportive professional services available in the community; once those patients are identified, caregiving professionals seek them out and work to convince them to use the services that these outreach workers can provide).

Somatic Treatments for Psychological Disorders

Somatic interventions for psychological disorders have existed since antiquity. A variety of early somatic therapeutic interventions for madness or melancholia existed, but because mental distress was often presumed to be of spiritual origin, many of these were performed in the context of religious rites. In Western cultures, penitence, self-mutilation, exorcism, and death (via drowning or the *auto-da-fé*—literally, an "act of faith") in religious rituals were used to expunge the evil influences that were believed to cause madness. In non-Western cultures, shamanistic rituals involving fasting, other forms of prolonged physical deprivation, or administration of potent psychotropic substances were employed not only as paths to individual enlightenment but also as treatment for those experiencing emotional distress.

A medical as well as a spiritual basis for somatic interventions also has a long history in Western cultures, however. Various subtypes of depression (e.g., "head melancholy," "hypochondriachal melancholy") had specific treatment recommendations, including opiates and other herbal agents. Saint John's wort, an herb still in use as an antidepressant treatment today, was one such recommendation. Somatic treatments included bloodletting, cupping, application of leeches, and purging (both "upward" and "downward"), all carefully described in Robert Burton's (1927) classic *Anatomy of Melancholy* first published in 1621.

Another excellent early example of a somatic intervention aimed at ameliorating psychological as well as physical conditions was the séance of Anton Mesmer. Mesmer was an 18th-century entrepreneur of sorts who purported to cure sufferers of nervous conditions by the application of "animal magnetism." Patients were gathered together in groups, generally around a central object such as a tree or a tub that was thought to be the repository of an electric or magnetic force. Individuals were linked to this object and to each other by grasping chains or cords that transmitted the curative force. Mesmer played mysterious music on a glass harmonica and suggested to patients the source of their ills.

Although his treatment enjoyed a period of great popularity in Europe, particularly among the privileged classes in Paris, within a few years it was debunked by scientists of the day who could not replicate the effects of animal magnetism. Mesmer was forced to flee from Paris and died in relative obscurity (Ellenberger, 1981; Gallo & Finger, 2000). His legacy is left in the term *mesmerizing*, which reflects the state of heightened suggestibility that led his patients to report the curative power of the séance. Mesmerism is considered to be the forerunner of modern clinical hypnotherapy.

Modern Somatic Treatments: Neuromodulatory Therapies

In more recent times, a number of somatic therapies have captured the attention of the psychiatric field. These can be loosely grouped under a category of treatments called *neuromodulatory therapies* (Moreines, McClintock, & Holtzheimer, 2011). As we shall see, few of these have withstood the test of empirical scrutiny and most, particularly those prevalent in the 20th century, have been consigned to a highly dubious position in the history of mental health treatment. In defense of somatic treatments, it is important to acknowledge that no single treatment, whether herbal, prescription medication, psychological, or somatic, has been demonstrated to be terribly effective in the long run. Response rates tend to be low, and rates of remission are high. Interventions that combine pharmacological and psychological treatments tend to yield higher rates of response, but even in these cases long-term response rates are usually disappointing.

PSYCHOSURGERY: PREFRONTAL LEUCOTOMY (LOBOTOMY)

The most notorious form of somatic treatment employed in modern psychiatry was the procedure known as *leucotomy*, commonly known as *lobotomy*. It was developed by a Portuguese psychiatrist, Egas Moniz, but achieved worldwide use via the aggressive promotion of a Washington, DC–based psychiatrist, Dr. Walter Freeman (see Valenstein, 1986, a must-read historical reference on lobotomy and other 20th-century somatic procedures). Despite its known debilitating aftereffects (including mental dulling and a state of psychological and physical apathy), lobotomy became, for a period in the 1940s and 1950s, one of the most widely used treatments for severe mental disease. Working under the assumption that the prefrontal cortex was both a nonessential element of the central nervous system and the origin of most nervous disorders, Freeman devised a procedure to sever white matter tracts between the prefrontal cortex (PFC) and other areas of brain. Because Freeman actually began by using ice picks, which he scored with markings to indicate depth of insertion, his procedure earned the sobriquet "ice pick therapy." Technically called leucotomes, these devices were inserted into the brain to rather indiscriminately cut white matter tracts extending to the PFC.

Freeman's technique gained popularity, despite the not unexpectedly high mortality rate due to bleeding, infection, or inadvertent destruction of vital subcortical areas. The acceptance of this procedure is perhaps not surprising, because it was developed during an era when few effective treatments for severe mental illness existed. The first antipsychotic medication was not introduced into widespread practice until 1954, and severe mental diseases did not lend themselves well to treatment by psychoanalytic psychotherapy, the predominant mode of treatment at the time. So, despite the obvious permanent disability that resulted from "successful" procedures (successfully treated patients were often docile and placid but frequently were significantly cognitively impaired and required permanent custodial care), lobotomy was relied on as a treatment for severe mental illness. Because records were poorly kept, it is unknown how many patients were subjected to this brutal treatment before increasing concern about its disastrous aftereffects led to its abandonment. The number, particularly in institutional populations, was likely considerable—probably around 20,000 (Malone, 2010).

OTHER COMMON PSYCHIATRIC PROCEDURES

We do not have space in this short chapter to review in depth a number of other common psychiatric procedures used before the advent of psychotropic drugs to control the manifestations of mental disease. Insulin coma therapy involved placing the patient into a hypoglycemic coma for several hours. Seizures, similar to those seen in electroconvulsive therapy (ECT), often resulted. Of these treatments, 40 to 60 were recommended for control of symptoms of schizophrenia. Other forms of prolonged coma of up to 10 days in duration were induced with high doses of barbiturates; this was thought to control symptoms of numerous disorders. A more current version of prolonged sleep therapy exists in "rapid withdrawal" from opiates, where opiate-dependent patients are placed in a drug-induced coma to spare them the discomfort of withdrawal. Because this treatment does nothing to prevent resumption of drug use, it is not recommended. "Seizure" therapies, the precursor of modern ECT, were common from the 1920s to the 1950s. In these treatments, various epileptogenic agents were administered to obtain the predictable changes in mental status that followed a seizure. Other treatments included "hydrotherapy" (spraying patients with pulses of hot or cold water) and "immobilization therapy" (wrapping patients in layers of wet sheets; Mora, 1967, and Valenstein, 1986, have fuller descriptions). Suffice it to say that none of these procedures has withstood the test of time, and none is currently viewed as either credible or humane.

PSYCHOSURGERY: ANTERIOR CINGULOTOMY AND CAPSULOTOMY

Psychosurgery was largely abandoned in the aftermath of Freeman's overzealous attempts to popularize lobotomy. In the more recent past, however, a limited form of psychosurgery has been used much more selectively to treat cases of severe obsessive–compulsive disorder (OCD) that is unresponsive to medications or behavioral treatment. In this procedure, known as *anterior cingulotomy*, the anterior cingulate gyrus is selectively lesioned using high-frequency radio beams (the gamma knife). Becau e these lesions are selective and the procedure does not involve craniotomy, side effects, although still present, are less pronounced than with more indiscriminant lesioning. Some patients report improvement in severe OCD after undergoing the procedure. For those with extremely severe and persistent symptomatology, it is possible (but not proven) that cingulotomy may be of benefit. Complete symptom resolution is rare, and different individuals respond at different rates. Long-term neuropsychological deficits, primarily in cognitive sequencing, image comparison, and deficits in attention, have been demonstrated (Cohen et al., 1999; Ochsner et al., 2001). Because of limited efficacy and concerns about permanent neurological damage, anterior cingulotomy is rare. A recent review examining 60 years of outcome data for psychosurgical procedures excluding lobotomy suggested that when used, anterior capsulotomy yielded the highest rate of improvement for GAD and OCD, whereas anterior cingulotomy (bilateral lesions to the anterior cingulate gyrus) was more effective in treating bipolar disorder, depression, and schizoaffective disorder. In this retrospective survey, addiction and schizophrenia had the lowest response rates to psychosurgery (Leiphart & Valone, 2010).

Recent interest has been shown in *deep brain stimulation (DBS)*, a technique that has a history of use in management of Parkinson's disease and other disorders. In this technique, electrodes are implanted in the brain (the ventral internal capsule and ventral striatum) and connected to an external battery pack. The rate of stimulation is adjusted for the individual patient. In 2009, the U.S. Food and Drug Administration (FDA) granted a humanitarian device exception approval for the use of DBS in refractory OCD (Malone, 2010). Malone also reported on a small series of patients with highly treatment-resistant depression who responded well to DBS, but this treatment remains experimental.

VAGUS NERVE STIMULATION

The FDA has approved the use of cervical vagus nerve stimulation (VNS) in the treatment of refractory epilepsy since 1997 and for treatment-resistant depression and major depression since 2005 (Al-Harbi & Qureshi, 2012). In this procedure, electrodes are implanted on the patient's left vagus nerve in the neck area. A pulse generator is implanted under the skin and attached to an external battery pack. The device is programmed to deliver regularly timed impulses to the vagus nerve. The patient with epilepsy can also deliver additional stimulation if the onset of a seizure is felt. Electrical stimulation of the vagus nerve results in a reduction in the frequency and severity of seizures for many (but not all) patients, and complete elimination of seizures in a few (perhaps 15%). The benefits of the device are cumulative; it typically becomes more efficient with use over time (Andrews, 2003). More recently, this device has been proposed as a treatment for depression on the basis of open-label trials (Kosel & Schlaepfer, 2003). This use, however, has been demonstrated only in small trials, and one trial comparing VNS to a sham procedure failed to show significant results for the active treatment at 10 weeks (Carpenter, Friehs, & Price, 2003). The mechanism through which VNS exerts its antidepressant effects (if any) is unknown but likely involves ascending stimulation of deep brain structures involved in the regulation of emotion.

ELECTROCONVULSIVE THERAPY

ECT is a common, albeit still controversial, psychiatric procedure involving the application of electrical current of varying amplitude and frequency to induce a seizure. It is believed to provide a more rapid response to treatment and greater short-term efficacy than other treatments for depression. Despite the generally enthusiastic endorsement of ECT by some clinicians, the absence of systematic studies on its short- and long-term negative side effects remains a troublesome gap in the literature. Baldly stated, the evidence base for ECT, both in terms of efficacy and negative consequences, continues to be insufficient.

It is hypothesized that the induction of a seizure represents the therapeutic component of ECT, although its exact mechanism of action is unknown. Some hypothesize that the memory loss that often follows ECT treatments is the therapeutic component, but research has not found a direct correlation between degree of memory loss and clinical improvement (McElheney, Moody, Steif, & Prudic, 1995). Alternatively, ECT may affect the production and activity of certain neurotransmitters in a similar fashion to antidepressants. Unlike earlier treatments based on seizure induction, modern ECT is performed under general anesthesia using a rapidly acting paralytic agent that prevents contraction of skeletal muscle (seizures induced without paralytic agents often resulted in broken teeth, fractured vertebrae, long bone fractures, and separation of muscle and tendon tissue from bone). An initial course of treatment for ECT is generally two to three procedures a week administered for 2 to 3 weeks, with follow-up, or maintenance, treatments given once or twice monthly for an indefinite period. Treatment with ECT generally results in improvement on most objective measures of depression, but its effects are transient and, as with other forms of treatment for depression, most patients will relapse without further intervention.

Although ECT is generally considered safe, its use remains controversial, with most concerns centering on memory deficits after treatment, and it does appear that some administrations of ECT may be more associated with memory deficits than others (Sackeim et al., 2007). It is important to note, as Sackeim et al. (2007) did, that despite the prevalence of ECT in the United States, with an estimated 100,000 patients treated per year, long-term prospective studies of the cognitive effects of ECT are essentially nonexistent, as is evidence supporting its long-term efficacy (Greenhalgh, Knight, Hind, Beverley, & Walters, 2005). Some researchers, citing shortcomings in the literature and the fact that many patients may respond to "sham" ECT treatments (Rasmussen, 2009), have argued that its use is not ethically justified (Read & Bentall, 2010; Stefanazzi, 2013). Proponents continue to advance ECT as the gold standard in treating depression, but ongoing scientific concerns and patient advocacy initiatives have led to legislation curtailing its use in some jurisdictions.

REPETITIVE TRANSCRANIAL MAGNETIC STIMULATION

ECT is an expensive procedure, requiring anesthesia, administration of drugs to block skeletal muscle seizure response, and postprocedure recovery. As we have seen, concerns persist about its long-term cognitive effects and efficacy, and many remain skeptical of its use. As noted, a central presumption in ECT has been that the evocation of a seizure is essential to its therapeutic action; a different form of brain stimulation, *repetitive transcranial magnetic stimulation* (rTMS; also referred to as simply transcranial magnetic stimulation or TMS) does not provoke seizures and has some efficacy in treating depression. Largely in response to concerns about negative effects of ECT, this and other less invasive treatments bearing some resemblance to ECT have come into use in the past 10 to 15 years. Many of the same methodological concerns seen in ECT studies (e.g., inadequate study design or long-term follow-up and a high response to sham interventions) also pertain to rTMS studies. Some authors have questioned whether brain stimulation that does not produce a seizure is truly an effective antidepressant treatment (Luber, McClintock, & Lisanby, 2013), but it is clear that non-seizure-producing brain stimulation, at least in some patients, produces a positive antidepressant response.

In rTMS, an electrode is placed on the scalp, generally over the area of the dorsolateral prefrontal cortex, and a strong magnetic current is subsequently applied. Like ECT, the procedure is repeated for a period of several weeks, generally daily in the case of rTMS. Unlike ECT, the aim is generally not to induce a seizure, although if a pulse of sufficient strength is applied, a seizure may result. Because patients treated with rTMS have been observed to improve without induction of a seizure, this observation casts doubt on the role of seizure as the therapeutic component of ECT. The use of anesthesia is not required, and patients are alert throughout the procedure. The treatment involves 6 weeks of applications of the device at 10 Hz to the left dorsolateral prefrontal cortex (Luber et al., 2013). It was hoped that rTMS would be an effective treatment against depression without causing the memory deficits seen in ECT, and in 2008, the FDA approved rTMS for the treatment of major depression not responsive to antidepressant medication. This approval is encouraging, but definitive evidence remains elusive. Just as in most studies of antidepressants, a strong placebo response is associated with rTMS, in most cases of similar size to that associated with antidepressant trials (Brunoni, Lopes, Kaptchuk, & Fregni, 2009). As is the case with other unimodal therapies, the total number of patients demonstrating true clinical improvement remains low (see Cusin & Dougherty, 2012, for an excellent, concise review of neuromodulatory treatments). Although the answer to this question has not been definitively settled, a well-designed trial (Luber et al., 2013), found small but significant differences between sham and actual rTMS; overall, however, only a minority of participants demonstrated clinically significant improvement.

MAGNETIC SEIZURE THERAPY

Because of potentially less harmful neurocognitive effects, magnetic seizure therapy (MST) is also being explored as an alternative to ECT. MST is a variant of rTMS, in that the same fundamental mechanism of transcranial magnetic therapy is used but at higher and more rapid rates of stimulation. MST, however, requires more powerful equipment to deliver the magnetic pulse than is available in most commercial rTMS devices. In MST, rTMS is administered to an anesthetized patient with sufficient power to induce a generalized seizure. The assumption is that there will be fewer negative neurocognitive effects (principally memory loss) resulting from the application of magnetic rather than electrical stimulation. Conclusions about its safety and utility await further trials, but it is an area of some current interest because of the possible safety benefits provided by this procedure over ECT. A review of 11 case series and trials concluded that MST largely lacked the neurocognitive deficits of ECT (reorientation after the procedure, retrograde and anterograde amnesia; McClintock,

Tirmizi, Chansard, & Husain, 2011). Another small, open label trial of MST was disappointing, with only five of the 13 patients completing the trial meeting response criteria (Fitzgerald et al., 2013). Thus, MST remains a purely investigatory form of treatment (Zyss et al., 2010).

PHOTOTHERAPY ("LIGHT BOX THERAPY")

Normal seasonal variations in the quantity of available natural light have been hypothesized to lead to sustained changes in mood, often clinical depression, in susceptible individuals. Although not all experts acknowledge the existence of seasonal mood disorders, several facts support the association between changes in ambient light and mood disorders. First, changes in circulating hormones (principally cortisol) and neurotransmitters (serotonin) have been found to be possibly different in some patients with and without the disorder (Joseph-Vanderpool et al., 1991). Second, seasonal depression is speculated to be more prevalent in northern latitudes, where changes in the amount of available light differs dramatically between seasons. Finally, seasonal variants of depression are also often associated with sleep disorders, and disruptions of circadian rhythm (sleep disorder) may also be responsive to phototherapy. Circadian rhythm disorders are also common in shift workers and travelers across several time zones (i.e., "jet lag"). Interestingly, in patients diagnosed with depression, a period of sleep deprivation has been demonstrated to result in at least transient improvement in mood (Berger, van Calker, & Riemann, 2003; Giedke, Klingberg, Schwärzler, & Schweinsberg, 2003).

The treatment of seasonal mood dysregulation with phototherapy is straightforward: The patient is exposed to bright light, usually generated by a series of fluorescent tubes contained in a portable box. These are available in different sizes and produce light of varying intensities, generally in the range of 2,500 to 10,000 lux, compared with normal room light of 100 to 150 lux. Whether a specific quantity of light is required to produce a therapeutic change is unknown, as is the mechanism of its effect. Theories relating to the production of the sleep-inducing hormone melatonin do not account for all the effects of phototherapy (Wyatt, 2000), and in general, results of investigations into bright light therapy yield equivocal results. A systematic review of bright light therapy for the management of insomnia in older adults was inconclusive (Montgomery & Dennis, 2002), but here as in other studies, the authors noted that the general absence of adverse side effects and potential efficacy in some patients suggests that it may be of potential benefit to some. Many recent reviews provide tepid endorsements for phototherapy for depression or its seasonal affective variant (Dirmaier et al., 2012). Many insurers regard phototherapy as experimental and do not cover this intervention.

EXERCISE THERAPY

There is intriguing, if incomplete, evidence that a structured program of physical exercise is an effective measure against depression. Like many unimodal therapies, by itself, exercise is probably not a sufficient treatment for patients with diagnosed depression, but here common sense should intervene and if not trump at least complement the results of scientific intervention. Exercise has salutary effects on general health; it is linked to at least short-term improvements in mood, temporary restriction of food intake, and numerous other beneficial factors. It is more than reasonable to include it in a multimodal approach to depression for those patients who can engage in it. Several meta-analyses of controlled and uncontrolled studies have demonstrated a positive effect derived from aerobic or nonaerobic exercise conducted two to three times weekly. However, when poorly designed or uncontrolled studies were removed from the analysis, the association, although apparently positive, was weaker (Lawlor & Hopker, 2001). At least one randomized trial has directly compared aerobic exercise, antidepressant medication (the SSRI sertraline, or Zoloft), and a combination of exercise and medication in older patients with depression (Blumenthal et al., 2001). This study found that although medication had a somewhat faster onset of action than exercise, at 4 months, patients in all groups reported equivalent improvement on standard measures of depression, and there was some evidence that those who continued with exercise beyond the end of the study period were at lower risk of relapse than those who did not (Babyak et al., 2000). The best available review of exercise in depression found modest but positive effects for exercise regimens for depression when compared with a control or no-treatment group (Rimer et al., 2012). Because exercise has beneficial effects on sleep hygiene, dietary regulation, and physical well-being, it is recommended that it be made an integral component of any treatment for patients with depression.

In sum, there appears to be a growing body of well-conducted studies demonstrating that exercise is of benefit in the management of depression, anxiety, and other nervous disorders. Whether exercise has any specific effect for any particular disorder is unknown. It is equally unknown whether there is a dose–response effect to exercise (i.e., does more exercise result in greater psychological improvement?) or what types of exercise are most beneficial, although a variety of both aerobic and nonaerobic protocols have been recommended. We do know, however, that exercise is associated with reports of enhanced well-being and objective measures of physical health. Furthermore, body mass index, physical health, and exercise are predictors of "successful" aging after age 60 (Vaillant & Mukamal, 2001). Moreover, levels of physical activity seem to be inversely correlated with depression from as early as childhood (Sallis, Prochaska, & Taylor, 2000).

Exercise programs for those with serious and persistent forms of mental distress, such as schizophrenia, should also not be ignored. Weight gain and diabetes are two complications resulting from the use of many newer antipsychotic medications, and a well-designed program of exercise, diet, and patient awareness is essential if the health consequences of these conditions are to be avoided.

Summary

This brief summary of psychosocial and somatic treatments for common mental disorders should, we hope, provide the reader with a general overview of techniques that have been or are currently used in clinical practice. Obviously, numerous treatments could not be discussed in one short book chapter, and readers are referred to other sources, such as Nathan and Gorman (2007), for more in-depth reviews. We hope readers will keep the following overarching principles in mind when considering these various interventions.

a. Psychosocial and somatic treatments for mental disorders remain frustratingly nonspecific. We often do not know the therapeutic component of either form of treatment, nor do we know whether manipulation of individual factors (e.g., a certain neurotransmitter, a certain cognitive or behavioral process) represents the curative element of either a somatic or a psychosocial treatment. There is some cause for optimism, however. We are increasingly able to formulate specific biological and psychological treatments for specific disorders, and as our knowledge advances, we should be able to further refine our therapeutic options.

b. Although we remain unable, in most instances, to determine the causality of a mental disorder (i.e., we do not really know if behaviors cause pathological changes in brain chemistry, if fundamental abnormalities in brain pathophysiology lead to aberrant behaviors, or if both mechanisms are involved), it is certain that brain and behavior are inextricably intertwined. In clinical terms, this sometimes, but not always, means that a combination of both somatic (often pharmacologic) and psychological treatments represents the optimal treatment for certain disorders, such as severe depression, mania, or other forms of psychosis. Certain disorders may respond to psychological interventions alone, but it is rare that somatic treatments are indicated as the sole intervention for any disorder.

c. In evaluating somatic and psychological treatments, it is vital to assess the strength of the evidence and the quality of the research in determining the potential efficacy of a treatment and its applicability to a specific condition. A few well-designed, randomized trials may boost our confidence in a particular treatment, but until these results have been replicated and their effects assessed in general clinical populations, our understanding remains incomplete.

References

Abbas, A., & Lieberman, J. (in press). Pharmacological treatments for schizophrenia. In P. E. Nathan & J. H. Gorman (Eds.), *A guide to treatments that work* (3rd ed.). New York, NY: Oxford University Press.

Al-Harbi, K. S., & Qureshi, N. A. (2012). Neuromodulation therapies and treatment-resistant depression. *Medical Devices, 5*, 53–65.

Andrews, R. J. (2003). Neuroprotection trek—the next generation. Neuromodulation I. Techniques—deep brain stimulation, vagus nerve stimulation, and transcranial magnetic stimulation. *Annals of the New York Academy of Sciences, 993*, 1–13. http://dx.doi.org/10.1111/j.1749-6632.2003.tb07506.x

Ayllon, T. (1968). *The token economy: A motivational system for therapy and rehabilitation.* New York, NY: Appleton-Century-Crofts.

Azrin, N. H., Sisson, R. W., Meyers, R., & Godley, M. (1982). Alcoholism treatment by disulfiram and community reinforcement therapy. *Journal of Behavior Therapy and Experimental Psychiatry, 13*, 105–112. http://dx.doi.org/10.1016/0005-7916(82)90050-7

Babyak, M., Blumenthal, J. A., Herman, S., Khatri, P., Doraiswamy, M., Moore, K., . . . Krishnan, K. R. (2000). Exercise treatment for major depression: Maintenance of therapeutic benefit at 10 months. *Psychosomatic Medicine, 62*, 633–638. http://dx.doi.org/10.1097/00006842-200009000-00006

Barlow, D. H. (2011). *The Oxford handbook of clinical psychology.* New York, NY: Oxford University Press.

Barlow, D. H., Allen, L. B., & Basden, S. L. (2007). Psychological treatments for panic disorders, phobias, and generalized anxiety disorder. In P. E. Nathan & J. M. Gorman (Eds.), *A guide to treatments that work* (3rd ed., pp. 351–394). New York, NY: Oxford University Press.

Barlow, D. H., Allen, L. B., & Choate, M. L. (2004). Toward a unified treatment for emotional disorders. *Behavior Therapy, 35*, 205–230. http://dx.doi.org/10.1016/S0005-7894(04)80036-4

Beck, A. T., Emery, G., & Greenberg, R. L. (2005). *Anxiety disorders and phobias: A cognitive perspective.* New York, NY: Basic Books.

Beck, A. T., Rush, A. J., Shaw, B. F., & Emery, G. (1979). *Cognitive therapy of depression: A treatment manual.* New York, NY: Guilford Press.

Berger, M., van Calker, D., & Riemann, D. (2003). Sleep and manipulations of the sleep–wake rhythm in depression. *Acta Psychiatrica Scandinavica, 108*(Suppl. 418), 83–91. http://dx.doi.org/10.1034/j.1600-0447.108.s418.17.x

Blumenthal, J. A., Babyak, M. A., Moore, K. A., Craighead, W. E., Herman, S., Khatri, P., . . . Krishnan, K. R. (2001). Effects of exercise training on older adults with major depression. *Archives of Internal Medicine, 159,* 2349–2356

Brunoni, A. R., Lopes, M., Kaptchuk, T. J., & Fregni, F. (2009). Placebo response of non-pharmacological and pharmacological trials in major depression: A systematic review and meta-analysis. *PLoS ONE, 4,* e4824. http://dx.doi.org/10.1371/journal.pone.0004824

Burton, R. (1927). *The anatomy of melancholy.* London, England: Chatto and Windus. (Original work published 1621)

Carpenter, L. L., Friehs, G. M., & Price, L. H. (2003). Cervical vagus nerve stimulation for treatment-resistant depression. *Neurosurgery Clinics of North America, 14,* 275–282. http://dx.doi.org/10.1016/S1042-3680(02)00121-3

Carr, A. A. (2009). The effectiveness of family therapy and systemic interventions for adult-focused problems. *Journal of Family Therapy, 31,* 46–74. http://dx.doi.org/10.1111/j.1467-6427.2008.00452.x

Carroll, K. M., Easton, C. J., Nich, C., Hunkele, K. A., Neavins, T. M., Sinha, R., . . . Rounsaville, B. J. (2006). The use of contingency management and motivational/skills-building therapy to treat young adults with marijuana dependence. *Journal of Consulting and Clinical Psychology, 74,* 955–966. http://dx.doi.org/10.1037/0022-006X.74.5.955

Cohen, R. A., Kaplan, R. F., Zuffante, P., Moser, D. J., Jenkins, M. A., Salloway, S., & Wilkinson, H. (1999). Alteration of intention and self-initiated action associated with bilateral anterior cingulotomy. *The Journal of Neuropsychiatry and Clinical Neurosciences, 11,* 444–453.

Craighead, W. E., Sheets, E. S., & Brosse, A. J. (2007). Psychosocial treatments for major depressive disorder. In P. E. Nathan & J. M. Gorman (Eds.), *A guide to treatments that work* (3rd ed., pp. 289–308). New York, NY: Oxford University Press.

Craske, M. G., & Barlow, D. H. (2007). *Mastery of your anxiety and panic: Therapist guide* (4th ed.). New York, NY: Oxford University Press.

Cusin, C., & Dougherty, D. D. (2012). Somatic therapies for treatment-resistant depression: ECT, TMS, VNS, DBS. *Biology of Mood and Anxiety Disorders, 2,* 14. Retrieved from http://www.ncbi.nlm.nih.gov/pmc/articles/PMC3514332

Dirmaier, J., Steinmann, M., Krattenmacher, T., Watzke, B., Barghaan, D., Koch, U., & Schulz, H. (2012). Non-pharmacological treatment of depressive disorders: A review of evidence-based treatment options. *Reviews on Recent Clinical Trials, 7*, 141–149. http://dx.doi.org/10.2174/157488712800100233

Ellenberger, H. (1981). *The discovery of the unconscious.* New York, NY: Basic Books.

Finney, J. W., Wilbourne, P. L., & Moos, R. H. (2007). Psychosocial treatments for substance use disorders. In P. E. Nathan & J. M. Gorman (Eds.), *A guide to treatments that work* (3rd ed., pp. 179–202). New York, NY: Oxford University Press.

Fitzgerald, P. B., Hoy, K. E., Herring, S. E., Clinton, A. M., Downey, G., & Daskalakis, Z. J. (2013). Pilot study of the clinical and cognitive effects of high-frequency magnetic seizure therapy in major depressive disorder. *Depression and Anxiety, 30*, 129–136. http://dx.doi.org/10.1002/da.22005

Gallo, D. A., & Finger, S. (2000). The power of a musical instrument: Franklin, the Mozarts, Mesmer, and the glass armonica. *History of Psychology, 3*, 326–343. http://dx.doi.org/10.1037/1093-4510.3.4.326

Giedke, H., Klingberg, S., Schwärzler, F., & Schweinsberg, M. (2003). Direct comparison of total sleep deprivation and late partial sleep deprivation in the treatment of major depression. *Journal of Affective Disorders, 76*, 85–93. http://dx.doi.org/10.1016/S0165-0327(02)00071-X

Greenhalgh, J., Knight, C., Hind, D., Beverley, C., & Walters, S. (2005). Clinical and cost-effectiveness of electroconvulsive therapy for depressive illness, schizophrenia, catatonia and mania: Systematic reviews and economic modelling studies. *Health Technology Assessment, 9*, 1–156, iii–iv. http://dx.doi.org/10.3310/hta9090

Hsu, S. H., & Marlatt, G. A. (2012). Addiction syndrome: Relapse and relapse prevention. In H. J. Shaffer (Ed.), *APA addiction syndrome handbook* (Vol. 2, pp. 105–132). Washington, DC: American Psychological Association.

Joseph-Vanderpool, J. R., Rosenthal, N. E., Chrousos, G. P., Wehr, T. A., Skwerer, R., Kasper, S., & Gold, P. W. (1991). Abnormal pituitary-adrenal responses to corticotropin-releasing hormone in patients with seasonal affective disorder: Clinical and pathophysiological implications. *The Journal of Clinical Endocrinology and Metabolism, 72*, 1382–1387. http://dx.doi.org/10.1210/jcem-72-6-1382

Keck, P. E., & McElroy, S. L. (2007). Pharmacological treatments for bipolar disorder. In P. E. Nathan & J. M. Gorman (Eds.), *A guide to treatments that work* (3rd ed., pp. 323–350). New York, NY: Oxford University Press.

Kosel, M., & Schlaepfer, T. E. (2003). Beyond the treatment of epilepsy: New applications of vagus nerve stimulation in psychiatry. *CNS Spectrums, 8*, 515–521.

Lawlor, D. A., & Hopker, S. W. (2001). The effectiveness of exercise as an intervention in the management of depression: Systematic review and meta-regression analysis of randomized controlled trials. *BMJ, 322*, 763–767. http://dx.doi.org/10.1136/bmj.322.7289.763

Lciphart, J. W., & Valone, F. (2010). Stereotactic lesions for the treatment of psychiatric disorders. *Journal of Neurosurgery, 113*, 1204–1211.

Leyfer, O., & Brown, T. A. (2011). The anxiety-depression spectrum. In D. H. Barlow (Ed.), *The Oxford handbook of clinical psychology* (pp. 279–293). New York, NY: Oxford University Press.

Litt, M. D., Kadden, R. M., Kabela-Cormier, E., & Petry, N. M. (2009). Changing network support for drinking: Network support project 2-year follow-up. *Journal of Consulting and Clinical Psychology, 77*, 229–242. http://dx.doi.org/10.1037/a0015252

Luber, B., McClintock, S. M., & Lisanby, S. H. (2013). Applications of transcranial magnetic stimulation and magnetic seizure therapy in the study and treatment of disorders related to cerebral aging. *Dialogues in Clinical Neuroscience, 15*, 87–98.

Malone, D. A. (2010). Use of deep brain stimulation in treatment-resistant major depression. *Cleveland Clinic Journal of Medicine, 77*, S77–S80.

McClintock, S. M., Tirmizi, O., Chansard, M., & Husain, M. M. (2011). A systematic review of the neurocognitive effects of magnetic seizure therapy. *International Review of Psychiatry, 23*, 413–423. http://dx.doi.org/10.3109/09540261.2011.623687

McElheney, M. C., Moody, B. J., Steif, B. L., & Prudic, J. (1995). Autobiographical memory and mood: Effects of electroconvulsive therapy. *Neuropsychology, 9*, 501–517.

Meyer, J. M., Davis, V. G., Goff, D. C., McEvoy, J. P., Nasrallah, H. A., Davis, S. M., . . . Lieberman, J. A. (2008). Change in metabolic syndrome parameters with antipsychotic treatment in the CATIE Schizophrenia Trial: Prospective data from phase 1. *Schizophrenia Research, 101*, 273–286. http://dx.doi.org/10.1016/j.schres.2007.12.487

Miklowitz, D. J., George, E. L., Richards, J. A., Simoneau, T. L., & Suddath, R. L. (2003). A randomized study of family-focused psychoeducation and pharmacotherapy in the outpatient management of bipolar disorder. *Archives of General Psychiatry, 60*, 904–912. http://dx.doi.org/10.1001/archpsyc.60.9.904

Montgomery, P., & Dennis, J. (2002). Bright light therapy for sleep problems in adults aged 60+. *Cochrane Database of Systematic Reviews, 2,* CD003403.

Mora, G. M. (1967). History of psychiatry. In A. M. Freedman & H. I. Kaplan (Eds.), *Comprehensive textbook of psychiatry* (pp. 3–34). Baltimore, MD: Williams & Wilkins.

Moreines, J. L., McClintock, S. M., & Holtzheimer, P. E. (2011). Neuropsychologic effects of neuromodulation techniques for treatment-resistant depression: A review. *Brain Stimulation, 4,* 17–27. http://dx.doi.org/10.1016/j.brs.2010.01.005

Mueser, K. T., & Duva, S. M. (2011). Schizophrenia. In D. H. Barlow (Ed.), *The Oxford handbook of clinical psychology* (pp. 469–503). New York, NY: Oxford University Press.

Muralidharan, A., Miklowitz, D. J., & Craighead, W. E. (in press). Psychosocial treatments for bipolar disorder. In P. E. Nathan & J. M. Gorman (Eds.), *A guide to treatments that work* (4th ed.). New York, NY: Oxford University Press.

Nathan, P. E. (2004). The evidence base for evidence-based mental health treatments: Four continuing controversies. *Brief Treatment and Crisis Intervention, 4,* 243–254. http://dx.doi.org/10.1093/brief-treatment/mhh021

Nathan, P. E., & Gorman, J. M. (2007). *A guide to treatments that work* (3rd ed.). New York, NY: Oxford University Press.

Ochsner, K. N., Kosslyn, S. M., Cosgrove, G. R., Cassem, E. H., Price, B. H., Nierenberg, A. A., & Rauch, S. L. (2001). Deficits in visual cognition and attention following bilateral anterior cingulotomy. *Neuropsychologia, 39,* 219–230. http://dx.doi.org/10.1016/S0028-3932(00)00114-7

Otto, M. W., & Applebaum, A. J. (2011). The nature and treatment of bipolar disorder and the bipolar spectrum. In D. H. Barlow (Ed.), *The Oxford handbook of clinical psychology* (pp. 294–310). New York, NY: Oxford University Press.

Paul, G. L., & Lentz, R. J. (1977). *Psychosocial treatment of chronic mental patients: Milieu versus social-learning programs.* Cambridge, MA: Harvard University Press.

Prochaska, J. O., & DiClemente, C. C. (1986). Toward a comprehensive model of change. In W. R. Miller & N. Heather (Eds.), *Treating addictive behavior: Processes of change* (pp. 3–27). New York, NY: Plenum Press. http://dx.doi.org/10.1007/978-1-4613-2191-0_1

Project MATCH Research Group. (1993). Project MATCH: Rationale and methods for a multisite clinical trial matching patients to alcoholism treatment. *Alcoholism: Clinical and Experimental Research, 17,* 1130–1145. http://dx.doi.org/10.1111/j.1530-0277.1993.tb05219.x

Project MATCH Research Group. (1998). Matching alcoholism treatments to client heterogeneity: Project MATCH three-year drinking outcomes.

Alcoholism: Clinical and Experimental Research, 22, 1300–1311. http://dx.doi.org/10.1111/j.1530-0277.1998.tb03912.x

Rasmussen, K. G. (2009). Sham electroconvulsive therapy studies in depressive illness: A review of the literature and consideration of the placebo phenomenon in electroconvulsive therapy practice. *The Journal of ECT, 25,* 54–59. http://dx.doi.org/10.1097/YCT.0b013e3181719b23

Read, J., & Bentall, R. (2010). The effectiveness of electroconvulsive therapy: A literature review. *Epidemiologica e Psichiatrica Sociale, 19,* 333–347.

Rimer, J., Dwan, K., Lawlor, D. A., Greig, C. A., McMurdo, M., Morley, W., & Mead, G. E. (2012). Exercise for depression. *Cochrane Database of Systematic Reviews, 11,* CD004366.

Sackeim, H. A., Prudic, J., Fuller, R., Keilp, J., Lavori, P. W., & Olfson, M. (2007). The cognitive effects of electroconvulsive therapy in community settings. *Neuropsychopharmacology, 32,* 244–254. http://dx.doi.org/10.1038/sj.npp.1301180

Sallis, J. F., Prochaska, J. J., & Taylor, W. C. (2000). A review of correlates of physical activity of children and adolescents. *Medicine and Science in Sports and Exercise, 32,* 963–975. http://dx.doi.org/10.1097/00005768-200005000-00014

Scott, J., Paykel, E., Morriss, R., Bentall, R., Kinderman, P., Johnson, T., . . . Hayhurst, H. (2006). Cognitive-behavioural therapy for severe and recurrent bipolar disorders: Randomised controlled trial. *The British Journal of Psychiatry, 188,* 313–320. http://dx.doi.org/10.1192/bjp.188.4.313

Spring, B., & Neville, K. (2011). Evidence-based practice in clinical psychology. In D. H. Barlow (Ed.), *The Oxford handbook of clinical psychology* (pp. 128–149). New York, NY: Oxford University Press.

Stefanazzi, M. (2013). Is electroconvulsive therapy (ECT) ever ethically justified? If so, under what circumstances? *HEC Forum, 25,* 79–94. http://dx.doi.org/10.1007/s10730-012-9182-0

Vaillant, G. E., & Mukamal, K. (2001). Successful aging. *The American Journal of Psychiatry, 158,* 839–847. http://dx.doi.org/10.1176/appi.ajp.158.6.839

Valenstein, E. (1986). *Great and Desperate Cures: The rise and decline of psychosurgery and other radical treatments for mental illness.* New York, NY: Basic Books.

Winters, K. C., Botzet, A., Fahnhorst, T., Arria, A. Dykstra, L. G., & Oliver, J. (2012). Social factors and the addiction syndrome. In H. J. Shaffer (Ed.), *APA addiction syndrome handbook* (Vol. 1, pp. 229–250). Washington, DC: American Psychological Association.

Wyatt, J. K. (2000). Seasonal affective disorder. In A. E. Kazdin (Ed.), *Encyclopedia of psychology* (Vol. 7, pp. 200–201). Washington, DC: American Psychological Association & Oxford University Press.

Yamada, K., Watanabe, K., Nemoto, N., Fujita, H., Chikaraishi, C., Yamauchi, K., . . . Kanba, S. (2006). Prediction of medication noncompliance in outpatients with schizophrenia: 2-year follow-up study. *Psychiatry Research*, *141*, 61–69. http://dx.doi.org/10.1016/j.psychres.2004.07.014

Zyss, T., Zieba, A., Hese, R. T., Dudek, D., Grabski, B., Gorczyca, P., & Modrzejewska, R. (2010). Magnetic seizure therapy (MST)—a safer method for evoking seizure activity than current therapy with a confirmed antidepressant efficacy. *Neuroendocrinology Letters*, *31*, 425–437.

Bruce K. McCormick

The Use of Medicine in the Treatment of Mental Disorders

8

D uring the 20th century, two events dramatically influenced our understanding of mental disorders and how they could be treated. The first half of that century saw the work of Sigmund Freud, who suggested that certain types of life experiences may bring about mental disorders. Although today many authorities are critical of some of Freud's original ideas, it is almost universally recognized that events in people's lives affect their behavior, and when those events exceed their ability to cope in a healthy manner, disorders of thought and behavior may result. The lasting legacy of Freud and the many others who built on his work is the use of psychotherapy to treat mental disorders. Today many approaches to psychotherapy are used in mental health treatment. An overview of the most prominent of these methods is presented in Chapter 7 of this book.

The second half of the 20th century included the discovery that certain bioactive chemical compounds can be of tremendous value in the management of symptoms of disordered thought and behavior. Indeed, in some cases, medicine was found to be so effective that people with illness so

http://dx.doi.org/10.1037/14672-008
Your Practicum in Psychology: A Guide for Maximizing Knowledge and Competence, Second Edition, J. R. Matthews and C. E. Walker (Editors)

severe that their survival required around-the-clock supervision in hospitals or institutions experienced improvement so dramatic that they could live in a normal home situation. Others, although still in need of supervision, recovered sufficiently to participate in work, recreational activities, and psychotherapy. The discovery that medicine can be an effective part of treatment brought about the recognition that biology as well as life experiences can contribute to the nature, severity, and perhaps even the cause of mental disorders. By the end of the 20th century, the majority of mental health professionals recognized that both psychosocial (i.e., environmental) and biological factors influence the presence and specific characteristics of mental disorders, and the use of *psychotropic*[1] medicine was commonly a part of comprehensive plans for mental health treatment. Now, during the early years of the 21st century, there is a growing body of research that shows our experiences not only coexist with our biological state but that life events can actually produce changes in the chemistry and physical structures of a person's body. These findings bolster support for treatment procedures that use an integration of biological and psychosocial interventions through a coordinated use of medicine and psychotherapy.

How Will Knowing About Medicines Be Helpful?

A basic knowledge of medicines used in mental health treatment can be of value to you as a psychology practicum student in several ways. In a comprehensive inpatient program such as a hospital, you may see how medicines and psychotherapy are used together in a treatment plan. You may have opportunities to join meetings with the many professionals involved in treating patients. These meetings are often called *staffings* or meetings of a *multidisciplinary team* or *treatment team*. Among the many things discussed during such staffings will be what medicines a patient is taking and whether those medications appear to be producing the desired results. It is common for the mental health care team to provide information about sleeping, eating, interacting with others, and whether the concerns that brought the patient to treatment are improving. Often the dose or type of medication a patient is taking will be maintained or changed depending on input from those meetings.

Knowing the basics of medicines can be useful in understanding how such decisions are made. Additionally, knowing the types of medicines a patient is taking may give a clue to the pattern of symptoms that person was experiencing or the kinds of behavior disturbance that

---

[1]*Psychotropic* literally means "mind altering."

individual was exhibiting before treatment was started. If you have an opportunity to interact with patients during your practicum, you may be able to tell that some of their thoughts and behaviors are affected by medicines. You also may notice some undesirable effects that result from the use of medicine, such as nausea, excessive thirst, or sedation.

It is likely that you will have an opportunity to observe one or more treatment settings. Some patients with serious, chronic, and difficult-to-treat mental disorders spend many months or years in long-term care. Many others may spend several days or a few weeks of acute inpatient care in a hospital until such time as their condition improves sufficiently that they can return home. Often it is the effectiveness of psychotropic medications that shortens hospital stays and allows individuals to remain or return home and be treated on what is termed an *outpatient basis*. That is, they live independently but have regular appointments at a treatment facility, often one or more times per week. During those appointments, the patients may participate in group or individual psychotherapy. In addition, they may review with their prescriber how the medications they are taking seem to be working and discuss any side effects or other problems they may be experiencing. These checkups to review the effectiveness of their medicines (often informally called *med checks*) allow examination of a patient's overall physical and mental health and provide an opportunity for any adjustments that might be needed in their prescription. Frequent medication checkups are necessary for many of the more potent psychotropic medications.

How Are Medicines Named?

The names given to medicines may sound strange or unusual. Adding to the potential for confusion is that most medicines actually have three types of names: a chemical name, a generic name, and a brand name.[2] The chemical name, which is an actual designation of the chemical composition of the drug, is not commonly used except by chemists involved in the research and development of drugs. The generic name, usually a much-shortened version of the chemical name, is a simpler and more easily remembered way to refer to the same substance. When a pharmaceutical company develops a compound, the company usually patents the new medicine and gives it a brand name that is exclusively used for the medicine when made by that company. When a patent expires and other companies can make the same medicine, it can have different brand names depending on the manufacturer. For example,

---

[2]A *brand name* is sometimes called a *trade name*.

the generic diphenhydramine is marketed under the different brand names of Benadryl, Caladryl, and even Simply Sleep.

To illustrate this admittedly complicated system of naming drugs, consider the example of a common medicine, a compound frequently used for relief from pain that has the chemical name N-acetyl-p-aminophenol. Although that name may not be readily known, you may recognize its generic name, *acetaminophen*, and almost certainly you know the brand name of Tylenol. The advantage of shortening a chemical name to easier generic and brand names is even more apparent with this example of a common psychotropic medicine that has the chemical formula of $C17H18F3NO \cdot HCl$, the imposing chemical name of (+)-N-methyl-3-phenyl-3-[(α,α,α-trifluoro-p-tolyl)oxy]propylamine hydrochloride, the generic name of fluoxetine, and the brand name of Prozac.

Why Three Names?

The foregoing examples show the advantages of using a name for medicines other than the cumbersome chemical name. Yet why have both generic and brand names? The answer has mainly to do with sales, marketing, and advertising. Any prescription drug for use with humans in the United States must first receive approval from the Food and Drug Administration (FDA). Before receiving FDA approval, the company that plans to sell a medicine must conduct extensive research to demonstrate that the product is effective for its intended use and how safe it is for consumers.

The research, development, manufacturing, and the testing of possible medicines often take several years and cost many millions of dollars. For companies to recoup money spent to bring a medicine to market and then make a profit, new prescriptions are usually patented. While the patent is in effect (usually for 17 years), only the company holding the patent may sell the drug. At the time it has exclusive rights to sell a medicine the pharmaceutical company will copyright a brand name, which unlike the patent, does not expire but continues to be legally protected for exclusive use by that company. When a patent does expire, other companies are allowed to manufacture the medicine and to market it (usually at a lower cost) under its generic name but not by its original name.[3] Often a medicine known by its brand name will gain

---

[3]Occasionally, a company will copyright more than one name for the same medicine. Usually this is done when the drug is marketed for more than one purpose. For example, Wellbutrin, which is marketed for depression, also has the brand name Zyban when it is marketed for smoking cessation.

acceptance from prescribers and consumers while the patent is in effect. The manufacturing company hopes that consumers will continue to select the brand name medicine even when the patent runs out. For example, the patent for Tylenol has long since expired, but many consumers still buy the brand medicine they know and in which they have confidence, ignoring generic preparations that are equally available and at a lower cost.

What Are Generic Medicines?

The term *generic medicines* refers to medications that, as explained earlier, are not marketed under the original brand name and that are usually sold by a company other than the one that originally developed and patented those compounds. Many of the newer psychotropic medications only exist as brand-name drugs, but several, such as citalopram (Celexa) and quetiapine (Seroquel) as well as many older, established medications, are available in a generic form. Generic medications are almost always lower in cost than brand-name medications. In actual practice, it is sometimes difficult to know if a particular patient is receiving a brand name or a generic drug, especially if one is unfamiliar with the names of each.

Formal writing style requires that brand names be capitalized and generics begin with lowercase letters. That convention is not always followed, however, and capitalization of generics is perhaps the most common error. Moreover, in casual conversations one may refer to a brand-name drug even though a generic will be used. For example, in treatment team meetings, a prescriber might suggest giving a patient "Seroquel," when that facility uses only the generic, quetiapine.

How Do Generic Medicines Compare With Brand-Name Medicines?

Most medicines that are taken by mouth (orally) include both active and inactive ingredients. Active ingredients are the actual chemicals that are the medicine; inactive ingredients include fillers, color, sometimes flavor additives, and other substances to hold or contain the active ingredients. The FDA requires that all generic medicines contain roughly the same amount of active ingredients as was in the original brand-name medicine; however, the inactive ingredients may be very different. In most cases, generic medicines, whether they are psychotropics or other types of prescription drugs, work equally well as the originals. Differences in inactive ingredients sometimes change, within limits, how quickly the medicines actually go to work in the body or how much of the active ingredient is actually available for use in the body.[4] Typically any such differences are small and biologically inconsequential; however, occasionally some individuals do respond better to brand-name than generic psychotropic medicines. To save money, many treatment facilities and many insurance companies insist on the use of generic medications when they are available.

How Do Medicines Work to Treat Mental Disorders?

The human brain is an organ made up of millions and millions of cells, mostly nerve cells, which are called *neurons*. The neurons in the brain send signals throughout the nervous system of the body and to muscles, glands, and organs. Nerve cells typically consist of a cell body with a *nucleus*; structures called *dendrites*, which receive signals from other parts of the body, including other neurons; and branches called *axons*, which send signals to other parts of the body.

Different areas of the brain and corresponding nerve pathways from the brain through the spinal cord reach all areas of the body and control and regulate most body functions, including breathing and heartbeat, voluntary movement and reflexes, and the functioning of organs and healing of injuries. Nerve signals in the brain also influence and are affected by thoughts, sensations, and emotions. Medicines that are used to treat emotional disorders typically work by altering the transmission of signals between neurons in the brain, usually by changing what happens at the microscopic spaces across which nerve cells send signals to other neurons or other cells of the body. These spaces are called *synapses*. Most medicines have a long and complicated trip, however, before they can enter the bloodstream and move to synapses to produce their desired effects.

---

[4]Generic medicines are required to have 80% to 120% actual availability of the active ingredients compared with brand-name medicines.

How Do Medicines Get to Where They Can Be of Use?

When thinking of medicines for the treatment of mental disorders, most people probably consider pills or capsules—that is, medications that are taken orally. Indeed the majority of (although certainly not all) psychotropic medicines are taken by mouth. Most of the absorbable things people ingest, including food and drugs, enter the bloodstream through the walls of the stomach and especially those of the small intestine. Approximately 80% of the blood from the small intestine then goes directly to the liver. The liver produces a complex system of enzymes that attempt to convert any substance not recognized as a nutrient, to a form that can be easily eliminated from the body. This process allows the body to rid itself of the minute amounts of toxins and other non-nutrients people may happen to ingest or otherwise absorb through their lives. The liver does not, however, distinguish between chemicals people may have unknowingly or accidentally ingested and chemicals they have taken for the treatment of illness. This means that soon after a person takes an oral medicine, the liver works to break down that medicine chemically so that it can be eliminated from the body. If the liver enzyme system is not able to bring about the complete elimination of a substance, it still transforms it so that it can later be converted to a more easily eliminated compound. Usually the transformation by the liver causes the substance to become more easily dissolved in water and therefore eliminated in the urine.[5] The substance that results from being changed (metabolized) by enzymes from the liver is called a *metabolite*.

Because metabolism can destroy medicines when they are taken by mouth, the amount of a medicine taken (the dosage) must be large enough so that a sufficient amount of the active ingredient remains in the bloodstream even after passing through the liver. However, some medicines, although effective in themselves, are metabolized by the liver to a form (called an *active metabolite*) that can be as or more effective than the original medicine. For example, two antidepressant medications, imipramine (Tofranil) and venlafaxine (Effexor), have active metabolites that last longer than the medicine before they are changed by the liver enzymes.[6] The stimulant lisdexamfetamine (Vyvanse) has no effect at all until it is metabolized to the active metabolite, dextroamphetamine.

---

[5]For this reason, urinalysis is often used to check for recent drug use.

[6]The active metabolites for Tofranil and Effexor are desipramine and desvenlafaxine, respectively.

Because the amount of medicine actually available to the body can be affected by metabolism and elimination, individual dosing may need to be increased or decreased for people with liver disease or impaired kidney function.

An alternative to using sufficiently large doses of a medicine to avoid having the medicine destroyed through metabolism is to avoid altogether the initial "first pass" of blood from the small intestine to the liver. This may be accomplished by administration of drugs through routes that do not involve the gastrointestinal tract. Alternatives to oral administration include *inhalation* (such as might be used for treating asthma or for rapid infusion of nicotine for smoking cessation), absorption through blood vessels in the rectum (as with suppositories), through tissue at the underside if the tongue (*sublingual*), or through the skin (*transdermal*). Some medicines are injected into muscle tissue (*intramuscular* or *IM*) or directly into the blood stream (*intravenous* or *IV*). Intramuscular injections of tranquilizing and antipsychotic medications have long been used to induce rapid sedation of highly agitated patients. An additional advantage of intramuscular injections is that many medicines prepared for that route of administration are rather thick (*viscous*) and can take days to be completely absorbed in the bloodstream, resulting in a sort of timed-release effect.

Even when a medicine has passed through (or bypassed) the liver, there are other obstacles to overcome before it reaches the neuronal synapses. Proteins in the bloodstream[7] have a strong chemical affinity for many medicines and active metabolites and bind with them, essentially "locking them up" before they reach their site of action. Sometimes as much as 70% or 80% of a medicine can be protein bound. Additionally, the brain is protected from being exposed to many foreign elements by what is called the blood–brain barrier, an anatomical structuring that makes it difficult for many types of molecules to pass directly into the blood supply to the brain. Some medicines, such as the class of tranquilizers known as benzodiazepines,[8] have a chemical structure that allows them to cross the blood–brain barrier rapidly and consequently produce their sedating effect quite rapidly. Other medicines with larger molecular structures have to rely on other much slower and less efficient means of passing the blood–brain barrier. Thus, the actions of liver metabolism, protein binding, metabolic activity, and kidney function, as well as the chemical structure of a drug, all determine the amount of medication and route of administration that might be needed for a given patient.

---

[7]Albumin, in particular, is one such protein

[8]Examples of benzodiazepines include alprazolam (Xanax), diazepam (Valium), and clonazepam (Klonopin).

How Do Medications Affect Nerve Transmissions?

Transmission of a signal through a given nerve cell occurs in one direction only and takes place through a change in electrical charge along the length of that neuron. Typically, a neuron's dendrites will receive sufficient stimulation to cause the nerve cell to fire (technically, to reach an *action potential*). The signal then travels the length of the neuron to the end of its axons. Beyond each axon is a small space called a *synapse*[9] that must be crossed for the signal to continue. Transmission of a signal across the synapse takes place by release from the axon of a few molecules of substances called *neurotransmitters* that cross the synapse and chemically bind to *receptor sites* on the receiving neuron (or other cell) that is to be stimulated. When enough receptor sites are stimulated at the same time, changes take place in the chemistry of the receiving cell that cause it to reach an action potential and transmit a signal (if it is also a nerve cell) or perform some other function (e.g., expand or contract if it is a muscle cell). This process of *synaptic transmission* involves submicroscopic structures and minute amounts of chemicals and can take place several times per second.

There are many known neurotransmitters and probably more yet to be discovered. Particularly relevant to brain functions involving what are considered emotional disorders are neurotransmitters such as *dopamine*, *serotonin*, and *norepinephrine*. *Acetylcholine* is another neurotransmitter that is often affected by psychotropic medications. A neurotransmitter that works outside the brain where neurons stimulate *end organs* such as the heart, muscles, glands, and blood vessels, acetylcholine is responsible for many of the side effects commonly experienced with psychotropic medicines.

After being released from the neuronal axon, neurotransmitters have but a brief opportunity to stimulate receptor sites before they are destroyed or removed from the synapse. Psychotropic medications usually work by increasing or by reducing a neurotransmitter's ability to stimulate receptor sites.

Normally, some neurotransmitters are chemically destroyed soon after they are released by molecules of enzymes, such as *monoamine oxidase* (MAO), which is naturally present in the synapse. A class of antidepressant medications called *monoamine oxidase inhibitors* (MAOI), as the name implies, inhibits the action of monoamine oxidase molecules by chemically changing them so that they can no longer destroy neurotransmitters.

---

[9]This space is also called a *synaptic cleft*.

Neurotransmitters can be removed from the synapse by binding with molecules that then transport them back into the axon from which they were released. The process of returning neurotransmitters to the axon is called *reuptake*. Many psychotropic medicines work by chemically blocking the bond between transporter molecules and neurotransmitters, thereby preventing reuptake of the neurotransmitters and allowing them to remain in the synapse, increasing the chance for stimulation of the receptor sites of the receiving cell. Medicines that function in this way are called *reuptake inhibitors* and are sometimes described by the specific neurotransmitters on which they act. For example, medicines such as fluoxetine (Prozac), sertraline (Zoloft), and citalopram (Celexa), used to treat depression, anxiety, and some other conditions, are called *selective serotonin reuptake inhibitors* (SSRIs) because they inhibit the reuptake, primarily, of the neurotransmitter serotonin. Likewise, a common antidepressant, venlafaxine (Effexor), is considered a serotonin and norepinephrine reuptake inhibitor (SNRI) because it inhibits the reuptake mainly of those two neurotransmitters. Medicines that increase the length of time neurotransmitters are present in the synapse, either by blocking reuptake or by preventing their destruction, make it more likely that enough receptor sites will be stimulated to send a signal to the receiving cell. Other medicines work by stimulating the release of extra neurotransmitters, and some actually enter the synapse and mimic neurotransmitters by themselves stimulating receptor sites. Medicines that function in those ways are called *agonists*.

Still other medications, called *antagonists*, block transmissions from neurons by binding with receptor sites, in effect locking out neurotransmitters so that the receiving cell cannot be stimulated. Whether by inhibiting the reuptake of a neurotransmitter, preventing its destruction by enzymes in the synapse, or acting as an agonist or antagonist, psychotropic medicines affect thoughts and moods through increasing and decreasing the complex pattern of nerve signals in the brain.

What Are Side Effects?

The desired improvements in behavior and subjective comfort that medicines produce, called *target effects*, result from changes in neuronal transmission at specific locations in the brain. However, because the bloodstream takes medicines throughout the body, medicines can cause unintended physiological changes by stimulating or blocking transmissions of neurons at locations that have nothing to do with the condition they are intended to treat. The unwanted results that come from the use of medicines are called *side effects*. Side effects can range from mild and inconsequential to so severe that even an otherwise effective medicine cannot be continued for a patient. A medicine may have to be discontinued because the side effects are excessively annoying, cause extreme discomfort, or in some cases, because they medically compromise the patient's physical health or survival.

Most psychotropic medicines have some associated side effects.[10] Which side effects are actually experienced depends not only on which neurotransmitters are influenced but also on the individual's specific body chemistry. For this reason, the side effects of medicines can differ greatly from one person to another. Some patients will have few mild side effects that subside in a few days, whereas others taking the same amount of the same medicine can experience much greater and prolonged discomfort. Examples of common side effects include sedation or drowsiness, changes in blood pressure, nausea or other stomach distress, headache, or increased or decreased salivation. Although common side effects of medicines are sometimes annoying, they are seldom of serious medical concern unless their discomfort causes patients to refuse to take the medication. Most medicines, however, have some side effects that, although quite rare, can be extremely serious and even life threatening.

In some cases, a major consideration in selecting which medicine would be best for a given patient requires balancing probable side effects with the expected benefit. For example, most medicines used to treat disorders such as schizophrenia can produce what are called *extrapyramidal* side effects, which include muscular rigidity, tremor, lethargy, and shuffling gait. Some of these antipsychotic medicines are less likely to produce extrapyramidal side effects but more likely to produce *anticholinergic* effects such as dry mouth, constipation, urinary retention, blurred vision, and mental confusion. Anticholinergic effects occur when transmission of the neurotransmitter acetylcholine is blocked. Another possible side effect from prolonged use of these medicines, called *tardive dyskinesia*, involves abnormal involuntary movements of the hands, trunk, and extremities, occasionally with associated facial contortions or grimaces. Usually tardive dyskinesia will stop with discontinuation of the medication; however, it can become a lifelong condition if the medicine causing it is not discontinued in time. Tardive dyskinesia often resulted from use of the earliest psychotropic medicines. Unfortunately, when medicines were first used to treat mental disorders, there were few available choices. When the benefits from medication were judged to be preferable to treatment without medicine, patients sometimes continued to

---

[10]Sometimes the difference between a target effect and a side effect depends on the reason a medicine is used. For example, diphenhydramine when taken as Benadryl for allergic reactions has the side effect of causing drowsiness. The same medicine as Simply Sleep has the target effect of drowsiness, and dryness of the mouth and nasal passages become side effects.

receive the same drugs for many years and developed permanent tardive dyskinesia. You may encounter such patients, particularly if you have an opportunity to observe a setting that serves persons who have a long history of treatment for psychotic disorders.

There are some side effects of medication that are relatively rare but that constitute serious, indeed sometimes deadly, conditions. *Neuroleptic malignancy syndrome* (NMS) is a potentially fatal condition that most often results from antipsychotic medication. The signs and symptoms of NMS include elevated body temperature, confusion, muscle stiffness, irregular heartbeat, and sweating. *Agranulocytosis*, a blood disorder, and *Stevens–Johnson syndrome*, a severe skin reaction, are both life-threatening conditions that can result from a variety of psychotropic medications. In the case of Steven–Johnson syndrome, the destruction of skin cells can be so severe that patients with that condition are sometimes treated in hospital burn units. The immediate treatment for these serious conditions is discontinuation of the offending medication and the initiation of supportive medical treatment. The many common and rare side effects that can result from psychotropic medications underscore the importance of frequent checks with the health care provider as well as the necessity for patients to follow their prescriber's directions closely.

How Are Medicines Developed?

As noted earlier in this chapter, it has only been about 60 years since the discovery that medicines can be of significant use in the treatment of mental disorders. Some of the most important of these discoveries have been accidental. For example, in 1952, two French physicians found that chlorpromazine (Thorazine), which had been developed with the hope that it would prevent lowered blood pressure during surgery—which it did not in fact do—greatly reduced the hallucinations and delusions associated with psychosis. Chlorpromazine became the first medicine found to be useful in the treatment of psychotic disorders such as schizophrenia.[11] Soon thereafter, a Swiss pharmaceutical company attempted to modify the chemical structure of chlorpromazine to produce an antipsychotic medicine with fewer side effects. The resulting drug, imipramine (Tofranil), did not work at all well for psychotic symptoms, but it was found to be an effective antidepressant medicine. Even more unexpected was the finding several years later that an ingredient that was being used as a filler for many tablets, valproic acid, was actually effective in treating seizure disorders.

---

[11]Prolonged use of chlorpromazine was responsible for many cases of tardive dyskinesia.

The early, accidental discovery of effective psychotropic medications started a flood of biochemical research that continues today with the goal of discovering additional medicines that are even more effective and that can treat a greater number of emotional conditions. Researchers today do not have to rely as heavily on accident and luck to determine the usefulness of medicines they are developing. Understanding of the human brain and how it works is greater than it was even a few years ago, and it is constantly expanding. Improved knowledge of brain function guides research toward the production of newer medicines. The actual effects of new medicines, in turn, give many clues to how the nervous system works. Certainly knowledge of the biological components of mental disorders has increased dramatically; however, there is still much that is not known. Indeed, biochemists typically are able to tell what a psychotropic medicine may do in the brain, but they are usually unsure exactly how and why it produces its effect. For example, medicines such as the SSRIs were developed as antidepressants, a function they often perform well, although researchers are not sure just why they work. Moreover, it was subsequently discovered that some of the SSRIs are also useful in treating conditions such as generalized anxiety, bulimia, and obsessive-compulsive disorder. The challenges for today and tomorrow will be to continue the study of the brain and to develop medicines that can effectively target selected brain functions while limiting unwanted effects on other unrelated biological processes.

What About Herbal Medicines?

The first medicines used by humans to treat illnesses came from plants and herbs that were naturally available. Plants often contain chemical compounds that can be useful in treating diseases. Indeed, many of the most commonly prescribed medicines today have as their active ingredients compounds that were first found in plants. Pharmaceutical companies often extract or synthetically produce those plant compounds to make modern drugs. Medicinal herbs have been used for treatment of mental as well as physical disorders. As an example, rauwolfia, an herb indigenous to India and the East Indies, was used for centuries to treat some mental disorders. In the mid-1900s, a U.S. scientist discovered a compound in rauwolfia called reserpine that was subsequently extracted and used as an early psychotropic.[12] Herbal medicine continues to be a

---

[12]Reserpine had many side effects and was soon replaced by other psychotropics such as chlorpromazine, but it continues to be used to treat some types of hypertension.

popular method of treatment in Eastern countries and central Europe. In recent decades, people in the United States have shown an increasing interest in herbal, or "natural," medicines. Today, the marketing of herbs, often in the form of tablets or capsules, is a multibillion-dollar industry.

There is no question that most herbal preparations have physiological effect on the body, but there are several concerns and misconceptions about the use of such substances. Many people falsely believe that because plants are natural, their use for medical treatment is safer than using pharmaceutical products. That assumption is often not the case. Certainly, oleander and hemlock are natural plants—and both are quite deadly when eaten. Plants and herbs can have an extremely complex chemistry. When they are ingested, the body is exposed to numerous chemical substances, some of which may have benefit, others that may be benign, and others that may be quite harmful. The exact chemical compounds or combination of compounds of an herb that produce a desired effect are often unknown. Likewise, dosage ranges for safety and effectiveness have not been clearly established for most herbal products. Recommended daily amounts, printed on the package labels, often come from speculation or tradition rather than rigid research.

Definitive scientific study of exactly which components of plants may be useful and how they work is growing as a result of consumer interest but remains limited at this time. In China and many other Eastern countries, the manufacture and sale of herbal preparations are regulated. In the United States, however, those products are marketed not as drugs but as "dietary supplements." That designation avoids FDA regulation, and, consequently, there is no governmental assurance of content, potency, quality, or even the absence of harmful impurities. Most important, herbals can interact with traditional pharmaceutical drugs. It is essential that patients inform their prescriber of any herbal, or other natural, substances they may be taking.

What Medications Are Commonly Prescribed for Mental Disorders?

One common and useful way to group psychotropic medicines is by the type of disorders they have been found to effectively treat. Although it is becoming increasingly common that many drugs are effective in treating more than one condition (see Table 8.1), psychotropic medications are still commonly grouped by their first or main use. Following are categories, brief descriptions, and examples of some of the more commonly used psychotropic medications. It is likely that you will find many of these medicines in use at the treatment programs you have an opportunity to observe.

ANTIDEPRESSANT MEDICATIONS

Tricyclic antidepressants, named for a molecular structure that all have in common (the molecular structure is three fused benzene rings), work by blocking the reuptake of the neurotransmitters epinephrine and serotonin. Although they take several days to be completely effective, the tricyclics are often effective in treating depression and are also of value in the treatment of anxiety. Many have been approved for use with children. Disadvantages include dry mouth and urinary retention,[13] potentially fatal overdose, and, in rare cases, cardiac (heart) toxicity. Examples include imipramine (Tofranil), desipramine (Norpramin), and amitriptyline (Elavil).

As described earlier, MAOIs produce their effect by blocking monoamine oxidase in the neuronal synapse so it cannot chemically destroy neurotransmitters. The MAOIs are also effective antidepressants, but when they are taken in combination with certain foods[14] or other medicines, they can produce life-threatening *hypertension* (high blood pressure) or other dangerous nervous system reactions. Examples of MAOI compounds include phenelzine (Nardil) and tranylcypromine (Parnate).

As noted earlier, SSRIs block the reuptake mainly of the neurotransmitter serotonin. The SSRIs have been found to be effective not only in the treatment of depressive disorders but also for generalized anxiety, obsessional disorders, panic disorders, and bulimia. It usually takes about two weeks for them to reach full effectiveness. Examples include fluoxetine (Prozac), sertraline (Zoloft), and escitalopram (Lexapro).

Other antidepressant medications have been developed that do not fit the traditional categories just described. Examples include venlafaxine (Effexor) and duloxetine (Cymbalta), both of which inhibit the reuptake of both norepinephrine and serotonin; vilazodone (Viibryd) which is a serotonin agonist at receptor sites and also affects

---

[13]Urinary retention as a side effect has allowed some tricyclics such as imipramine (Tofranil) to be used to treat nocturnal enuresis (bed-wetting).

[14]Specifically, MAOIs are particularly dangerous when taken in combination with tyramine, a substance that occurs naturally in many foods.

TABLE 8.1

Examples of Commonly Used Psychotropic Medications

Brand name (generic name)	Conditions approved by the FDA to treat						
	Anxiety disorders	Depression	Bipolar disorder	Schizophrenia	ADHD	Alzheimer's dementia	Other uses
Antidepressants							
Prozac, Seraphim (fluoxetine)	X	X					Premenstrual dysphoric disorder
Zoloft (sertraline)	X	X					
Celexa (citalopram)	X	X					
Lexapro (escitalopram)	X	X					
Wellbutrin, Zyban (bupropion)		X					Smoking cessation
Viibryd (vilazodone)		X					
Effexor (venlafaxine)	X	X					
Cymbalta (duloxetine)	X	X					Chronic pain
Antipsychotics							
Seroquel (quetiapine)		X[a]	X	X			
Abilify (aripiprazole)		X[a]	X	X			
Geodon (ziprasidone)			X	X			
Zyprexa (olanzapine)			X	X			
Saphris (asenapine)			X	X			
Latuda (lurasidone)			X	X			

Medication		Other indications
Mood stabilizers		
Lithium	X	Schizoaffective disorder
Depakote (valproic acid)	X	Seizure disorders
Lamictal (lamotrigine)	X	Seizure disorders
Psychostimulants		
Ritalin (methylphenidate)	X	Narcolepsy
Concerta (methylphenidate)	X	
Dexedrine (d-amphetamine)	X	Obesity Narcolepsy
Adderall (mixed amphetamine salts)	X	
Vyvanse (lisdexamfetamine)	X	
Benzodiazepines		
Xanax (alprazolam)	X	Seizure disorder
Valium (diazepam)	X	Alcohol withdrawal
Klonopin (clonazepam)	X	Epileptic seizure Seizure disorders
Ativan (lorazepam)	X	Epileptic seizure Insomnia
Antidementia agents		
Aricept (donepezil)	X	
Namenda (memantine)	X	

Note.   ADHD = attention-deficit/hyperactivity disorder.
[a]In combination with other medications.

feedback channels so that more serotonin is released from axons; and bupropion (Wellbutrin), a norepinephrine and dopamine reuptake inhibitor.

ANXIOLYTIC (ANTIANXIETY) MEDICATIONS

Benzodiazepines are tranquilizers that provide temporary relief for anxiety. As noted earlier, the benzodiazepines easily cross the blood–brain barrier, so they work rather quickly. They are often used for acute anxiety attacks or as short-term treatment to allow the other long-term medicines to take effect. These medicines are also sometimes used to treat withdrawal symptoms during alcohol detoxification.

The body can develop a tolerance to benzodiazepines, and their prolonged use may actually cause depression. These medicines are relatively safe in overdose, but even modest amounts can be fatal when taken with alcohol. Examples include diazepam (Valium), clonazepam (Klonopin), and alprazolam (Xanax).

Buspirone (BuSpar) is an antianxiety medication that works in a complex way by blocking feedback channels in neurons so that they continue to release serotonin. Tricyclic antidepressants and SSRIs, as noted earlier, are also effective in the long-term treatment of anxiety.

ANTIPSYCHOTIC MEDICATIONS

Medications termed *typical antipsychotics* are used to treat conditions such as schizophrenia. They are usually effective in reducing symptoms such as hallucinations and delusional thought. These medications generally reduce neural transmission by blocking dopamine receptors at receiving neurons (i.e., they are dopamine antagonists). All can produce extrapyramidal or anticholinergic side effects, and all have a risk of tardive dyskinesia with prolonged use. Typical antipsychotics are further classified as having *low potency* or *high potency*.[15] Low-potency antipsychotics such as chlorpromazine (Thorazine) and thioridazine (Mellaril) are less likely to cause extrapyramidal motor side effects, whereas high-potency antipsychotics such as trifluoperazine (Stelazine), thiothixene (Navane), and haloperidol (Haldol) tend to have fewer or milder anticholinergic side effects.

---

[15]Typical antipsychotics are grouped as high or low potency. Both are equally effective treatments; the difference is in the amount of medication needed to reach therapeutic effect. It takes more of a low-potency medication to have the same treatment effect as a high-potency preparation.

Atypical antipsychotics are newer medications that function somewhat differently from the traditional medications (hence, "atypical"). In some cases, these new medications produce fewer or milder side effects, and some may bring about improvement not found with typical medicines, such as enhanced emotional expression, social interest, and motivation. Examples include the dopamine and serotonin agonists risperidone (Risperdal), lurasidone (Latuda), ziprasidone (Geodon), and aripiprazole (Abilify). Another atypical antipsychotic, clozapine (Clozaril), which is mainly a dopamine antagonist, has gained much attention because it not only reduces abnormal behavior in schizophrenia but also promotes more normal emotional expression. Moreover, Clozaril does not seem to produce extrapyramidal side effects. Unfortunately, Clozaril can cause seizures, and it is more likely than most medicines to produce agranulocytosis. The potential severity of those side effects limits the medicine's utility and necessitates strict and regular laboratory monitoring of its use.

MOOD STABILIZERS

Mood stabilizers are medicines used to treat conditions such as bipolar disorders in which a patient may experience periods of depression and excessive elation (mania), usually separated by periods of relatively less disturbance. The typical medicine used to treat severe cases of such cycling mood disorders is lithium (e.g., Eskalith, Lithonate). Unlike most medicines, lithium is a metal and is therefore not metabolized by the liver. Blood levels of lithium must reach a certain level to be effective; however, excessive amounts of lithium can produce toxicity and even death. Lithium levels in the blood can change rather rapidly depending on diet, exercise, and other medicines one may be taking. Therefore, close monitoring of blood levels is necessary with lithium. Some cyclic mood disorders respond well to treatment with antipsychotic medications. Additionally, a number of medicines developed to control seizures have been found to be effective mood stabilizers. Examples include carbamazepine (Tegretol), divalproex (Depakote), and lamotrigine (Lamictal).

PSYCHOSTIMULANTS

Psychostimulants, as their name implies, stimulate neural transmission in the brain. Most of these agents work by blocking the reuptake of dopamine. These medications are used to treat conditions such as the sleep disorder narcolepsy and attention-deficit/hyperactivity disorder. Some years ago, they were often prescribed as diet aids because they also reduce appetite; however, that use is now uncommon because more effective medicines are available and because psychostimulants can be abused and may produce psychological addiction. Examples include dextroamphetamine (Dexedrine, Vyvanse), methylphenidate (Ritalin, Concerta, and Metadate), and amphetamine and dextroamphetamine (Adderall).

How Does a Prescriber Know Which Medicine Is Best for a Patient?

The examples provided here do not include all possible conditions for which psychotropic medications may be used, and they list only a few typical examples of the many medications that are available for use. With so many choices, how do prescribers know which medicines to use for which patients? In addition to considering factors such as a patient's age, overall health, and medical status, many prescribers consider subtle aspects of the emotional disorder and evaluate factors such as possible side effects when selecting a particular psychotropic medicine. Even with the most careful examination, however, the use of psychotropic medicines unavoidably includes an element of trial and error.

There is no guarantee that any medication will produce the desired results for a given patient. Likewise, individual differences in body physiology can cause unwanted side effects for any medication. The usual procedure is to prescribe a medicine thought likely to be effective and then closely monitor how well the patient tolerates it and determine whether it is producing the desired improvement. It is this monitoring that often takes place during treatment staff meetings and at med checks. It is not at all uncommon to find that medications will need to be changed or supplemented with the addition of other medicines. It is clear that the need for ongoing study of the biological components of mental disorders and the ways in which medicines can work continues.

Medicine or Psychotherapy?

It is not surprising that the discovery of medicines' effectiveness in treating mental disorders has caused some to question the need for psychotherapy. Does the finding that biological agents can change mood, emotion, and behavior mean that one should abandon psychotherapy in favor of only physiologically based treatment? The majority of mental health professionals would argue against such a one-sided approach to treatment. Although it is true that biology is linked to mental functioning, it would be incorrect to assume that all mental disorders necessarily result from biological causes. In many situations, even if medication is helpful, it may be that relative effectiveness in responding to and coping with life events has caused rather than resulted from the changes in physiology.

As we learn more about mental disorders, we are discovering intricate interactions between our biology and our environment. For example, although it is now believed that individuals can have a biological predisposition for some mental disorders such as schizophrenia, environmental factors appear to play a big part in determining whether that disorder will come about and what course it will take. Similarly, conditions such as posttraumatic stress disorder are clearly triggered by environmental events, but we now know that there may be a physiologically based vulnerability for such a reaction. Conditions such as reactive depression can often be treated quite effectively without the use of medication, and many anxiety disorders seem to respond best when psychotherapy and medication are used together. Even when there is reason to suspect a biological cause for a mental illness, psychotherapy may shorten the severity and duration of that condition and help patients comply with treatment and cope with their disorders. Both medication and psychotherapy can be of tremendous value in the treatment of mental disorders. Often, treatment is not a matter of choosing between medicine and psychotherapy but rather deciding how best to include both methods into an integrated plan of mental health care.

Summary

During the past 60 years, an ever-increasing number of medicines that can greatly improve disordered thought and behavior have been developed. Medication is now routinely used as part of an overall treatment program in most mental health settings. Knowledge of the basics of medicines and familiarity with the types of medications used in mental health treatment, as well as their side effects, are important in understanding a comprehensive plan of treatment.

Knowledge of how each drug produces its effects in the body and ongoing study of how the brain works help prescribers in selecting the proper medicines for each patient. Our understanding of the biological components of mental disorders has increased dramatically, yet much remains unknown.

Additional Readings

Johnson, J., & Preston, J. D. (2012). *Clinical psychopharmacology made ridiculously simple* (7th ed.) Miami, FL: MedMaster.

Julian, R. M., Advocat, C. D., & Comaty, J. E. (2011). *A primer of drug action* (12th ed.). New York, NY: Worth.

Preston, J. D., O'Neal, J. H., & Talaga, M. C. (2013). *Handbook of clinical psychopharmacology for therapists.* Oakland, CA: New Harbinger.

Stahl, S. M. (2012). *Essential psychopharmacology: Neuroscientific basis and practical applications* (4th ed.). Cambridge, England: Cambridge University Press.

Online Resources

http://www.webmd.com/drugs/index-drugs.aspx
http://www.webmd.com/vitamins-supplements/default.aspx
http://www.nlm.nih.gov/medlineplus/druginformation.html
http://www.nlm.nih.gov/medlineplus/druginfo/herb_All.html

Free Smartphone Apps

Medscape.com
Epocrates.com

Jean C. Elbert

Special Issues in Working With Children | 9

I n this chapter, I provide introductory information for those undergraduate students contemplating future study or work with preschool and school-age children and who may be planning a formal practicum experience or volunteer work in a child setting. Such placements typically include public or private schools, day-care facilities, hospitals, pediatric or mental health clinics, and hospitals or residential settings. I begin with a review of basic information regarding normal development and then provide emphasis on challenges experienced by children who demonstrate emotional or behavioral problems. This information will help you have a better foundation to understand what you see in the applied setting. A predominant frame of reference for understanding behavioral and emotional disturbance (*developmental psychopathology*) in the child is that it is normal development gone awry; that is, failure in certain aspects of development often represents a precursor to subsequent emotional and behavioral problems. It is beyond the scope of this chapter to provide detailed and specific information, and I assume

http://dx.doi.org/10.1037/14672-009
*Your Practicum in Psychology: A Guide for Maximizing Knowledge and Competence,
Second Edition,* J. R. Matthews and C. E. Walker (Editors)

that you will receive information regarding the practices of a particular setting, together with appropriate supervision in working with a particular group of children. However, I provide general comments regarding suggested ways for you to develop rapport, interact, and respond to problematic behaviors when working with children.

Brief Review of Developmental Issues

THE PRESCHOOL CHILD

Development of Motor, Cognitive, and Language Skills

Table 9.1 provides an overview of the expected milestones in development of preschool children, covering physical as well as cognitive development (Schickendanz, Schickendanz, Forsyth, & Forsyth, 2001). By age 1, most children learn to walk and then begin running and climbing on playground equipment such as ladders and jungle gyms. They are throwing a ball overhand by age 3, and by ages 4 to 5, most are able to ride a tricycle. Fine motor control develops somewhat later; preschool children are usually able to button clothes, string beads, and use a "fist" grip to manipulate markers at 3 or 4. Most children are tying their shoes by age 5 (Kail, 2002; Schickendanz et al., 2001). Observing and interacting with preschool children in a variety of activities will provide you with many examples of physical and motor development.

Before age 5 children have what is known as *preoperational* thinking, which is illogical, inflexible, and tied to specific contexts. Young preschool children are initially "egocentric" and believe that others perceive the world as they do. They often confuse appearance with reality, do not yet appreciate that thoughts differ from reality, and do not understand that others can have false beliefs (e.g., conclude that someone who is smiling must be happy). By age 4, the understanding of what others know (*theory of mind*) begins to develop, and you can foster this by reading picture books to children, discussing various points of view, and encouraging them to comment on their own thoughts or experiences related to the story (Kail, 2002; Schickendanz et al., 2001). Activities like these will provide many examples of both the child's language and cognitive development (e.g., the degree to which a child can participate in a conversation about the story, as opposed to merely pointing and labeling pictures).

In normally developing preschool children, language develops rapidly, and they will begin to show large increases in vocabulary.

TABLE 9.1

Milestones in Preschool Development

	Area of Development			
Age	Physical	Cognitive	Language	Social-Emotional
3 years	Demonstrates true run with both feet leaving ground; walks upstairs alternating feet; walks downstairs using marked-time climbing; can take off most clothing	Begins to demonstrate preoperational thinking; knows conventional counting words up to five; can solve nesting cup problem by reversing two cups or by insertion	Understands *in, on,* and *under;* speaks in more complete sentences; distinguishes graphics that are writing versus pictures; begins to overgeneralize rules for creating verb tenses and plurals	May begin preschool; uses physical aggression more than verbal aggression; can remember a prohibition when the parent is absent
3 years, 6 months	Can hop a few steps on preferred foot; can button large buttons; can put on easier clothing	Cannot easily distinguish false beliefs; can count five objects before making a partitioning error	Might use syllable hypothesis to create written words; rereads favorite storybooks using picture-governed strategies; often uses scribble writing	Has difficulty generating alternatives in a conflict situation; learns aggressive behavior rapidly if these means succeed
4 years	Appears thinner because of longer trunk; can walk a curved line; walks downstairs alternating feet; can gallop; can cut straight line with scissors	Can make a row of objects equal to another row by matching one to one; understands false beliefs	Creates questions and negative sentences using correct word arrangement; might create "mock" letters	Watches, on average, 2 to 4 hours of TV per day

(continued)

TABLE 9.1 *(Continued)*

Milestones in Preschool Development

Age	Area of Development			
	Physical	Cognitive	Language	Social-Emotional
4 years, 6 months	May begin to hold writing tool in finger grip; leans forward more when jumping from a height, can button smaller buttons	Knows conventional counting up to 15; understands false beliefs	Often reverses letters when writing; understands *beside, between, front,* and *back*	Self-control often depends on removal of temptation
5 years	Can stop and change direction quickly when running; can hop 8 to 10 steps on one foot	Selects own view in three-mountain task; creates classes of objects based on a single defining attribute	Understands passive sentences; may begin to use invented spellings	Inhibitory or effortful control should be well-established for familiar prohibitions
5 years, 6 months	Can connect a zipper on a coat; may be able to tie shoes	Can count 20 objects without making a partition-ing error; may display conservation of number	May begin to make print-governed reading attempts with favorite books	

Note. From *Understanding Children and Adolescents* (4th ed., p. 403), by J. A. Schickendanz, D. I. Schickendanz, P. D. Forsyth, and G. A. Forsyth, 2001, Boston, MA: Allyn & Bacon. Copyright © 2001 by Pearson Education. Reprinted with permission.

Young children initially learn vocabulary through direct association: by attaching a word with something concrete that they can see or touch. Later they begin to infer word meaning from both context and word order, with concrete nouns and verbs representing their earliest vocabulary. Words such as prepositions (e.g., *in, on, under*) appear later, with *beside, between, in front of,* and *behind* not emerging before 4 to 5 years. In young children, language is often restricted to the "here and now." By age 4, children with sufficient language stimulation begin to follow along with simple stories that have picture cues, rhyming words, and language that they have heard many times. A feature of language development at this stage is the beginning sensitivity to the *phonology* of speech, that is, the sounds that make up words; by age 3, most children should be able to recognize and produce the sounds represented in their native language. This "play" with language (rhyming, taking words apart, and substituting sounds) develops naturally in many children, and engaging them in wordplay is important in encouraging language development. Perhaps more important, this play with sounds in words becomes one of the most important factors in early reading development: Those children who do not develop the sensitivity to sounds in words are known to be at much greater risk for difficulty in mastering beginning reading skills (Kail, 2002; Schickendanz et al., 2001).

Adequate language development is critically important for cognitive and social development as well as later school performance. If you are working with young preschool children, you should be aware of the factors that enhance language development. These include (a) using simple sentences with a slow rate of speech; (b) demonstrating joint attention, for example, commenting on what the child is attending to and encouraging interactive conversation; (c) following the child's lead during play interactions rather than directing; (d) reading to the child, choosing books with multiple repetitions, directing the child to associate words with pictures, and engaging the child in language play by inviting him or her to think of words that rhyme (e.g., "Let's think of words that start with the same sound as . . ."); and (e) asking "what and where" questions and actively engaging the child in a story. The process of language acquisition unfolds quite readily in most young children with adequate stimulation. However, for some children with otherwise normal development, speech and language is delayed. Such children cannot find the words to express their needs, leading to considerable frustration, distress, and sometimes, emotional outbursts. Many such children with diagnosed expressive language disorders are known to be at risk for both learning disabilities (because later reading and writing skills build on a foundation in oral language), and emotional disorders (involving frustration, social anxiety, or noncompliance). In children from different linguistic and cultural backgrounds, second-language learning obviously develops more slowly, and they tend to mix vocabulary from both languages. However, by preschool age, bilingual children typically are able to separate the two languages, and by school entry, many are proficient in both languages and even begin to surpass monolingual children in some language skills (Kail, 2002). For those children who have not learned English before school entry, research suggests that they do best when given instruction in English while simultaneously being taught their other subjects in their native language (Padilla et al., 1991).

Social and Emotional Development

To better understand the behavior of young children, you should be aware of those critical elements of development that shape healthy, positive social relationships. First, both a child's biological traits (nature) and the environment created by parents, extended family, caretakers, teachers, and significant others (nurture) combine to jointly influence emotional development and social behavior in children. One primary aspect of these influences is *attachment*, the emotional bond that exists between the infant and primary caregiver. This bond emerges as parents respond to signals of their infant's distress, and these early experiences with parenting set the stage for development of trust in others. Attachment typically develops by the middle of the first year of life and is characterized by responding differently to familiar and unfamiliar people and showing wariness of strangers. The primary attachment person provides a secure base from which the infant can explore the environment. When working with toddlers or preschool children, you should have some basic understanding of the patterns of attachment, which typically develop between 12 and 18 months. On the basis of observations of children's reactions to their mothers' absence and to the introduction of a stranger, several patterns of attachment have been reported. Children with a *secure* attachment may be moderately distressed by their mother's absence but are usually comforted when she returns. These children tend to be more social and are better apt to develop empathy. *Insecure–avoidant* attachment describes those young children who tend to have poor exploration, who are often highly distressed at their mother's absence, and who then may actually resist efforts at comfort when she returns (Kail, 2002). Important for later emotional development is the extensive body of work showing that mothers who respond to their infants abruptly, who are unresponsive, or who pace their behavior to their own needs and schedules tend to foster the development of an anxious or ambivalent attachment characterized by excessive anger, clinging, or avoidance behavior on the part of the infant (Campbell, 2002). An excellent way of understanding attachment patterns in preschool children is to observe the interactions between children and their working parent(s) when the child is dropped off in a day-care setting. Although most children will require some time to adjust to new caretakers, there are some children who will be highly stressed by separation, are difficult to console, and may show moderate to extreme irritability.

The parents' ability to interpret and adjust to their young child's signals is often a predictor of the child's later behavior. Insecurely attached infants tend to cry more, play less often, have more frequent tantrums, and show aggression, emotional dependence, and need for support as children (Kail, 2002; Schickendanz et al., 2001). Other evidence for the later effects of disturbed attachment comes from examples of children raised in institutional settings in which bonding with caretakers has not been adequately fostered (e.g., in recent years exemplified by the experience of the many children adopted from Eastern European orphanages). We know that many of these children respond indiscriminately to others and fail to form lasting relationships. This issue of attachment is certainly important for the increasing number of young children in day care. A large national study indicated that child care, per se, does not appear to affect the development of secure mother–infant attachment (National Institute of Child Health and Human Development, 1997). However, infants whose mothers are insensitive and unresponsive to their needs are more likely to develop insecure attachment when placed in poor quality child care. Thus, if you were to seek a practicum experience in a child-care setting, you would do well to inquire about the extent and quality of staff training and the child-to-adult ratio.

Finally, although disturbed attachment is a significant general risk factor for later disturbances in emotional responses and problem behavior, both positive and negative changes in the parents' situation (e.g., increase or reduction in life stressors, mental health problems, and individual stability) will clearly influence the attachment relationship.

A second major influence on a child's development is *temperament*, a child's consistent mood and individual style of interaction with the environment. Infants and toddlers differ with respect to how strongly they react emotionally, how easily they become calm again, their general physical activity level, and their ease and preference in being with people. Early studies of infants and preschool children (e.g., Kagan, 1989) identified three general types of temperament in infants that appear to be fairly stable in young preschool children: "easy" (adaptable), "slow to warm up," and "difficult" (having more intense moods, frequent crying, higher levels of irritability, and slow to accept change). Infants with a difficult temperament have been shown to frequently withdraw from new experiences, display a negative mood, and be slow in adapting to new situations. Such infants are more difficult to parent and are at risk for problems in controlling their behavior. Sensitive parenting helps many difficult infants outgrow this phase. However, those with "negative emotionality" and those whose parents are impatient or intolerant are at considerable risk for later depression and behavioral problems (Garrison & Earls, 1987; Kail, 2002; Schickendanz et al., 2001).

An important aspect of temperament is *self-regulation*—the process through which young children actively try to control their emotions, motor activity levels, and attention. Some experts believe that the development of self-control may be the most important variable in later social and behavior problems. The child who has poor control of emotions and behavior is more apt to have a later psychiatric diagnosis and may also be at major risk for being either victim or perpetrator of physical abuse. For example, poor control of bodily functions is a frequent precursor to later serious eating and elimination disorders (e.g., obesity, anorexia and bulimia, and enuresis and encopresis). You should be aware that obesity is now recognized as being one of the most significant health problems in the United States, with more than 15% of children over age 6 being overweight. The American Academy of Pediatrics (Krebs & Jacobson, 2003) has recommended that those involved in the care of children can play an important role in preventing childhood obesity by encouraging parents to instill healthy eating patterns, routinely promote physical activity, include unstructured play, and limit the child's sedentary time in watching television and videos.

By age 2 to 3 years, children typically begin to learn which behaviors are acceptable and which are unacceptable. This is when most children have developed the cognitive and language skills to respond to verbal commands and to exercise self-control. Young children begin to mimic a parent's directives and respond to reward and punishment, which then leads to internalizing the parent's values. You can see this in young preschool children who may actually verbalize a parent's command (i.e., "No, No!"). When does the young child develop conscience? Although some 3-year-old children begin to say, "I'm sorry," it is not until later that they are able to use true self-appraisal. This aspect of development becomes extremely important; those children who don't develop the ability to appraise their own behavior are at risk for excessive anxiety, guilt, later obsessive-compulsive behaviors, and depression, or alternatively, acting out and antisocial behaviors (Wenar & Kerig, 2000).

Developing Rapport With Preschool Children

A child's temperament and comfort with new people will vary, but it is important for you to learn to "read" a child's signals. For example, when approaching children for the first time, if they avert eye contact and appear shy, it is important to provide time for these slow-to-warm-up children to adjust. Offering them an interesting toy, commenting on what they are doing (e.g., "nice digging in the sand"), and following their lead rather than directing them are good ways to initiate contact.

In contrast, direct questions or commands may be intimidating to some children. Children are typically quite sensitive to facial expression; a pleasant smile and quiet demeanor may be encouraging to the child, whereas a loud voice or laughter can intimidate the shy child. When first meeting a child, it is often helpful to join an activity including another familiar child or adult, thus allowing a shy child a chance to "look over" the new person. You will also need to be sensitive to different cultural expectations that influence a child's behavior. For example, making direct eye contact varies across cultures; children from Native American and some Latin American and Asian cultures are not socialized to make direct eye contact in the same way as children from the dominant Caucasian culture and may be taught to believe that this is impolite.

THE SCHOOL-AGE CHILD

Development of Motor, Cognitive, Language, and Academic Skills

Table 9.2 provides an overview of growth and development in the school-age child. Physical growth slows, with the average child's height increasing by 2 to 3 inches per year and weight by 5 to 7 pounds per year. Girls tend to begin their preadolescent growth spurt at age 10 to 11, with boys maturing somewhat later, at the beginning of their teens. We noted previously that obesity often has its roots in preschool; however, this stage of rapid physical development in school-age children increases the risk for obesity. Overweight children are often rejected by peers and tend to have lowered academic performance, poor self-esteem, and increased behavior problems and are at increased risk for depression. Finally, poor weight control in children clearly puts them at risk for food binging and purging and serious eating disorders, particularly in young preadolescent girls (Schroeder & Gordon, 2002).

Some children will have difficulty with gross motor control, balance, and physical coordination, and you should be sensitive to these weaknesses, particularly if you are to be involved in directing children's sports or physical activity. Fine motor skills show accelerated development in 6- to 8-year-olds. By early school age, children develop a more mature grip and develop the fine motor skills necessary for writing; it is also at this age that children with fine motor difficulty are identified. In elementary school, children begin involvement in organized play, which provides opportunities for development of motor skills. Organized sports, jumping rope, bicycling, and throwing all support gross motor development, whereas marbles, Legos, and arts and crafts help to increase fine motor development (Kail, 2002; Schickendanz et al., 2001).

School-age children make significant gains in cognitive development: They first begin to use mental operations to solve problems, and

TABLE 9.2

Milestones in School-Age Development

Age (years)		Area of Development		
	Physical	Cognitive	Language	Social-emotional
6	Has 90% of adult-size brain; reaches about two thirds of adult height; begins to lose baby teeth; moves a writing or drawing tool with the fingers while the side of the hand rests on the table top	Begins to demonstrate concrete operational thinking; demonstrates conservation of number on Piaget's conservation tasks; can create series operationally rather than by trial and error	Might use a letter-name spelling strategy, thus creating many invented spellings; appreciates jokes and riddles based on phonological ambiguity	Feels one way only about a situation; has some difficulty detecting intentions in situations in which damage occurs; demonstrates Kohlberg's preconventional moral thinking
7	Is able to make small, controlled marks with pencils or pens because of more refined finger dexterity; has longer face; continues to lose baby teeth	Begins to use some rehearsal strategies as an aid to memory; becomes much better able to play strategy games; may demonstrate conservation of area	Sorts out some of the more difficult syntactic difficulties, such as *ask* and *tell*; more conventional speller; more fluent reader	May express two emotions about one situation, but these will be same valence; demonstrates Kohlberg's conventional thinking; understands gender constancy
8	Plays jacks and other games requiring considerable fine motor skill and good reaction time; jumps rope skillfully; throws and bats a ball more skillfully	Still has great difficulty judging if a passage is relevant to specific theme; may demonstrate conservation of specific area	Sorts out some of the more difficult syntactic difficulties, such as *ask* and *tell*; more conventional speller; more fluent reader	Expresses two same-valence emotions about different targets; understands that people may interpret situations differently but thinks it is because of different information

	Physical	Cognitive	Language	Social/Moral
9	Enjoys hobbies requiring high levels of fine motor skill (sewing, weaving, and model making)	May demonstrate conservation of weight		Can think about own thinking or another person's thinking but not both at same time
10	Girls may begin to menstruate	Begins to make better judgments about relevance of a text; begins to delete unimportant information when summarizing		Can take own view and view of another as if a disinterested third party
11	May begin preadolescent growth spurt if female	May demonstrate conservation of volume	Begins to appreciate jokes and riddles based on syntactic ability	Still has trouble detecting deception; spends more time with friends
12	Has reached about 80% of adult height if male, 90% if female; has all permanent teeth except for two sets of molars; plays ball more skillfully because of improved reaction time; begins to menstruate	Shows much greater skill in summarizing and outlining; may begin to demonstrate formal operational thinking		May begin to demonstrate Kohlberg's postconventional moral thinking

thinking becomes more logical; for example, they are not as bound by physical appearances and develop the important ability for *perspective taking*. Between ages 7 to 12, children begin to understand that others have different ideas, feelings, and behaviors from their own. This ability to take another's perspective is critically important in developing healthy social skills. Cognitive development involves the child's growing ability to *process information*, which can be viewed as a hierarchy including the following levels from simple to complex: (a) *perception*, the ability to recognize differences in bits of sensory information, beginning with recognition of faces to later visual discrimination of letters and numbers (*u/n* and *bid*) and recognizing different sounds in spoken words (*ban* and *pan*); (b) *memory*, the ability to retain and store what is heard or seen for higher level processing; and (c) *conceptualization*, higher level thinking and logical reasoning. Children's memory skills improve rapidly during the elementary school years as they begin to use more effective strategies to aid memory: rehearsal, elaboration, chunking and organizing information, and linking new information to their own previous experience. Inadequate development in any of these cognitive processes can reflect various types of *learning disabilities* that subsequently affect the child's development of the academic skills of reading, written language, and math. If you are working with children on their schoolwork, you can assist them by teaching some strategies for remembering information.

Language and communication skills greatly expand in school-age children. Their vocabulary increases when they begin to grasp multiple meanings and root words that help to expand concepts (e.g., happy and then unhappy, happiness, and happier). School becomes a child's major "work," and school success becomes a major factor in developing self-esteem. Learning to read becomes prominent and is a skill that involves the integration of many subskills. Understanding that reading involves getting meaning from the printed word initially requires the perceptual abilities to recognize, distinguish, and label letters of the alphabet, learning specific letter–sound correspondence, and recognizing that in English there is not perfect correspondence between letters and sounds. Good vocabulary and oral language background are essential for children to understand that reading is a *psycholinguistic guessing game* in which one's previous oral communication skills (depth and breadth of vocabulary and understanding word endings) aid in making decisions about unknown written words (Kail, 2002; Schickendanz et al., 2001). It is important to mention that the particular method of reading instruction is now known to be important in the ease with which children develop reading skill. Although methods of teaching reading have varied over time, research now clearly demonstrates that direct and systematic instruction in the structure and phonology of written words (e.g., their letter–sound correspondence) is essential in teaching children to recognize ("decode") written words. With frequent exposure to words, children learn to recognize familiar spelling patterns (e.g., "ight") and associate those with known words, which then allows them to sound out and recognize unfamiliar words. Following this initial word recognition stage, reading comprehension skill is strongly associated with the child's ability to understand spoken language (Shaywitz, 2003). Depending on the particular city or state, bilingual education classes may be available so that a child is able to learn new information in his or her native language or be assisted by a translator while learning English as a second language.

Written language is often considered to be the most complex communication task. It presumes knowledge of correct spelling, understanding the rules of grammar and formal sentence construction (that is, the ability to appropriately organize and sequence words within a sentence and sentences within a paragraph), and, at a higher level, to organize ideas. Thus, most children with learning disabilities or children with English as a second language will have difficulty in this area. In learning math, children progress from using a counting strategy for simple computation to using mental operations involving memory. By third or fourth grade, most children have memorized addition and subtraction "math facts."

Social and Emotional Development

An important aspect of healthy social development in the school-age child is the growth of *social cognition*, the ability to think about a situation from another's point of view and thereby understand the other person's behavior and also how he or she might feel—that is, *empathy*. Showing concern for others and communicating through both body language and spoken language are important ingredients in social acceptance. Popular children tend to be skilled in both the language and social aspects of communicating; they are able to join into others' play and conversation, are good at appraising how their behavior affects others, and are more likely to share and cooperate. In contrast, those children with poor verbal or nonverbal communication skills are often left out, ignored, teased, or rejected (Kail, 2002; Schickendanz et al., 2001). Peer acceptance clearly factors into the child's emotional stability. Rejected children often have histories of inconsistent parental discipline and parents whose own social skills are poorly developed; thus, they likely have had poor models for developing appropriate social skills. The development of negative behaviors varies with age and gender in children. Younger children are more likely to use bullying behaviors; by school age, girls are more apt to use verbal aggression and gossip, whereas boys tend more toward physical aggression.

The development of self-esteem typically is shaped during school age when children are able to be more introspective and begin to compare themselves and their skills with peers'. Those with healthy self-esteem can be objective about their abilities in different areas, such as school-work, sports, and music. They may be aware that they don't excel in all areas; yet they are generally able to maintain healthy self-esteem. In contrast, children with poor self-esteem are unable to be objective, judge themselves harshly, and view poor skill levels (i.e., in academics or athletics) to mean they have less value as a person. Self-esteem is based in part on how children are viewed by those around them; those with nurturing, accepting parents and teachers are more likely to have healthy self-esteem. Parents who set rules, provide structure and discipline, and reward compliance tend to have children with higher self-esteem. Children with low self-esteem are known to be at risk for a variety of developmental problems, including poor peer relationships and depression (Wenar & Kerig, 2000). If you are working with school-age children with low self-esteem, several aspects of child care are important in enhancing self-esteem: (a) providing an atmosphere in which verbal and physical aggression are not tolerated, (b) using opportunities to reinforce the importance of effort and fair play (e.g., "I really liked how you helped out there!"), and (c) commenting to a self-critical child, "You are being quite hard on yourself."

Developing Rapport With School-Age Children

Before meeting children, it will be helpful for you to learn something about them: their interests, likes and dislikes, and particular strengths and weaknesses. With children who are shy or who have limited language communication, you should refrain from excessive questioning. Such children will feel more comfortable when they are invited to choose an activity or game, and the choice of activity may reveal a child's skill level, competitiveness, and level of self-confidence. If you may be involved in tutoring children, you will want to encourage and reward attempts without being judgmental or reinforcing negative self-appraisal (e.g., "Good trying; that was a really hard one"). Most children are able to relate to someone who is accepting and lets them take the lead but who also is able to set clear limits regarding aggressive behaviors. It is also important to be aware of cultural differences among school-age children. For example, more direct physical interaction may be accepted in African American children but be less accepted in Asian or Native American children.

Issues Regarding the Family Context

A number of issues related to the context of the family are important to understand in working with children, among them parent discipline, parent conflict, divorce, and blended families. The process of change and adaptation surrounding parents' conflict and divorce can obviously have major consequences for the child and family, particularly when this is prolonged (Schroeder & Gordon, 2002). A child may have to deal with the loss of a parent, adapt to remarriage, and adjust to a foster parent or family. In addition, as the custodial parent, mothers often experience reduced income, which may create stress for both parent and children. The possibility of ongoing parental conflict and custody arrangements are additional stressors. A child's age, temperament, and ability to regulate feelings (anger, sadness, happiness, and fear) are all relevant factors in how well the child will cope with parents' divorce. Younger children are more apt to try to control parents' disputes, older children tend to take sides, and the largest fraction of children often appear to cope by avoidance and withdrawal. When divorced parents remarry and construct new "blended" families, these most often include a stepfather because mothers are more often granted custody of children. Whereas school-age boys may benefit from a positive relationship with an involved stepfather, girls are more apt to sense a disruption in the close relationship with their mothers, often making adjustment more difficult for them (Schroeder & Gordon, 2002).

Finally, parents and siblings may play a large role in cultivating aggressive behavior in children. Families in which parents use physical punishment and siblings respond to conflict with physical fights clearly serve as models for aggressive behavior to the child. In addition to physical punishment, parents who are coercive, unresponsive, and not emotionally engaged or invested in their children are likely to have aggressive children.

Children With Special Challenges: Introduction to Childhood Disorders

The following sections deal briefly with several of the most common types of developmental disorders and emotional and behavioral disorders in children. I refer you to Batshaw (2002) for a comprehensive review of children's neurodevelopmental disorders and to Mash and Wolfe (2002) and Gelfand and Drew (2003) for reviews of major childhood emotional and behavioral disorders. In addition, websites including information about children and adolescents are included in a list of online resources at the end of this chapter.

Many potential child practicum sites involve programs for exceptional or challenged children, and you would benefit from background information regarding primary delays and disorders in development that place some children at particular risk. Exhibit 9.1 lists the primary

---

EXHIBIT 9.1

Definitions of Common Childhood Disorders

Mental retardation: Children may experience significant delay in cognitive development that is typically assessed by an intelligence quotient (IQ) of below 70, which is accompanied by similar delays in adaptive functioning (how effectively the child can cope with ordinary life demands). Such cognitive delays are often accompanied by similar delays in physical and language development. There is wide variation in a child's functioning, ranging from children who function quite well in school and the community to others whose physical and cognitive impairments require high levels of care.

Communication disorders: Children may experience delay or disorder in oral language development, that is, the ability to comprehend (receptive language) or to produce speech (expressive language). There are several types of expressive disorder characterized by the child who (a) has difficulty with the motor pattern in articulating sounds or words, reducing the intelligibility of speech *(phonological disorder);* (b) stutters; or (c) has difficulty in using proper grammar and word order (syntax) or processing *(semantics).*

Specific learning disability: Children may experience significant delays in achievement of age-appropriate academic achievement in reading (word recognition and comprehension), writing (spelling and written language), or math, which are not *primarily* a function of mental retardation. The most frequent type of learning disability is *dyslexia*, a specific difficulty in mastering word-decoding skills. This disorder often has a genetic basis and is characterized by difficulty in phonological awareness, the understanding that words are composed of sequences of sounds. Children with oral language disorders often also exhibit disabilities in reading and written language. Children with math disabilities often have problems with spatial orientation and associated visuomotor disorders.

Sensory disorders: Children may experience impaired vision or hearing acuity that may range from mild visual problems correctable by glasses or mild hearing loss correctable by sound amplification or hearing aids to total deafness or blindness. Although children with severe sensory impairment require highly specialized educational settings and training, children with milder impairments may be expected to have mild to moderate difficulty in various aspects of communication/language and thinking/reasoning.

Physical and motor impairments: Children may experience a wide variety of fine and gross motor skill disorders, ranging from mild finger dexterity to severe *cerebral palsy* (brain injury from birth, which may result in generalized impairment in the part of the brain controlling large- and small-muscle movement and coordination). Such children may require a wheelchair, be unable to speak, and have little use of coordinated hand and finger movements but may have quite normal thinking, reasoning, and language comprehension abilities.

Pervasive developmental disorders (PDD): Children may experience developmental disorders characterized by abnormalities in social functioning, language, and communication and unusual behaviors and interests. *Autism* is the more severe form of PDD that is caused by disorder in brain development that results in generalized impairment in complex information-processing abilities, most often with severe impairments in language development. Once thought to be rare, the incidence of *autistic spectrum disorders* has been found to be steadily increasing, with a sizeable fraction of children functioning within the mentally retarded range of ability. Children with *Asperger's* disorder have a milder form of the disorder, which includes difficulties in social interaction and unusual, restricted, and stereotyped patterns of behavior but with relatively intact cognitive and communication skills. Some children with PDD have highly developed but isolated skills in reading, math, and music, and are regarded as savants

EXHIBIT 9.1 *(Continued)*

(children who have generalized developmental delays but specialized abilities in only selected areas of their development).

Emotional and behavioral disorders: Children with psychiatric disorders experience a variety of problems related to the ability to regulate emotional experience and to control their behavior. Childhood disorders are typically divided into two categories: *internalizing* disorders that involve distress for the child (e.g., anxiety and depression), and *externalizing* disorders that involve outward-directed behaviors (e.g., overactive, oppositional, or aggressive behaviors). Management and treatment of these disorders typically involves psychotherapy or behavior management approaches, and the various behavioral approaches often have well-supported evidence for their effectiveness.

childhood disorders, each of which is also a recognized category of special education. Thus, children who meet eligibility criteria for any of these disorders must be provided appropriate special education services in the "least restrictive environment"—that is, they are to be included with normally achieving peers to the extent possible.

Children with a specific learning disability represent the largest of these categories and include children who, despite adequate intelligence, experience significant difficulty in mastering basic academic skills of reading, math, and written language. Those children with reading disability (*dyslexia*) represent the largest category of learning disabilities, and research in the past 10 years has shown that brains of individuals with dyslexia do not process information as efficiently as do normal readers; moreover, this disability is known to be inherited in many individuals. Learning disability has traditionally used a *discrepancy model* for diagnosis, based on the assumption that there must be a significant discrepancy between a child's assessed intelligence and his or her actual level of academic achievement. However, this model has been fraught with problems, primary among them that children not meeting arbitrary criteria for discrepancy are often ineligible to receive needed specialized instruction until they have experienced several years of failure. The federal law that defines learning disability and the criteria for special education eligibility was revised in 2004. As an alternative to requiring that a child must demonstrate a significant discrepancy between intelligence and achievement, it is possible for school systems to diagnose a learning disability if a child fails to respond to research-based instruction (Individuals With Disabilities Education Improvement Act, 2004). This change will help to mandate appropriate early instruction as well as to make needed services available to a child early in elementary school. Federally sponsored research has clearly demonstrated that dyslexic children need carefully sequenced instruction in *phonological awareness* together with highly structured, systematic instruction in word decoding. It is expected that early diagnosis and early and appropriate instruction for such children may result in many fewer children diagnosed with dyslexia, or reading disability.

Although it is beyond the scope of the chapter to discuss the different categories of disability, you should be aware that any child with a disability may often cope with significant feelings of frustration, lowered self-esteem, and, not infrequently, associated behavior disorders. Finally, there is considerable (20%–30%) overlap between learning disability and attention-deficit/hyperactivity disorder (ADHD). The nature of this overlap is not clear, although there may be some shared genetic variation; significant attentional disorders may interfere with mastering reading, or alternatively, persistent academic failure may lead to restlessness and inattention in the classroom.

COMMON EMOTIONAL DISORDERS IN CHILDREN: INTERNALIZING DISORDERS

The term *internalizing* refers to conditions that primarily produce stress in the child and have less obvious impact on others: for example, the child who experiences worry or stress, is overly anxious, or is sad. Preschool children are most frequently fearful of strangers, animals, being hurt, and the dark. A shy or inhibited (slow-to-warm-up) child experiences more than usual anxiety and discomfort when separated from the parent. When working with these children, you should know that they will need considerable time to adjust to new surroundings and adults. For some young children, separation from the parent can precipitate extreme panic and distress (i.e., prolonged crying and extreme irritability). When day care is necessary for such a child, introduction to a new setting and caregiver must be gradual. As a caregiver, you should ask the parent to provide a familiar toy or blanket and a favorite snack as "transitional" objects to help comfort the child. In developing rapport with such a child, you will want to let the child take the lead and respect his or her need to "warm up." For young children placed in day care, slowly introducing activities, speaking softly, and showing patience often helps to calm a fearful child. In situations in which the child shows marked distress on separation from the parent (e.g., prolonged crying and extreme irritability), the parent–child relationship likely needs to be addressed by a professional—for example, by teaching the parents effective means to comfort their child while similarly providing the needed encouragement to trust other caretakers.

For a school-age child experiencing diagnosable anxiety or depression, recognized treatments by psychologists typically involve psychotherapy, with *behavioral therapy* and *cognitive behavioral therapy* approaches demonstrated to be most successful. Many children with specific fears and phobias require skilled treatment in *desensitizing* them; for example, children with irrational animal phobias are taught to master fear by means of developing a *fear hierarchy*, or graded sequence of things they fear, followed by gradually exposing them to feared animals in small increments. This process is coupled with teaching children methods to reduce the physical symptoms of anxiety through relaxation resulting in *systematic desensitization*. Child therapists practicing cognitive behavioral therapy believe that a child's thoughts, beliefs, and feelings are important and require as much modification as the child's environment. Excessive separation anxiety in school-age children can often be severe, for example, leading to the child's refusal to leave home or go to school (Mash & Wolfe, 2002).

Children who constantly appear unhappy and who show little enthusiasm for normal age-appropriate activities often have mood disorders (depression) that can affect many areas of their functioning. Such children often feel inadequate, are preoccupied with their own inner feelings, and may experience physical changes such as loss of appetite and fatigue. These are often the children who have poor regulation of their emotions and poor skills in coping with new situations (Gelfand & Drew, 2003). Recognizing these symptoms in a child, you should ask supervisors about making an appropriate referral to a mental health professional.

COMMON BEHAVIORAL DISORDERS IN CHILDREN: EXTERNALIZING DISORDERS

In contrast to internalizing problems, children with externalizing problems tend to direct their behaviors outwardly—that is, toward other people. Depending on a child's individual temperament, the development of autonomy (the "terrible twos") is a normal process for toddlers and preschool children. However, when this process goes awry, the irritability and negativism may become extreme, resulting in "disruptive behavior disorders" in children (American Psychiatric Association, 2000). Such children exhibit problems that annoy and disrupt others: temper outbursts, arguing, deliberately annoying others, and noncompliance, which may be consistent with *oppositional defiant disorder*. Interventions for these children typically involve special programs to train social and cognitive skills (aimed at remediating deficient problem-solving skills) and to train parents in methods of behavior management. A subset of these children with high levels of aggression may meet diagnostic criteria for *conduct disorder* in which clearly antisocial behavior occurs (e.g., stealing, fire setting, involvement with drugs, physical aggression, and gang-related activity). Such children clearly are in need of highly structured therapeutic programs and may be referred for management in residential facilities administered through the juvenile justice system.

Many young children with disruptive behavior disorders also exhibit the core symptoms for ADHD: inattention, impulsivity, and overactive behaviors (American Psychiatric Association, 2000). Of the school-age population, 3% to 5% is estimated to have this disorder, which is more prevalent in boys than in girls. Their impulsivity frequently leads these children to behave inappropriately, talk out of turn, and have difficulty waiting. Such behavior often provokes reprimands from others (i.e., peers, parents, and teachers who often inadvertently reinforce inappropriate behaviors by their negative attention). Although the majority of children with ADHD display the characteristic impulsiveness and difficulty in modulating their behavior, a smaller subset of children diagnosed with ADHD have a *primarily inattentive* subtype. In contrast to the hyperactive child, these children often appear "spacy," disorganized, and "hypoactive," or slow to respond. Similar to those with hyperactivity, these children seem not to listen and often have difficulty processing and understanding language; unlike hyperactive children, they are more apt to exhibit internalizing disorders of anxiety or depression.

Symptoms reflect an interaction of biology (e.g., temperament), which sets the risk, and environment (e.g., how parents, families, teachers, and others respond to the child's behavior), which can serve to both increase and reduce the symptoms. The primary treatments for ADHD include medication, parent training programs, and behavioral interventions for children (see Gelfand & Drew, 2003, for discussion of stimulant medications). Although medications may effectively reduce symptoms of ADHD, they are not a "cure" for the disorder, which must be managed by modeling and reinforcing the child's appropriate behaviors. Thus, the preferred and more comprehensive approach to working with the child with ADHD also includes behavior-based interventions: "contingency management," structured to provide specific consequences for the child's behavior (rewards for compliance and punishment for noncompliance). For most children with ADHD, behavioral management involves setting up well-designed behavioral contracts in which behaviors are carefully specified, followed by rewards for compliance. Frequently the rewards are points or tokens (the "token economy" system) that are redeemable in favorite activities tailored to the child (e.g., a video game, time with a favorite toy, or spending money). Exhibit 9.2 provides some practical suggestions if you are involved in working with children who have symptoms of ADHD (Mather & Goldstein, 2001).

The child with extreme oppositional or aggressive behaviors clearly requires specialized management. One behavioral approach for treating young children that has a record of success by professionally trained

EXHIBIT 9.2

Suggestions for Working With Children With Attention-Deficit/Hyperactivity Disorder (ADHD)

1. Be positive. This involves giving directives to the child (e.g., "I want you to sit in this chair" vs. "Stop teasing Jamie").
2. Give clear directions. Make instructions simple and brief, and have the child repeat them.
3. State the rules. Have a brief list of rules (written for school-age children who can read) for expected procedures in the particular child practicum setting; go over them with the child, and ask him or her to repeat them.
4. Provide cues. For older school-age children in a classroom or doing seat work, external cues have been found to be helpful in assisting children to monitor their on-task behavior (e.g., running a tape on which a beep sounds at programmed intervals and having the child make a check on a chart when he or she was on task).
5. Structure and minimize transitions. The child with ADHD does best when the environment is formal, focused, and structured.
6. Provide a consistent routine. A consistent schedule and plan for children with ADHD is much preferable to varying the sequence of activities.
7. Keep things changing. Within the consistent routine, the child with ADHD functions best when given multiple shortened work periods together with opportunities for choices of both tasks and reinforcers.
8. Offer feedback. Immediate, specific, and labeled feedback for compliance (e.g., "I like the way you sat down in your seat right after I asked you to").
9. Prepare the child for changes. Specifically mention any change in routine and the amount of time remaining for a specific activity.
10. Use preventive strategies. Anticipate potential problems by considering the task demands and the child's skills and develop preventative rather than reactionary strategies.

Note. From *Learning Disabilities and Challenging Behaviors: A Guide to Intervention and Classroom Management* (pp. 71–75), by N. Mather and S. Goldstein, 2001, Baltimore, MD: Paul H. Brookes Publishing Co. Copyright 2001 by Paul H. Brookes Publishing Co. Adapted with permission.

therapists with extensive training is *parent–child interaction therapy* (Eyberg, 1988; Hembree-Kigin & McNeil, 1995). Although it is emphasized that this treatment method requires highly specialized training, some of the principles followed may be useful in dealing with disruptive behaviors. Giving children *negative attention* for disruptive behavior (e.g., verbal reprimands) may actually serve to increase the behavior; alternatively, it is important to clearly describe or demonstrate the desired behavior, then reward the child for compliance. The following practices are useful in modifying difficult behavior: (a) practicing minding by making *direct* commands and describing *specific* behavior, followed immediately with *labeled praise* for compliance (e.g., "Thanks for putting your bike in the garage when I asked you to; good minding!"); (b) demonstrating and modeling the skills; (c) using *selective ignoring* of such inappropriate behaviors as whining, nagging, and tantrums; (d) imitating and praising appropriate play; and (e) *using strategic attention* (e.g., for playing *gently*, using an *indoor* voice, sharing, and taking turns). For students working with children who demonstrate seriously aggressive or destructive behaviors, it is paramount that you be provided with specialized training in methods of safe restraint and that you receive careful supervision in using such methods. Hembree-Kigin and McNeil (1995, p. 68) recommended a brief wrist restraint in which the caretaker gives a briefly stated rule (e.g., "no hurting"), averts his or her eyes while gently holding the child's forearms for approximately 20 seconds, and then says, "I'm going to let you go now; remember, no more hurting." You would then draw the child into more a prosocial activity by initiating appropriate play. It is emphasized that you *must* receive clear permission from the particular governing agency to use any method of physical restraint of a child.

TREATMENT SETTINGS FOR CHILDREN

You will find that potential practicum sites for gaining experience with children will vary greatly and include a wide variety of settings, both inpatient or residential (children's hospitals, pediatric units in general hospitals, and residential treatment centers) and outpatient (private or public schools, day-care centers, after-school programs, Head Start programs, private preschool programs, outpatient child development and child mental health clinics, child study centers, or with mental health providers in private practice settings). If you are planning a practicum experience, it is recommended that you meet with an undergraduate advisor who frequently sponsors such student placements and who may have a list of prospective sites in the area. The following issues should be considered when beginning to seek a practicum experience with children: (a) the age range of children (preschool, school age, or adolescents), (b) whether the experience will involve actual interaction with children versus observation or errand running, (c) the extent of training and supervision that will be provided in the setting, and (d) the amount and quality of previous experience with children expected by the site.

Lyman and Campbell (1996) have provided a thorough discussion of residential and inpatient treatment settings for children and youth with emotional and behavioral problems. Child mental health treatment settings reflect a continuum of care, from least to most restrictive. Outpatient settings might involve 1 to 3 hours weekly of private individual psychotherapy, family therapy, and behavioral therapy, with school and community activities minimally affected. In-home interventions involve direct treatment in the child's home: establishing a treatment, modeling behaviors, and instructing parents in the procedures. Examples include crisis intervention and the growing number of private agencies that provide intensive behavioral treatments for young autistic children.

These latter services most often involve *discrete trial training*—that is, systematically shaping appropriate behaviors with primary reinforcers such as food, verbal praise, or physical contact. Such experience is excellent background if you may be planning graduate study in areas such as clinical child or school psychology. However, you should be aware that the degree and quality of training can be quite variable, and you would be advised to inquire about the nature and extent of training and supervision. College students are often used as assistants in day treatment and in regular education, special education, and after-school therapeutic programs. Some children are placed in residential or inpatient care for brief periods (generally less than 2 weeks) to stabilize them during a crisis; others may be removed from home and placed in foster care. Group homes are often operated as part of child-care agencies and employ "house parents."

LEGAL AND ETHICAL ISSUES

Finally, it is important that as a practicum student involved with children and youth, you are aware of the professional code of ethics (American Psychological Association, 2010; see also http://www.apa.org/ethics) including *informed consent, confidentiality, duty to protect*, and *duty to report* (Brems, 2002). Specific procedures may differ across various practicum settings (pediatric hospital, psychiatric facility, therapeutic clinic, or day care), and you should be informed of the specific practices in a particular setting. However, there are some general principles of ethical conduct and legal requirements in working with children.

Signed informed consent indicating that the parent (custodial parent in the case of divorce) is informed of all relevant information regarding the evaluation and treatment of his or her child is necessary before mental health treatment. This includes videotaping or audiotaping and observation, risks and benefits of treatment, and the limits of confidentiality and duty to report—that is, mandated reporting of information relating to harmful neglect or abuse of a child.

A therapist or agency has a *duty to warn* a potential victim if a client has acknowledged the threat of harm to others (see Chapter 4, this volume, for a discussion of the duty to warn). Although this would typically not be relevant with child clients, it could apply in the case of adolescents. Finally, parents of children are guaranteed the security and privacy of information regarding themselves and their children. Agencies involved with children must disclose how information regarding children and families will be used, develop specific procedures for how privacy regarding diagnostic and therapeutic practices will be protected, and state how long personal records and files will be maintained and how and when they will be destroyed.

Summary

Experience in working with both normally developing children and adolescents as well as those who present challenges of development and behavior is now expected for students applying for admission into many applied graduate programs. If you are planning to enter such fields as clinical child psychology, school psychology, applied developmental psychology, or social work, experience in working with a wide age range of children and adolescents is highly desirable. In this chapter, I outlined some of the primary aspects of normal physical, cognitive, language, and social-emotional development and provided a brief introduction to those children exhibiting learning and behavior disorders. It is my hope that with this introduction, together with additional readings, you may be better informed in selecting a practicum setting that suits your goals and interests. This introduction outlines such important skills as developing rapport, engaging children, and appreciating how appropriate behaviors are reinforced by adult praise and encouragement. It is also important that you become an educated consumer of potential training experiences—that is, that you are conscious of the need for supervision, particularly with children with serious emotional or behavioral disorders, and that you have an appreciation of ethical standards in the care of children.

Online Resources

American Academy of Child and Adolescent Psychiatry: http://www.aacap.org

American Academy of Pediatrics: http://www.aap.org

Child Development Institute: http://childdevelopmentinfo.com

Children and Adults With Attention-Deficit/Hyperactivity Disorder (CHADD): http://www.chadd.org

Council for Exceptional Children: http://www.cec.sped.org

Education Resources Information Center (ERIC): http://eric.ed.gov

Individuals With Disabilities Education Improvement Act (H.R. 1350) https://www.congress.gov/bill/108th-congress/house-bill/1350

Learning Disabilities Online: http://www.ldonline.org

National Center for Learning Disabilities: www.ncld.org

National Information Center for Children and Youth With Disabilities: http://www.parentcenterhub.org/resources

References

American Psychiatric Association. (2000). *Diagnostic and statistical manual of mental disorders* (4th ed., text rev.). Washington, DC: Author.

American Psychological Association. (2010). *Ethical standards of psychologists and code of conduct (2002, Amended June 1, 2010)*. Washington, DC: Author. Retrieved from http://www.apa.org/ethics/code/index.aspx

Batshaw, M. L. (2002). *Children with disabilities* (5th ed.). Baltimore, MD: Brookes.

Brems, C. (2002). *A comprehensive guide to child psychotherapy* (2nd ed.). Boston, MA: Allyn & Bacon.

Campbell, S. B. (2002). *Behavior problems in preschool children* (2nd ed.). New York, NY: Guilford Press.

Eyberg, S. (1988). Parent–child interaction therapy: Integration of traditional and behavioral concerns. *Child & Family Behavior Therapy, 10*, 33–46. http://dx.doi.org/10.1300/J019v10n01_04

Garrison, W. T., & Earls, F. J. (1987). *Temperament and child psychopathology* (Vol. 12). Newbury Park, CA: Sage.

Gelfand, D. M., & Drew, C. J. (2003). *Understanding child behavior disorders* (4th ed.). Belmont, CA: Wadsworth.

Hembree-Kigin, T. L., & McNeil, C. B. (1995). *Parent–child interaction therapy*. New York, NY: Plenum.

Individuals With Disabilities Education Improvement Act. (2004, November 17). *Strengthening and renewing special education: The Individuals With Disabilities Education Improvement Act* (H. R. 1350 Conference Report). Retrieved from http://archives.republicans.edlabor.house.gov/archive/issues/108th/education/idea/1350confsummary.htm

Kagan, J. (1989). Temperamental contributions to social behavior. *American Psychologist, 44*, 668–674. http://dx.doi.org/10.1037/0003-066X.44.4.668

Kail, R. V. (2002). *Children*. Upper Saddle River, NJ: Prentice Hall.

Krebs, N. F., & Jacobson, M. S., & the American Academy of Pediatrics Committee on Nutrition. (2003). Prevention of pediatric overweight and obesity. *Pediatrics, 112*, 424–430. http://dx.doi.org/10.1542/peds.112.2.424

Lyman, R. D., & Campbell, N. R. (1996). *Treating children and adolescents in residential and inpatient settings*. Thousand Oaks, CA: Sage.

Mash, E. J., & Wolfe, D. A. (2002). *Abnormal child psychology*. Belmont, CA: Wadsworth.

Mather, N., & Goldstein, S. (2001). *Learning disabilities and challenging behaviors: A guide to intervention and classroom management*. Baltimore, MD: Brookes.

National Institute of Child Health and Human Development, Early Child Care Research Network. (1997). The effects of infant childcare on infant–mother attachment security: Results of the NICHD Study of Early Child Care. *Child Development, 68,* 860–879.

Padilla, A. M., Lindholm, K. J., Chen, A., Duran, R., Hakuta, K., Lambert, W., & Tucker, G. R. (1991). The English-only movement. Myths, reality, and implications for psychology. *American Psychologist, 46,* 120–130. http://dx.doi.org/10.1037/0003-066X.46.2.120

Schickendanz, J. A., Schickendanz, D. I., Forsyth, P. D., & Forsyth, G. A. (2001). *Understanding children and adolescents* (4th ed.). Boston, MA: Allyn & Bacon.

Schroeder, C. S., & Gordon, B. N. (2002). *Assessment and treatment of childhood problems* (2nd ed.). New York, NY: Guilford Press.

Shaywitz, S. (2003). *Overcoming dyslexia.* New York, NY: Knopf.

Wenar, C., & Kerig, P. (2000). *From infancy through adolescence* (4th ed.). *Developmental psychopathology* Boston, MA: McGraw-Hill.

Sara H. Qualls, Daniel L. Segal, and Kimberly E. Hiroto

Special Issues in Working With Older Persons

10

W e are delighted that you are considering doing clinical work with older adults as part of your practicum or internship training! We hope the information in this chapter gives you some important insights into the challenges and opportunities associated with growing older and some tips to help you prepare for success with your clinical training experiences. We represent perspectives from early, mid-, and late-career *geropsychologists* (psychologists who specialize in work with older adults) who have loved working in this field and have devoted ourselves to drawing in, and training, the next generation, which we hope includes you.

In this chapter, we provide an overview of possible roles and the settings in which students may find practica, and orient you to the information and skills you need in preparation for work with older adults. We hope that the information herein will help you appreciate the growing importance of a career in geropsychology.

http://dx.doi.org/10.1037/14672-010

Your Practicum in Psychology: A Guide for Maximizing Knowledge and Competence, Second Edition, J. R. Matthews and C. E. Walker (Editors)

Why Choose a Practicum With Older Adults?

As you begin your training and work with older adults, we encourage you to reflect on what draws you to the aging population. Many psychologists decide to specialize in working with older adults because of having important relationships with older adults (e.g., parents or grandparents) in their own family of origin. Some of these psychologists witnessed older family members aging with grace and dignity. By witnessing such exemplars of "successful aging," they have positive images of aging in mind. Other psychologists decide to focus on this area of practice because they had a close relationship with an older adult who experienced significant decline and disability in later life, for example, a grandmother who suffered from some form of dementia. By witnessing extremely difficult aspects of aging (as in this example, a disease process that is not a normal part of aging), some professionals chose this area of specialty out of a passion to help those older adults whose aging process is exceptionally complicated.

Yet another group of professionals who decide to focus on older adults do so for more pragmatic reasons, like the exceptional career opportunities for work in an emerging field such as geropsychology. You likely have several reasons for choosing to work with the older adult population that may not have been mentioned here. Regardless, we encourage you to think about what draws you to this type of work, so you can begin to map out a training plan (and possible career trajectory) that is personally satisfying and meaningful to you, working with a population that you truly enjoy.

Demographic Shifts: Growing Need and Career Opportunity

Practicum students who will be working with older adults should be aware of the important demographic patterns affecting much of the world. Indeed, the older adult population is booming in all of the developed countries as people are living longer, healthier lives. The United States, in particular, is in the midst of a longevity revolution, primarily because of the massive numbers of baby boomers progressing into later life. Beginning in 2011, the oldest of the boomers began turning 65 years old. From now through 2030, approximately 10,000 people each day will reach their 65th birthday. This population bulge will have a profound impact on the demographics of our nation. For example,

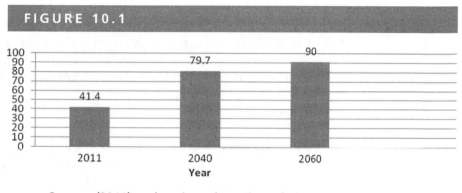

FIGURE 10.1

Current (2011) and projected number of older adults in the United States (in millions). Data from the Administration on Aging, U.S. Department of Health and Human Services (2012).

Figure 10.1 shows the dramatic shift from 2011, when the older adult population (persons age 65 years old and older) numbered 41.4 million, representing 13.3% of the population (roughly one in eight individuals) to projections for 2040 and 2060. Because of the boomer cohort, it is projected that by 2040, approximately 21% of the U.S. population will have passed their 65th birthday, representing about 79.7 million people. By 2060, the number of older adults is projected to be 92 million (Administration on Aging, U.S. Department of Health and Human Services, 2012).

The gender gap among the older adult population (65 years old and older) in the United States is notable because women tend to outlive men. For example, in 2011, there were 23.4 million older women and 17.9 million older men, representing a sex ratio of 131 women for every 100 men. This ratio becomes even more pronounced with advancing age, ranging from 112 women for every 100 men in the 65- to 69-year age group to a high of 203 for the 85 years and older age group. The fastest-growing subpopulation of older adults is the oldest-old group (those age 85 years and older), who are also the most frail. In the United States, the oldest-old group is projected to increase from 5.7 million people in 2011 to 14.1 million people in 2040. The projected older adult population is also expected to become significantly more ethnically and culturally diverse (Administration on Aging, U.S. Department of Health and Human Services, 2012), prompting the need for more diversity and multiculturally informed training for all mental health professionals who serve older adults.

With the rise in the older adult population, the number of older adults who suffer from a diagnosable mental disorder will also increase (Segal, Qualls, & Smyer, 2011). According to the recent Institute of Medicine (2012) report on the mental health and substance use workforce for older adults, approximately 14% to 20% of older adults suffer from a mental disorder, including depressive disorders, anxiety disorders, schizophrenia and other psychotic disorders, and dementia-related behavioral and psychiatric problems. An even greater percentage of older adults experience significant symptoms of mental disorders and subsequent reduced quality of life, even though the symptoms do not meet a diagnostic threshold. The growth of the number of older adults in the United States with significant mental health and substance abuse problems indicates that the need for psychologists who specialize in working with older adults (professional geropsychologists) will grow substantially over the next several decades (Institute of Medicine, 2012).

Population Heterogeneity

"If you have seen one older adult, you have seen one older adult." This adage is one we find to be true, because later life is when our population is most heterogeneous. You may be surprised to learn that the population of 6-year-olds has less variability on almost any dimension we might choose (e.g., height, weight, functional skills, blood pressure) than the population of 80-year-olds. Students desiring a career working with older adults need broad exposure to many populations of older persons to gain a true appreciation of this heterogeneity.

Most people associate the onset of aging with age 65, which was established in legislation during the Great Depression as the age at which adults become eligible for Social Security retirement benefits. Of course, aging starts at birth, so no chronological age defines one as *aged*. Furthermore, knowing a person's chronological age provides little information about any dimension of life (e.g., marital status, health, mobility).

In this section, you will be invited to reflect on your experiences interacting with older adults. In light of the broad variability in aging populations, this is a moment in which to consider *which* older adults you have experienced. What health status? Social history? Race and ethnicity? Gender? Social class? Sexual orientation? Ability level? These are but a few dimensions on which older adults represent almost endless variation. Your family experience was in a particular social location (e.g., African American, middle-class, educated) with a particular health status (e.g., grandmother with dementia) whose needs were met in a particular way (e.g., your family provided care until her last few months when she lived in a memory unit of an assisted living facility). Look around to consider the wide range of older adults with whom you might want to gain new experiences.

Compelling and Interesting Roles for Psychologists

As you consider pursuing professional opportunities focusing on older adults, note that there are many important roles for geropsychologists. Two of the most popular roles for geropsychologists are those of clinician and researcher, although psychologists also have important roles in setting public policy, administration of programs, and even in development of technologies to maximize independence.

PROFESSIONAL SERVICES

Professional geropsychologists focus on the diagnosis, assessment, and treatment of older adults with mental health disorders or problems. In many cases, geropsychologists work with the family members of older adults to help them manage the burdens of caregiving for an ill older adult, for example, someone with dementia or severe physical disabilities. Some of the most popular settings for clinical work include outpatient private practice settings (either as a solo practitioner or as part of a group practice) and working as a geropsychologist in the federal VA Health System, which employs thousands of mental health professionals who serve our aging veterans in both outpatient and inpatient settings across the United States.

Another important venue of practice is in long-term care (LTC) settings, such as nursing homes. Although the vast majority of older adults live independently in the community, those with the most severe forms of physical and mental health problems (most notably some form of dementia or other chronic mental disorder like schizophrenia) cannot effectively or safely live at home or at other supportive environments (like a congregate living facility) and thus are placed in nursing homes designed to meet their serious care needs. Working with older adults in these settings requires specialized training, knowledge, competencies, and skills (Hyer & Intrieri, 2006; Molinari, 2000; Norris, Molinari, & Ogland-Hand, 2002; Rosowsky, Casciani, & Arnold, 2009). Clinical work in LTC settings is especially challenging because clients are often affected by a multitude of impeding factors, including financial, medical, social, cognitive, and psychiatric issues. Psychologists in these settings typically provide evaluation, consultation and training to staff members regarding how to deal with poorly adjusted or behaviorally aggressive or otherwise problematic residents, and they also provide direct mental health services to the residents.

Yet another popular setting for clinical work is in medical settings (e.g., university-affiliated teaching hospitals), where psychologists play important roles serving medically ill older adults who are in need of mental or behavioral health services. Although sometimes lumped under a behavioral health label, two distinct sets of services may be offered in health settings. Mental health services address mental disorders. Behavioral medicine or behavioral health services help people manage their health conditions more effectively. For example, older adults coping with cancer or being evaluated for an organ transplant may also have a mental disorder that requires treatment during this challenging time, or they may need behavioral strategies to maximize self-management of a medical condition.

An increasingly popular setting for geropsychological practice is integrated care—for example, a primary care medical clinic, where psychologists serve as part of the team of health care professionals who attend holistically to the client's mental and physical needs in the same setting without necessarily having to refer the client to a specialty mental health setting located outside of the hospital or clinic (American Psychological Association Presidential Task Force, 2008). In these settings, geropsychologists typically function as consultants to medical professionals and provide direct behavioral health assessment and psychotherapy services to older adults (usually in a brief, short-term treatment model).

Geropsychologists may overlap with other psychologists working in health care as well. Neuropsychologists who specialize in work with older adults evaluate cognitive strengths and weaknesses to assist with diagnosis of diseases or effects of traumatic brain injury or stroke and to inform legal decisions about competence to maintain legal rights. Almost all geropsychologists garner some neuropsychological evaluation training that positions them to help implement the findings of a neuropsychological evaluation report. Psychologists also may support persons and families through the dying process with mental and behavioral health services if they affiliate with hospice and palliative care services (Qualls & Kasl-Godley, 2011). Health psychologists have intensive specialty in working with medical disorders, another area of work which geropsychologists often need to do.

Professional geropsychologists (counseling or clinical, or applied developmental) have a broad range of service opportunities that overlap many specialties within psychology as well as across other fields such as nursing, medicine, social work, and even physical, occupational, or speech therapies. In some settings the geropsychologist is the only person who can provide those services, and so she or he builds the professional capacity to do so, whereas in other settings the geropsychologist pulls together data from many specialties to inform assessment and intervention plans.

RESEARCH

An extensive range of research topics are being pursued with the intent of understanding aging and supporting a high quality of life for all of us as we age (Schaie & Willis, 2011). Some researchers focus on understanding basic processes associated with aging. For example, active areas of psychological investigation include cognitive, social, and emotional changes with aging. Other researchers focus on more applied topics, such as mental health and aging, as they study the nature of psychopathology in later life, the assessment of psychopathology, and the effectiveness and applications of psychological therapies for older adults (Lichtenberg, 2010; Segal et al., 2011; Zarit & Zarit, 2007). There are many popular scientific journals that focus on aging issues and geropsychology, and these are listed in Exhibit 10.1. Professional organizations maintain websites that provide useful information (see Exhibit 10.2 for a selective listing). In particular, note the availability of a new online repository of information on training, GeroCentral, and its website (http://www.gerocentral.org).

How Do I Prepare to Work With Older Adults?

Working with older adults often involves critically examining your individual and collective cultural values about aging and aging processes. Consider your beliefs about and prior experiences with older adults, particularly those closest to you. How do you and your family typically communicate with older adults? Does your language change as you describe a 65-year-old compared with an 85-year-old or a 100-year-old person? If so, why? Would you interact similarly were this person 45 years old? How might your demeanor change when speaking with your friend, professor, or your parent? When you consider the quality and quantity of life experiences collected over 65, 85, or 100 years, would your language use and approach to interacting with this person change? Why or why not? Sitting with these questions and reflecting on your responses can help develop even greater insight into your beliefs and assumptions of older adults and how previous experiences have affected your perspective. This remains important because working with clients in life stages that we have yet to experience involves a degree of humility, self-awareness, and a critical shift in our view of the world. The first part of this section includes practical tips for making these shifts to aid in communication, whereas later sections focus

---

EXHIBIT 10.1

A Sampling of Psychology Journals that Focus on Aging or Geropsychology

- *Aging and Mental Health*
  http://www.tandfonline.com/toc/camh20/current
- *Alzheimer Disease and Associated Disorders*
  http://journals.lww.com/alzheimerjournal/pages/default.aspx
- *American Journal of Geriatric Psychiatry*
  http://ajgponline.org
- *Clinical Gerontologist*
  http://www.tandfonline.com/toc/wcli20/current#.UgAaHazOA8k
- *Educational Gerontology*
  http://www.tandfonline.com/toc/uedg20/current#.UgAa4azOA8k
- *Gerontology & Geriatrics Education*
  http://www.tandfonline.com/toc/wgge20/current#.UgAfMKzOA8k
- *GeroPsych: The Journal of Gerontopsychology and Geriatric Psychiatry*
  http://www.hogrefe.com/periodicals/geropsych/
- *International Journal of Aging and Human Development*
  http://www.baywood.com/Journals/PreviewJournals.asp?Id=0091-4150
- *International Journal of Geriatric Psychiatry*
  http://onlinelibrary.wiley.com/journal/10.1002/%28ISSN%291099-1166
- *International Psychogeriatrics*
  http://journals.cambridge.org/action/displayJournal?jid=IPG
- *Journal of Aging Studies*
  http://www.journals.elsevier.com/journal-of-aging-studies
- *Journal of Applied Gerontology*
  http://jag.sagepub.com
- *Journal of Gerontology: Psychological Sciences*
  http://psychsocgerontology.oxfordjournals.org/
- *Journal of the American Geriatrics Society*
  http://onlinelibrary.wiley.com/journal/10.1111/%28ISSN%291532-5415
- *Psychology and Aging*
  http://www.apa.org/journals/pag/
- *Research on Aging*
  http://roa.sagepub.com/
- *The Gerontologist*
  http://gerontologist.oxfordjournals.org

---

on role negotiations and the practice of setting appropriate boundaries and maintaining privacy.

INTERPERSONAL COMMUNICATION

You may bring to your practicum a habit of speaking to older adults in a distinct way that is less than helpful, sometimes referred to as *elderspeak*. Elderspeak refers to the quality and content of communication toward older adults that can be infantilizing and indicate signs of disrespect and

---

EXHIBIT 10.2

Professional Organizations and Resources for Geropsychology

- American Psychological Association (APA) Division 12, Section II (Society of Clinical Geropsychology). Website: http://www.geropsychology.org
- APA Division 20 (Adult Development and Aging). Website: http://www.apadivisions.org/division-20
- APA Office on Aging. Website: http://www.apa.org/pi/aging
- Council of Professional Geropsychology Training Programs (CoPGTP). Website: http://www.copgtp.org
- GeroCentral. Website: http://www.gerocentral.org
- National Coalition on Mental Health & Aging (NCMHA). Website: http://www.ncmha.org
- Psychologists in Long Term Care (PLTC). Website: http://www.pltcweb.org/index.php

---

condescension. This quality of communication often sounds like "baby talk," including a higher-pitched voice, singsong quality of speech, and use of words like "precious," "adorable," "cute," and "little"—adjectives typically reserved for young babies and toddlers. Affectionate names such as "honey" or "dear" are other forms of elderspeak. Sometimes, this form of communication reflects cultural and regional differences, and often persons engaging in elderspeak are nurturing and well intentioned. Of key import is the recipient's perception of elderspeak. Although some may perceive it as a form of affection, others may perceive it as infantilizing, disrespectful, and irritating. Indeed, even persons with severe dementia and limited verbal communication demonstrate signs of agitation when caregivers use elderspeak toward them (Williams, Herman, Gajewski, & Wilson, 2009; Williams, Kemper, & Hummert, 2004).

SENSORY AND PHYSICAL CHANGES

Normative, age-related changes in sensory abilities can affect daily functioning in many ways, including receptive and expressive communication. For example, changes in hearing (particularly reduced ability to hear higher pitched tones) and vision can significantly and adversely affect a person's ability to follow conversations, navigate in new environments, or feel confident in social situations. Not all older adults experience these changes, so information about the challenges each individual is facing is important to have before interacting. Often, the providers are the ones who need to adjust to the changing needs of our older clients, being cognizant of visible and invisible deficits (e.g., unsteady gait and cognitive impairment, respectively) and how to best accommodate for these challenges. We must balance awareness of a client's challenges with caution in making assumptions that the person wants or needs assistance. Providers want to encourage the client to do the task on his or her own, offering help when asked, or if safety or dignity requires it.

Following are brief tips for how to accommodate sensory deficits in older adults. Although not comprehensive, we hope this section will serve as a launching point for you to think even more critically about how sensory changes can affect communication and the level of resiliency and flexibility needed for clients to adjust to these changes.

Decreased vision can reflect normative (e.g., myopia) or non-normative (e.g., macular degeneration, cataracts, glaucoma) age-related changes (Fozard & Gordon-Salant, 2001). It behooves providers working with older adults to be aware of visual challenges in their clients, and providers may need to ask basic questions such as whether the client needs corrective lenses and whether their current prescription suits their needs. Following are some tips for accommodating visual changes in older clients to facilitate ease of communication:

1. Increase the brightness in the room and reduce glare (if using a computer).
2. Use high-contrast colors when presenting printed material or graphics (e.g., dark text or bright pictures on light background).
3. Increase the font size on printed materials.
4. If navigating multilevel environments, use brightly colored tape or paint to highlight steps and prevent tripping (e.g., with vision changes, older adults may have some difficulty recognizing changes in ground level if the step is the same color as the ground).
5. Create large-print or large-graphic signage with high-contrast colors (e.g., signs for male and female bathrooms that have bright white silhouettes of a male or female figure against dark blue backgrounds).

If working in environments where clients have significant visual impairments, it is helpful to be aware of their level of vision to discuss with them the level of assistance they may or may not need. If offering help to a client with visual impairment, do so verbally, and offer your arm for them to reach out and hold rather than touching them first and potentially startling them. Offering them assistance is typically preferred rather than assuming the client needs help. Ask clients if they can adequately see and read printed materials. If your client appears to be having difficulty with written information, try to assess whether he or she has difficulties with seeing the print or reading it. Some older adults may not be literate and have understandable difficulty notifying a provider. Asking subtle questions without inducing shame can be helpful (e.g., "May I help you with reading that questionnaire? Some people have difficulty reading this. Would you like some help?"). Providing your client with the option of completing paperwork (or other written material) himself or herself or having you read it to them can also circumvent your client's potential discomfort addressing vision or reading challenges.

Much like vision, hearing changes can be normative (e.g., changes in pitch sensitivity) or nonnormative (e.g., tinnitus) age-related changes (Fozard & Gordon-Salant, 2001). Some older clients may need hearing aids, although this does not guarantee adequate hearing, because they may choose not to wear them or the quality of the hearing aid or its calibration may undermine sound quality. Although hearing aids serve their function, they unfortunately do not match the natural ability of the ear to filter out irrelevant background noise (e.g., the hum of overhead lights, the ticking of a clock). Consequently, when working with persons using hearing aids, the following tips are useful:

- Reduce background noise significantly.
- Speak slowly, enunciate clearly, and use a lower-pitch voice.
- Avoid turning your back while talking with clients so that your lips are always visible to the listener.

Clarifying your client's listening preferences while developing rapport allows you to know how to best communicate. You can offer useful suggestions for ways in which your client can adjust to these changes, and by doing this demonstrate respect for his or her needs and preferences. Ask your client if he or she can adequately hear and understand you. Offer to speak louder or slower, or lower the pitch of your voice. Inquire whether your client hears better out of one particular ear, and situate yourself accordingly. Sometimes clients cannot afford hearing aids or may lack access to audiology services. In that case, consider using a "pocket talker," which your agency may already have. This device consists of headphones connected to a microphone into which you speak. The client adjusts the volume according to his or her preferences. This can greatly enhance a person's comprehension and allow him or her to track and contribute to the conversation.

With age come additional changes in balance and manner of walking (i.e., posture and gait; Ketcham & Stelmach, 2001). Taking these changes into consideration can demonstrate nonverbal signs of respect. For example, slowing your walking speed or matching your client's pace has practical implications: It can decrease the chances that your client will potentially trip, fall, get short of breath, or feel disrespected while attempting to keep pace with you. Additionally, slowing your rate of walking also demonstrates your willingness to adjust your style to meet another person's needs. Similar to working with clients with low vision, one should offer to help a client rather than assume that the client wishes for or needs assistance (e.g., struggling to get out of a chair, navigating rooms in a wheelchair or with a walker). Assess your physical environment from the perspective of your client and determine whether the room needs adjusting for safety precautions. Simple accommodations may be needed, such as removing a chair to make room for a wheelchair, decreasing the risk of a fall by providing chairs with armrests and without wheels, or removing throw rugs or ensuring rugs are flat to reduce trip hazards.

ROLE NEGOTIATIONS

Your roles as a practicum trainee may be tightly prescribed or may be a new experience for the agency. In the latter case, procedures to integrate practicum students may not be established before your arrival. A key task early in your practicum is to become clear about roles and expectations, as discussed in Chapter 1. If you are entering a training clinic for an initial practicum, your role may be well established as a psychologist-in-training. However, other community settings where you may be placed may not have a clear role that reflects your psychology identity. For example, in a nursing home, you may be perceived as a nice young volunteer who can help staff implement activities. Either role (or myriad others) may constitute a wonderful practicum for you and is likely to engage you in excellent learning. You are likely to fit in better and meet your own learning goals if you ascertain clearly at the beginning about where you fit and what you are expected to be doing. This section provides a framework for thinking of your role, its limits, and ways of managing emergent needs.

A starting point in clarifying your role is to understand the organizational chart of the agency or setting, and where you fit in it. Who is your direct supervisor? What department is he or she in? What is the role of that department in the overall organization? To whom does your supervisor report? Answering these questions will help you make sense of what you are asked to do (and not do), and who can provide guidance to you.

Undergraduate students are often placed in nonprofessional roles for the purpose of gaining exposure to older adults with a particular set of needs and the settings in which they seek services. Perhaps you are an activity aide in a senior housing campus or a "social work" intern in a skilled nursing facility (title is dictated by state regulations but may be an appropriate place for a psychology trainee). Before starting your placement, you need to identify your supervisor, and how that person fits into the overall purpose of the setting. Ideally, you will have a job description for your role, with clear expectations defined and clear lines of reporting.

If you are a graduate student trainee working under a psychologist supervisor for the purpose of learning professional skills, keep in mind that you work under the license of your supervisor. This is important because should something happen within the context of your relationship with your client, your supervisor is ultimately responsible. It is imperative that you respect this relationship because your supervisor entrusts you to work ethically under his or her guidance. Usually it is the student's responsibility to inform clients of your role as a trainee and that you are under the supervision of a licensed psychologist with whom you will discuss pertinent information that arose in session.

You may wish for a certain degree of autonomy in your internship. Negotiating this balance often requires an explicit conversation with your supervisor to clarify your role and the limitations therein. For example, what is your exact job description (or memorandum of understanding in some circumstances), what are your expected work hours, and whom do you contact in case of an emergency? In addition to these questions, some other basic questions that may arise include the following:

- How do I introduce myself to new clients? Do I have a business card?
- What contact information should I provide? As noted in Chapter 1, never provide your personal contact information (phone number, personal e-mail, address).
- How should I dress during my visits with clients? Do I take my own car (if visiting clients in their homes)? Is there mileage reimbursement?
- What are your (supervisor's and/or agency's) expectations of me?
- What are my training goals? How will I know I am making progress toward them? (Tip: The more specific and measurable, the better.)

DOS AND DON'TS OF SERVICE DELIVERY

There are many gray areas in professional practice, just as there are certain do's and don'ts when working with others—in this case, older adults. Clarifying with your supervisor your specific role and expectations during internship will help elucidate the parameters of your job. Here we outline some basic do's and don'ts.

Do:

- Introduce yourself and clarify your role as a practicum trainee under the supervision of a licensed psychologist (or social worker, etc.),
- explain the limits of confidentiality with your client (e.g., duty to warn, child or elder abuse), and
- discuss in supervision any concerns you have about your client's welfare (or that of a child or other older adult).

Don't:

- Take on new responsibilities without consulting with your supervisor;
- give medical or psychological advice without speaking first with your supervisor even if you have expertise in that area (remember, you are working under your supervisor's license);
- offer rides to your client (or accept rides) or run errands for your client unless that is explicitly identified as part of your job duty;
- share private information about one client with another, even if they know each other;
- share private information with another staff member who is not intimately involved in your client's care and/or has no need to know (e.g., the administrative assistant working on your team but without direct client contact);
- take pictures of your client without first receiving written consent from your client or legal guardian and assent from your client (if your client lacks decisional capacity for this);
- meet with or interact with your client or his or her friends and family members outside of work, including via social networking sites (e.g., Facebook, Twitter); or
- give your client a gift, including but not limited to money, gift certificates, souvenirs, tokens of appreciation, food.

How do you handle having a favorite, or less favorite, client? Being in the helping profession, often we wish to help some clients more than others. This is something to discuss with your supervisor because it is a great learning opportunity. For example, strong fondness for a client can be a sign that this specific person evokes something in you that goes beyond the therapeutic relationship (e.g., your client resembles your beloved grandmother). Such responses are termed *countertransference* in clinical psychology (Kane, 2002). It remains an ethical and legal imperative that you not cross boundaries with your client (becoming friends) or with anyone in your client's social or familial network (e.g., befriending or becoming romantically involved with your client's grandson). Although it may feel anxiety provoking to think of all the "don'ts" on this list (and those not mentioned), perhaps the best guide is your intuition and professional judgment (American Psychological Association, 2010). If you find yourself in a compromising position, ask yourself, "What would my colleagues or supervisor do?" Listen to your intuition, and check your gut reaction. If you have a second thought, it is best to refrain from the activity and check with your supervisor, unless it is an urgent matter, which we discuss next.

HANDLING EMERGENT NEEDS

On rare occasions, you may face emergency client needs. Addressing such situations warrants attention to increase your preparation and sense of readiness for your internship. Your initial role negotiations need to include clarification of how you respond to older adults who are at risk.

Urgent health needs may arise, ranging from finding pills on the floor, to learning of medication nonadherence, to learning of elder abuse. The role established at the beginning of your internship or practicum needs to outline how you handle emergency situations. In some roles, you will be expected to inform your supervisor quickly, and she or he will initiate any action needed. In others, you may need to proceed with action. For example, if you find pills on the floor or learn of medication nonadherence, your supervisor (or you, if authorized) would first ask your client or caregiver about what may be happening. Are they aware of the problem? Does this happen frequently? What are the medications for, has the person taken them regularly, and if not, why? Consider your relationship, if any, with your client's primary care physician or medical team. Do you have the right to contact them (often this entails a form, signed by the client, authorizing you to release his or her relevant information)? Many other risk issues may arise, and you need to be clear on what role you are expected to take and certain that you have proper training in agency policy, state statutes (e.g., for elder abuse reporting), and professional ethics commensurate with the role assigned to you. Many settings where students work with older adults are in the field, so to speak, with no one down the hall to ask. Thus, preparation for the unexpected is particularly important in geropsychology.

In short, practicum is designed to stretch you, but not beyond what is professionally appropriate. Many of our trainees have felt uncomfortably unprepared to handle a crisis, but actually had all of the necessary training to implement an appropriate response. If you want or need added guidance, be sure to request this from your supervisor. However, also trust your supervisor to prepare you and support you, and if you are guided to handle something independently that scares you, you need to trust their assessment of your skills and jump in—with a lot of support.

BOUNDARIES

As mental health providers, regardless of level of training, we have various ethical and legal responsibilities. As psychologists (including psychologists in training), we adhere to our state and national guidelines, which include the American Psychological Association (APA) "Ethical Principles of Psychologists and Code of Conduct" (including 2010 amendments; hereafter referred to as the Ethics Code; see http://www.apa.org/

ethics/code/index.aspx). Additionally, it behooves students to be aware of rules and regulations of your academic program and internship agency. Identify any inconsistencies between these and work with your supervisor, professor, or both to clarify or reconcile discrepancies to reduce confusion.

As stated previously, it is of utmost importance that you remain aware of your role with the client and not cross or test boundaries. For example, a mental health provider would not typically call a client's daughter for them if the client is functionally able to do so, but would instead work with the client to make this call on his or her own (review the section on do's and don'ts for more examples). Sometimes providers feel particularly close to one client more than others (e.g., thinking of them outside of work, feeling a sense of kinship with this person). If you find yourself feeling emotionally and even physically drained after work, or having difficulty separating your professional and personal life, these may be signs of compassion fatigue or burnout (Figley, 2002). Consider increasing self-care activities to help rejuvenate yourself and create better work–life balance. Also be sure to discuss your feelings and reactions with your supervisor, who will help you understand and manage them.

It can be challenging to maintain a personal yet professional relationship with someone. For this reason, consulting with colleagues and supervisors is helpful. Often a particular client evokes something in us that other clients do not. Perhaps he or she reminds us of a beloved grandparent or their story harkens back to our own family of origin. It remains crucial that we as providers remain aware of what we bring into the room and clearly separate our personal feelings and issues from those of our clients. This helps clarify the motivating factor for different statements, actions, etc. (e.g., Whose anxiety are you treating? Are you asking this question for yourself or for your client?). Delineating your problems from those of your client is crucial to doing ethical and good quality work.

THE HEALTH INSURANCE PORTABILITY AND ACCOUNTABILITY ACT AND PROTECTED HEALTH INFORMATION

You may have heard the acronyms HIPAA and PHI used in various settings. HIPAA stands for Health Insurance Portability and Accountability Act of 1996, which created laws and regulations for sharing and maintaining the privacy of an insured person's protected health information (PHI). This typically refers to electronic communication (e.g., e-mail, fax) but also includes oral and written forms of communication (e.g., using a client's full name in public and discussing his or her health problems). The PHI refers to individually identifiable health information, including name, demographic information; past, present, or future health conditions (medical or mental); types of health care services received (including psychotherapy); and past, present, or future forms and amounts of payment. Health care and insurance agencies and their business associates, including psychology trainees, are responsible for adhering to HIPAA (for more information, see http://www.hhs.gov/ocr/privacy/hipaa/understanding/summary).

Given rules and regulations like the HIPAA Privacy Rule and the APA Ethics Code, it can seem difficult to know how to discuss your work with others without disclosing too much information. It helps to discuss your work in broader rather than specific terms. You can judiciously use real-life examples, but consider how much information to disclose, especially if you live in a small community where sharing certain information could compromise your client's privacy. Discussing your role with others obviously depends on your internship position and the type of work you do. Your client may share personal information with you regardless of your role. Typically the work can become personally meaningful, raising the question of how to discuss this with others.

As a provider, you may want to process compelling and poignant experiences on your own or with your family, friends, and partner. How do you do this without compromising the privacy of your client? It depends on the purpose of processing. If you are processing to better understand your client, this is best done with your supervisor in the service of gaining greater insight into your client. If the purpose of processing is to reflect on your own experiences, the focus turns toward you and sharing a client's confidential information falls to the background. Processing of this sort typically involves reflecting on your own thoughts and feelings, perhaps drawing on interactions with your client but with a focus on your internal experiences.

Engaging in your own counseling can be one way of processing personal experiences. Although you cannot share personally identifiable information of clients with your own counselor, this environment allows you space to reflect on your experiences in ways that facilitate self-awareness and growth. Therapy may also elucidate underlying factors why you may have stronger responses to one client and not another, and further enhance your work.

Additional means of processing experiences include journaling, creating a support group with a contracted therapist, and talking with friends, family, professors, and partners about your experiences, feelings, and thoughts. Solitary reflection can allow you time to sit with your thoughts and feelings and process your experiences of growth and challenge. Talking with others, whether in a peer-run support group, a process group, or confiding in family and friends can facilitate greater insight into and discovery about yourself, and enrich your professional experiences as well.

How Do I Use the Training?

We hope your initial exposure to work with older adults stimulates you to pursue further training with this important population. For those of you who are heading into graduate school in clinical or counseling psychology, there are several doctoral programs that have a specific emphasis in geropsychology. In these programs, you will acquire a broad range of competencies and skills that serve as the foundation for professional practice and research focusing on older adults. These competencies are discussed next.

As we noted earlier, geropsychology is a recently defined specialty field (Knight et al., 2009), but one for which some important events have recently happened that signify its growing maturity. In 2007, the National Conference on Training in Professional Geropsychology was held in Colorado Springs, Colorado, at the base of beautiful Pikes Peak. The aim of this conference was to develop an aspirational training model for competent geropsychologists, which culminated in the publication of the Pikes Peak model for Training in Professional Geropsychology (Knight, Karel, Hinrichsen, Qualls, & Duffy, 2009). The Pikes Peak model delineates aspirational attitude, knowledge, and skill competencies for geropsychology practice. If you decide to progress in geropsychology professional training, you will find it helpful to read more about the model, and study the self-assessment tool that provides a comprehensive listing of the content and skills in which you will want to find training.

Another important outcome of the National Conference was the formation in 2007 of the Council of Professional Geropsychology Training Programs (CoPGTP; http://www.copgtp.org). CoPGTP includes member programs that provide training in geropsychology at the predoctoral, internship, postdoctoral, and postlicensure levels. In addition, CoPGTP supported the development of the Pikes Peak Geropsychology Knowledge and Skill Assessment Tool (Karel, Emery, Molinari, & CoPGTP Task Force on the Assessment of Geropsychology Competencies, 2010), which is available at the CoPGTP website. This assessment tool allows for self-rating of numerous competencies aligned with the Pikes Peak model and has emerging evidence for its utility and validity (Karel et al., 2012). More recently, the APA Commission for the Recognition of Specialties and Proficiencies in Professional Psychology approved geropsychology as a specialty area of practice. With such recognition, leaders in the field of geropsychology received approval for board certification in geropsychology through the American Board of Professional Psychology. This mechanism allows psychologists who are deemed competent in foundational and functional competencies related to older adults to be credentialed as a specialist in geropsychology. As you can see, these are exciting times to join the field of professional geropsychology, and as we noted earlier, there is a tremendous need for geropsychology specialists.

Students who want to conduct research on aging as geropsychologists can also find great value in a practicum. Although the scientific literature offers tremendous information about aging, nothing one reads in books substitutes for direct observation of the phenomenon of interest. Students of cognition will find it helpful to have witnessed how healthy, independent older adults effectively adapt to normal age-related changes in cognition and to have witnessed and worked with profoundly cognitively impaired older adults who may struggle to adjust to seemingly small changes. Similarly, social psychological researchers who typically interface with older adults in a controlled laboratory setting also benefit from observing older adults within their normal daily patterns as a source of researchable ideas. Experience across settings helps researchers minimize unfounded generalization from lab-based data to the general population.

Conclusion

Geropsychology offers a wide range of career opportunities that are intellectually engaging, offer productive contributions to society, and are personally satisfying. Practicum and internship experiences are excellent strategies for exploring those while in undergraduate or graduate programs in psychology. With society aging rapidly, the need for this field will grow exponentially during your career lifetime, so exploring opportunities in this area is wise and will potentially help you define your career. The heterogeneity of the aging population invites the possibility of engaging in multiple practica to capture more of the fascinating possibilities.

References

Administration on Aging, U.S. Department of Health and Human Services. (2012). *A profile of older Americans: 2012*. Washington, DC: Author. Retrieved from http://www.aoa.gov/Aging_Statistics/Profile/2012/docs/2012profile.pdf

American Psychological Association. (2010). *Ethical principles of psychologists and code of conduct (2002, Amended June 1, 2010)*. Retrieved from http://www.apa.org/ethics/code/principles.pdf

American Psychological Association, Presidential Task Force on Integrated Health Care for an Aging Population. (2008). *Blueprint for change: Achieving integrated health care for an aging population.* Washington, DC: Author.

Figley, C. R. (2002). Compassion fatigue: Psychotherapists' chronic lack of self care. *Journal of Clinical Psychology, 58,* 1433–1441. http://dx.doi.org/10.1002/jclp.10090

Fozard, J. L., & Gordon-Salant, S. (2001). Changes in vision and hearing with aging. In J. E. Birren & K. W. Schaie (Eds.), *Handbook of the psychology of aging* (5th ed., pp. 241–266). San Diego, CA: Academic Press.

Hyer, L., & Intrieri, R. C. (2006). *Geropsychological interventions in long term care.* New York, NY: Springer Publishing Company.

Institute of Medicine. (2012). *The mental health and substance use workforce for older adults: In whose hands?* Washington, DC: National Academies Press.

Kane, M. N. (2002). Awareness of ageism, motivation, and countertransference in the care of elders with Alzheimer's disease. *American Journal of Alzheimer's Disease and Other Dementias, 17,* 101–109. http://dx.doi.org/10.1177/153331750201700206

Karel, M. J., Emery, E. E., & Molinari, V., & the CoPGTP Task Force on the Assessment of Geropsychology Competencies. (2010). Development of a tool to evaluate geropsychology knowledge and skill competencies. *International Psychogeriatrics, 22,* 886–896. http://dx.doi.org/10.1017/S1041610209991736

Karel, M. J., Holley, C. K., Whitbourne, S. K., Segal, D. L., Tazeau, Y. N., Emery, E. E., . . . Zweig, R. A. (2012). Preliminary validation of a tool to assess competencies for professional geropsychology practice. *Professional Psychology: Research and Practice, 43,* 110–117. http://dx.doi.org/10.1037/a0025788

Ketcham, C. J., & Stelmach, G. E. (2001). Age-related declines in motor control. In J. E. Birren & K. W. Schaie (Eds.), *Handbook of the psychology of aging* (5th ed., pp. 313–348). San Diego, CA: Academic Press.

Knight, B. G., Karel, M. J., Hinrichsen, G. A., Qualls, S. H., & Duffy, M. (2009). Pikes Peak model for training in professional geropsychology. *American Psychologist, 64,* 205–214. http://dx.doi.org/10.1037/a0015059

Lichtenberg, P. A. (2010). *Handbook of assessment in clinical gerontology* (2nd ed.). San Diego, CA: Elsevier Academic Press.

Molinari, V. (Ed.). (2000). *Professional psychology in long term care.* New York, NY: Hatherleigh.

Norris, M., Molinari, V., & Ogland-Hand, S. (Eds.). (2002). *Emerging trends in psychological practice in long term care.* Binghamton, NY: Haworth Press.

Qualls, S. H., & Kasl-Godley, J. E. (2011). *End-of-life issues, grief, and bereavement: What clinicians need to know.* Hoboken, NJ: Wiley.

Rosowsky, E., Casciani, J. M., & Arnold, M. (2009). *Geropsychology and long term care: A practitioner's guide.* New York, NY: Springer Science + Business Media.

Schaie, K., & Willis, S. L. (2011). *Handbook of the psychology of aging* (7th ed.). San Diego, CA: Academic Press.

Segal, D. L., Qualls, S. H., & Smyer, M. A. (2011). *Aging and mental health* (2nd ed.). Hoboken, NJ: Wiley.

Williams, K. N., Herman, R., Gajewski, B., & Wilson, K. (2009). Elderspeak communication: Impact on dementia care. *American Journal of Alzheimer's Disease and Other Dementias, 24,* 11–20. http://dx.doi.org/10.1177/1533317508318472

Williams, K., Kemper, S., & Hummert, M. L. (2004). Enhancing communication with older adults: Overcoming elderspeak. *Journal of Gerontological Nursing, 30,* 17–25. Retrieved from http://www.communicationcache.com/uploads/1/0/8/8/10887248/enhancing_communication_with_older_adults_-_overcoming_elderspeak.pdf.

Zarit, S. H., & Zarit, J. M. (2007). *Mental disorders in older adults: Fundamentals of assessment and treatment* (2nd ed.). New York, NY: Guilford Press.

Janet R. Matthews and C. Eugene Walker

Mental Health Professions

11

S ome of the earlier chapters of this book have mentioned health care professionals with whom many psychologists work. At times it is difficult to determine the person's professional identity based on the activities you observe. In this chapter, we provide more information about some of these professions. If you are an undergraduate student, you may wish to explore some of these professions as an alternative to a career as a psychologist. If you are a psychology graduate student, you may find yourself working with many of these professionals. Having a better understanding of their training will increase your ability to work collaboratively with them.

Optimal treatment for individuals with emotional problems requires a wide range of services. Service providers are trained in many mental health professions. Over the years, cost-cutting reductions in staff have blurred the lines in terms of who provides which type of service. Similar cost considerations have led many treatment centers to rely heavily on the use of medication rather than psychological treatments, which often require more professional time. Although such

http://dx.doi.org/10.1037/14672-011
Your Practicum in Psychology: A Guide for Maximizing Knowledge and Competence,
Second Edition, J. R. Matthews and C. E. Walker (Editors)

measures do keep costs down, they do not necessarily provide the best treatment for those in need of care. Increasingly, optimal care for many disorders involves a combination of medication and behavioral treatment. Unfortunately, funding for the latter is often limited. Nevertheless, prospects for financial remuneration are only one consideration in choosing a career. Other considerations include personal satisfaction with the contributions you are able to make, your values, your philosophy of the good life, and similar considerations. You may be willing to accept a lower income level, as long as it is sufficient for meeting life's needs, to achieve other meaningful goals for your life. There is an old saying to the effect that, at any point in life, you are what you are at the expense of what you might have been. We constantly must make choices about what we want to do with our time and energy.

As you read this chapter, you will learn some general information about the training and professional activities of many professions. For those students who want further information about any of these professions, we provide resources at the end of the chapter. A degree in psychology can provide a good foundation for pursuing most of these professions. Each facility has different staffing needs and budgetary support. Thus, you will not necessarily meet people from each of the professions we are describing. You may also meet people who have different titles at your placement and yet seem to be doing the type of work we describe here. This situation is related to the blurring of jobs. Depending on the nature of your facility, you may also meet people from health professions we have not described. Because there are so many professions involved today in the provision of health care services, we cannot cover all of them in this book. We have selected those professions with whom our students most often have interactions. Other professions may be found by doing an Internet search of mental health professions and allied health care providers. We suggest that you interview some of these people to find out what training they have had and what their role is, and obtain their perspective on their own job satisfactions and frustrations. It is important to learn not only about the tasks and rewards of a career but also the types of things that can make a professional upset with his or her role. Although you do not want to dwell on the negative side of any career, you do want to have some idea about whether you will have difficulty with certain facets of it. For example, if a particular position requires a considerable amount of paperwork with tight deadlines, and you already know that you are not comfortable with tight timelines, this is probably not the job for you. Be sure to be respectful in your questioning and let interviewees know you are interested in knowing more about the different professions as you plan for your future career or how to work more effectively with them as you move into your role as a psychologist. The information you receive may well help you decide on what you want to do professionally. Whether you choose one of these other professions as your primary profession or just learn more about interdisciplinary options, you may find this information useful.

Psychologists

Psychologists in mental health settings are generally clinical or counseling psychologists. Theoretically, clinical psychologists are trained to work with more severe forms of mental illness, while counseling psychologists work with less severe emotional problems and attempt to help people optimize their ability to cope with life problems. In practice, however, these distinctions are artificial, and there is almost total overlap in the functioning of the two specialties in job settings. These psychologists have a doctoral degree (PhD, doctor of philosophy; PsyD, doctor of psychology; or EdD, doctor of education) in psychology, with specialization in the areas of personality, psychopathology, diagnostic evaluation, treatment of people with emotional disturbances, methods of scientific research, and related areas. The clinical or counseling psychologist must complete 4 years of undergraduate training, usually with a major in psychology, and at least 4 or more years of graduate training in psychology. During graduate training, in addition to relevant courses, students in psychology work in treatment settings such as hospitals and clinics under the supervision of experienced psychologists. This part of graduate training provides a series of integrated practica. These experiences form the foundation for the next phase of your training. You then complete a year of internship before receiving the doctoral degree, and then undergo an additional year or more of supervision after the doctoral degree is awarded. At this point, the psychologist-in-training can be licensed to offer services on an independent basis to the public as well as use the term *psychologist*. The title of psychologist is restricted to doctorally trained professionals who have a license to practice the profession in that state, territory, or Canadian province.

When a psychologist moves from one state to another, she or he must obtain a new license and is not permitted to use the title in the new state until meeting that jurisdiction's requirements. Some states have reciprocity agreements with others and recognize licenses issued by each other. Individuals with master's level training in psychology often qualify for certification or licensing in various areas of counseling but may not refer to themselves as psychologists. In some states, professionals who work for state agencies are exempt from this title limitation. Some common titles for master's level practitioners in the

United States are *licensed professional counselor, psychological assistant,* and *marriage and family therapist.* We discuss some of these professions later in the chapter.

Clinical and counseling psychologists are trained and experienced in the basic sciences pertaining to diagnosis and treatment of emotional disturbances. In addition, they have a significant amount of training in research methods and procedures, which enables them to conduct research that adds to our understanding of mental illness and its treatment. This background also helps them evaluate published clinical research as part of continuing to improve their approach to their practice. A major difference between those psychologists with a PhD and those with a PsyD is the balance between the research and applied portions of their training. The PsyD programs place greater emphasis on the applied work, such as practica, than on the science of psychology. Psychologists trained in PsyD programs have received training in the broad background of psychology in addition to their practical experiences. Psychologists trained in PhD programs are more likely to have been required to produce a research dissertation as part of their doctoral training requirements than those from the PsyD programs. In the PsyD programs, the research requirement might be met through an empirical research project, but it is more likely to be an intensive case study or a publishable quality literature review.

In addition to psychologists who identify themselves as clinical psychologists, you may also encounter those who provide more specialized services in terms of activities and/or populations. For example, with the growing population of older people, as noted in Chapter 10, you may interact with clinical geropsychologists. If you are working with potential cases of people with neurological complications, you are likely to meet clinical neuropsychologists. Clinical health psychologists work with people who have a range of physical disorders. Forensic clinical psychologists work in a range of areas within the legal system including, but not limited to, evaluation of individuals' ability to stand trial or continue to handle, for example, their own finances.

Psychiatrists

Psychiatrists are physicians who specialize in treating mental illnesses. After graduating from medical school, these physicians do a residency where they are trained to work with people whose behavior is sufficiently distressing to them or to others to be labeled a mental illness. The general psychiatry residency usually lasts 4 years after completing medical school. Some psychiatrists specialize by the age of the patients they see, such as working with children (child psychiatry) or the elderly (geropsychiatry). Such specialty training often requires 1 or more additional years of training after the general psychiatry residency. Some psychiatrists specialize in particular types of disorder, such as depression. Like their colleagues in other fields of medicine, some psychiatrists elect to have general practices where they see a range of both ages and disorders.

Within the U.S. mental health system, psychiatrists may serve as medical director, program director, hospital administrator, and consultant to special programs. Traditionally, psychiatrists have emphasized the use of medication for the treatment of the more severe mental illnesses such as the psychoses. Historically, the development and administration of psychotropic medication has been cited as a major reason for the deinstitutionalization movement. Before these medications were available, many patients exhibited such disordered behavior that they could expect to spend most if not all of their lives as inpatients. They were sent to long-term care facilities, often located great distances from their homes. Thus, it was difficult for family members to participate in their treatment or even to visit them regularly. Today, patients with these same behaviors may be given medication, stabilized on it, and released to outpatient treatment in a week or less.

Over time, medications have also been developed to treat less severe forms of disordered behavior. Television ads for antianxiety and antidepressant medications are now common. Thus, although psychiatrists are trained to prescribe as well as to perform more traditional forms of psychotherapy, they often find their practices consisting of mental status evaluations, prescription of medications, and evaluation of medication dosage level. Few psychiatrists currently spend a significant amount of their time doing psychotherapy. This is generally left to other professionals such as psychologists, counselors, and social workers. If you happen to live in one of the states where specially trained psychologists may also prescribe medication (at the time of this writing, Louisiana and New Mexico), you may wish to observe how they combine this activity with those we described earlier.

Social Work

In July 2002, the International Federation of Social Workers adopted a new definition of their profession. According to this definition:

> The social work profession promotes social change, problem solving in human relationships and the empowerment and liberation of people to enhance well-being. Utilizing theories

of human behaviour and social systems, social work intervenes at the points where people interact with their environments. Principles of human rights and social justice are fundamental to social work. (http://ifsw.org/policies)

Social workers receive their postbaccalaureate training in social work. This profession has its own body of knowledge and code of ethics. Most professionals working in psychiatric settings as social workers have an MSW degree (master's of social work) and are then certified after practicing for 2 years (3,000 hours) under the supervision of an experienced social worker and passing a national test. Social workers may also enter the profession with a bachelor's degree, and a small number have doctoral degrees in social work. Those with doctoral degrees have more training in research and are generally interested in academic and research careers. When you read a chart note signed by a social worker who has the initials BCSW after his or her name, that means the person is a board-certified social worker. LCSW refers to a licensed clinical social worker, and ACSW stands for accredited clinical social worker. These are equivalent to BCSW.

Social workers are trained to conceptualize emotional problems from the perspective of how they interact with the person's social functioning. To be able to do this, they are trained to consider how factors such as poverty, racism, and unemployment affect mental health and how one's mental health determines the role one plays in daily life. They tend to view a patient's problems in the context of the family or community rather than from an individual basis the way the *Diagnostic and Statistical Manual of Mental Disorders* system is designed.

Academic training in social work includes courses in behavioral science, research, social work theory, and therapeutic interventions. In addition, a major part of the training is supervised fieldwork. This fieldwork is done in facilities such as community agencies and, when the student is interested in becoming a psychiatric social worker, psychiatric hospitals. Social work has been one of the leading professions in the use of supervised fieldwork as part of the educational process. In contrast to the training of psychologists, social workers do not have a focus on formal psychological testing procedures, although certain forms of assessment, mostly based on interview, are part of their education. Similarly, research training is included in social work programs, but it does not receive the emphasis it does in psychology programs.

Traditionally, social workers were the members of the mental health team who took the patient's history and made arrangements for follow-up care in the community after discharge from the hospital. They may also do follow-up home visits to check on the patient after discharge from the hospital. They receive training in working with a range of community agencies and thus may help patients receive various community services.

Today, social workers are also primary therapists for patients, serve as unit administrators, and maintain independent private practices. They work with individuals, groups, families, and communities. Their interventions include assessment and diagnosis of emotional problems, crisis intervention, psychosocial and educational interventions, and both brief and long-term psychotherapy. For example, according to Minnesota statutes (2001, § 148B),

> Social work practice is the application of social work theory, knowledge, methods, and ethics to restore or enhance social, psychosocial, or biopsychosocial functioning of individuals, couples, families, groups, organizations, and communities, with particular attention to the person-in-environment configuration.

In Minnesota, for example, social workers who are licensed to practice at the independent level both diagnose and treat emotional disorders.

Social work appears to be a growing profession. Trull and Prinstein (2013) noted that social workers at the beginning of the 21st century were providing about half of all mental health services in the United States. Enrollment in social work training programs has grown to support this profession. Some of these programs now offer the doctoral degree as well, while others provide the option of taking a joint degree in such other professions as law or public health.

Counselors

Different titles are used for counselors depending on state law where they practice. Some common professional titles are licensed professional counselor (LPC); marriage, family, and child counselor (MFCC); and licensed mental health counselor (LMHC). There are a number of others in various states. Educationally, these individuals most often have a master's degree requiring 1 or 2 years of study after the undergraduate degree followed by supervised practical experience. Their bachelor's degree may have been in any of the behavioral sciences or even unrelated areas such as English literature, chemistry, or history. These individuals have a specialty license from the state to provide counseling services to individuals, groups, and families. Regardless of the type of setting, some mental health facilities also have specialty counselors known as pastoral counselors. Because this term tends to be used across various states, we are providing additional information about this profession. This example illustrates one of the roles counselors may have within the mental health service delivery system.

Pastoral Counselors

Today there are more than 3,000 counselors in the United States who identify themselves as pastoral counselors. Some of these counselors are members of the clergy of various religions, but others are individuals who have received graduate education integrating theology and psychology. According to the American Association of Pastoral Counselors,

> pastoral counseling has evolved from religious counseling to pastoral psychotherapy which integrates theology and other faith tradition knowledge, spirituality, the resources of faith communities, the behavioral sciences, and in recent years, systemic theory. (http://www.aapc.org/about-us/brief-history-on-pastoral-counseling.aspx)

Pastoral counselors provide individual, group, and family counseling on both an inpatient and outpatient basis. Their approach to emotional problems is to discuss them within a spiritual context.

A 1992 Gallup poll of 1,000 people reported that 66% of the respondents preferred to receive counseling from a person who represented their spiritual values. Thus, it is not surprising that people experiencing distress seek assistance from their clergy. Many members of the clergy have neither the time nor the training to provide extensive work with these individuals. Pastoral counselors are one alternative for people who wish to have the clinical services they receive include a spiritual component. Depending on the pastoral counselor, reading scripture, prayer, and other religious activities may be combined with more traditional forms of psychotherapy. To provide a more standardized form of training for pastoral counselors, the American Association of Pastoral Counselors (see the website listed at the end of this chapter for information) accredits training programs for pastoral counselors and is currently developing a national licensing exam for them. In mental health facilities, the chaplain may include pastoral counseling as a part of his or her duties or may choose to limit practice to traditional religious duties.

Psychiatric Nursing

Psychiatric nursing is a specialty area within the nursing profession. Although a person can become a registered nurse (RN) with a specialized 2-year degree, today many of the psychiatric nurses working in hospitals have not only a bachelor's degree, based on 4 years of training, but also a master's degree, which requires an additional 2 years. There arc also specialty training programs in which people who have under-graduate degrees in related fields, such as psychology, can enter nursing programs and gain the added training to join this profession. Psychiatric nurses are often employed in inpatient psychiatry settings. They function as unit coordinators and administrators as well as staff members. They often work closely with the psychiatrist on managing the dosage of psychotropic medication prescribed by the psychiatrist. They may also provide individual, group, and family psychotherapy. During their specialty training, they learn about psychiatric diagnosis and psycho-therapy much the same way as other mental health professionals.

Creative Arts Therapists

A general term often used to describe therapists with a range of specialties within the arts is *creative arts therapist*. The term *expressive therapy* is also sometimes used. The National Coalition of Arts Therapies Associations includes six specialty groups: art, dance and movement, drama, music, poetry therapists, and psychodramatists. We have provided website addresses for many of these professions at the end of this chapter so that readers can get information about training programs and career options. Although many hospitals have one staff member who provides services overlapping many of these specialties, each has its own organization and curriculum. We provide brief descriptions of a few of them to illustrate these fields.

ART THERAPY

The belief that the creative process involved in making various art products allows one to express and deal with emotions is the basis for art therapy. Art therapists do patient assessment, treatment, and research in psychiatric settings. They also provide consultation to other professionals in these settings. Art therapy is conducted with individuals, groups, families, and communities. Art therapists must have a solid foundation in human development and psychological theory. Most art therapists have master's degrees. The first graduate degree programs in art therapy appeared in the 1970s. By 2014, there were 35 nationally accredited master's degree programs in art therapy (http://www.arttherapy.org/aata-educational-programs.html). To be listed as a registered art therapist, the person must have successfully passed a national examination.

Historically, mental health professionals have studied patient artwork to better understand both patient pathology and treatment reaction. Like-wise, art educators found that people's spontaneous art often symbolically reflected personal issues. These two streams of interest contributed to the development of formal training programs in art therapy. Art therapists use both talking about art and its actual production as parts of therapy. They may select specific media, such as charcoal or ceramics, for the patient depending on his or her problems. With increased technology, art therapists are also using videotaping and computer graphics to help their patients express emotional needs (Wadeson, Durkin, & Perach, 1989). Art therapy has been found to be useful with such diverse problems as eating disorders (Ki, 2011) and work with traumatized combat veterans (Lande, Tarpley, Francis, & Boucher, 2010).

DANCE THERAPY

Dance or movement therapy is the psychotherapeutic use of movement to assist in emotional expression and integration by the patient. Its foundation is in the expressive nature of dance, which allows patients to experience themselves through their bodies. Among the goals of dance therapy are catharsis, mood elevation, and improvement of self-esteem and body image. Training for this profession is on the graduate level with undergraduate coursework in psychology providing a good basis for it. Graduates of approved master's degree programs in dance/movement therapy may become registered as DTR (dance therapist registered). Dance therapy is used on both an individual and group basis in both inpatient and outpatient mental health treatment settings.

DRAMA THERAPY

Drama therapy uses both processes and products of theater to relieve patient symptoms and assist in personality integration. Drama therapists help patients express feelings, gain insight, and facilitate growth. Many drama forms are used. Although patients may play standard roles in published plays, more often they are encouraged to reenact previous traumatic life events and to role-play effective coping behaviors. Other techniques include puppetry, mime, improv and similar theatrical modalities. A pioneer in this field was J. L. Moreno, who coined the term *psychodrama* and developed many of the techniques still used today (Ehrenwald, 1976). Drama therapists are trained in theories of personality and developmental psychology in addition to the theater arts.

MUSIC THERAPY

Modern music therapy started in the 20th century at Veterans Administration hospitals. Musicians were visiting the veterans to play for them. When the professional staff noted patient improvement following these visits, they asked that some musicians be hired as regular hospital employees. It soon became apparent that these new employees needed education regarding the etiology and characteristics of the patients' problems. Thus, suitable college curricula were developed. Today certified music therapists (CMT) have at least a bachelor's degree in music therapy or its equivalent from an approved training program. Their training includes a 900-hour clinical internship. The first music therapy degree program was founded in 1944 at Michigan State University. Since that time, both master's degree and doctoral degree programs have been established.

Their approach to treating emotionally disturbed people is a combination of many forms of psychotherapy combined with various music modalities. Just as psychologists differ in their theoretical orientation and methods of doing therapy, so do music therapists. Music therapists use their relationship with the patient to help the patient address problems in much the same way that psychologists, social workers, and others do. Although they use various forms of music in their work, music therapists do not need to have a professional level of music ability. They do, however, need to have some musical ability as well as an appreciation of different forms of music. The patient does not need to have any musical ability to benefit from this form of treatment.

Music therapy has been used with patients of all ages. It has been used with a range of mental disorders, including Alzheimer's disease, substance abuse, and neurodevelopmental disorders. Music therapists assist in both the assessment and treatment process, and music therapy is used in both individual and group sessions. The techniques may involve receptive listening to music, performance of various forms of music, music improvisation, and discussion of the lyrics of songs. The music therapist helps the patient explore personal feelings, practice problem solving, and make positive emotional changes.

Music has been found to assist in stress reduction. Because stress is a common component of emotional problems, its reduction is a useful part of the treatment program. To illustrate the use of music therapy in a clinical setting, we provide some brief examples. Consider an early approach Rogers (1993) developed for use with children who have been sexually abused. In this approach, different musical instruments are designated as representing different people in the child's life. The child helps the music therapist select which instruments represent which people. The music therapist uses the size of the instruments as well as their relative placement and which are played with which others to help understand the child's trauma. This approach is quite similar to the use child psychologists make of toys when working with children. In more recent work, music therapy combined with cognitive behavioral therapy has been found to lead to an increase in the experience of positive emotions without the use of substances in a study with adults diagnosed with substance use disorder (Baker, Gleadhill, & Dingle, 2007). Similarly, a double study in which the assessors did not know whether the patients had received music therapy along with standard treatment or only standard treatment found greater symptom reduction in a group of hospitalized patients with a primary diagnosis of schizophrenia or schizophrenic-like psychosis (Gold, 2007).

Occupational and Recreational Therapy

Therapists in these two specialties use their skills not only to assist in the assessment and treatment of emotional problems but also to provide patients with the opportunity to develop new interests that can be used throughout their lives. Both of these professions work with people across the life span on both an inpatient and an outpatient basis.

OCCUPATIONAL THERAPY

The occupational therapist helps the patient learn new ways to approach the job setting so that it is not experienced as overwhelming. She or he helps patients learn time management skills, how to work productively with others, and how to enjoy leisure time. In some cases, the occupational therapist may help the patient change employment settings because the current one does not meet the patient's emotional needs. For example, some inpatients may not be able to return to former positions because those jobs are no longer available.

Currently, people serving as occupational therapists may have a bachelor's, master's, or doctoral degree. Recently, the American Occupational Therapy Association (AOTA) established qualifications for this title. Starting January 1, 2007, new occupational therapists must have education beyond the undergraduate degree. A list of accredited programs can be found on the AOTA website listed at the end of the chapter.

RECREATIONAL THERAPY

The recreational therapist involves the patient in selected active experiences such as games, sports, and other activities intended to aid in recovery and promote wellness in the future. The website of the largest organization of recreational therapists, the American Therapeutic Recreation Association, states that "recreational therapy utilizes various activities as a form of active treatment to improve the physical, cognitive, emotional and social functioning and to increase independence in life activities of persons disabled as a result of trauma or disease" (https://www.atra-online.com). These activities are designed to teach positive self-esteem and encourage interpersonal relations to facilitate growth. Participation in these activities may also allow the patient to feel sufficiently comfortable to talk about issues not yet revealed in more traditional forms of therapy. The recreational therapist may then share this information with the patient's primary therapist. There are national standards for certification as a recreational therapist. They are available on the website cited at the end of the chapter.

Summary

In this chapter, we introduced readers to a range of mental health professions. There are many others that might have been included. We did not provide an exhaustive description of any of them but rather attempted to illustrate each field as it currently functions. Students who wish to explore these related professions further are encouraged to visit some of the websites listed next and to do their own Internet searches for additional professions. Below, we also provide the titles of two books that contain such career information. One of these books deals with issues faced by students doing graduate study in any of the helping professions, and the other addresses various career paths within psychology. Once again, these are just two of the many books available.

Websites

- http://www.arttherapy.org (American Art Therapy Association)
- http://www.aapc.org (American Association of Pastoral Counselors)
- http://www.ADTA.org (American Dance Therapy Association)
- http://www.musictherapy.org (American Music Therapy Association)
- http://www.aota.org (American Occupational Therapy Association)
- http://www.psych.org (American Psychiatric Association)
- http://www.apa.org (American Psychological Association)
- http://www.atra-online.com (American Therapeutic Recreation Association)
- http://www.psychologicalscience.org (Association for Psychological Science)
- http://www.ifsw.org (International Federation of Social Workers)

- http://www.nadt.org (National Association for Drama Therapy)
- http://www.poetrytherapy.org (National Association for Poetry Therapy)
- http://www.naswdc.org (National Association of Social Workers)
- http://www.ncata.com (National Coalition of Arts Therapies Associations)

Further Reading

Students who are considering careers in one of the mental health fields may want to do further reading in addition to asking questions of the professionals with whom they are interacting in the course of their field placement experience. The following sources may be helpful starting points.

Echterling, L. G., Cowan, E., Evans, W. F., Staton, A. R., Viere, G., McKee, J. E., . . . Stewart, A. L. (2008). *Thriving: A manual for students in the helping professions* (2nd ed.). Boston, MA: Lahaska Press.

The information in this book is designed for students in graduate school for any of the helping professions. Chapters address personal issues faced by students who are in the process of integrating their personal and professional identities. The book also provides ethics codes for several of the helping professions as well as references on counseling.

Davis, S. F., Giordano, P. J., & Licht, C. A. (2009). *Your career in psychology: Putting your graduate degree to work.* Hoboken, NJ: Wiley-Blackwell.

The information in this book is for those completing graduate degrees who are searching for a good career match. It includes chapters on the applied areas of forensic psychology, clinical neuropsychology, and school psychology, as well as preparation for licensure.

Sternberg, R. J. (Ed.). (2006). *Career paths in psychology: Where your degree can take you* (2nd ed.). Washington, DC: American Psychological Association.

This book describes a number of careers in psychology. Psychologists provide information about what they do on a regular basis in their jobs and how you get started doing the type of work they do.

References

Baker, F. A., Gleadhill, L. M., & Dingle, G. A. (2007). Music therapy and emotional exploration: Exposing substance abuse clients to the experiences of non-drug induced emotions. *The Arts in Psychotherapy, 34,* 321–330. http://dx.doi.org/10.1016/j.aip.2007.04.005

Ehrenwald, J. (1976). *The history of psychotherapy: From healing magic to encounter.* New York, NY: Aronson.

Gold, C. (2007). Music therapy improves symptoms in adults hospitalised with schizophrenia. *Evidence-Based Mental Health, 10,* 77. http://dx.doi.org/10.1136/ebmh.10.3.77

Ki, P. (2011). Exploring the experiences of participants in short-term art-based support groups for adults living with eating disorders. *Canadian Art Therapy Association Journal, 24,* 1–13.

Lande, R. G., Tarpley, V., Francis, J. L., & Boucher, R. (2010). Combat trauma art therapy scale. *The Arts in Psychotherapy, 37,* 42–45. http://dx.doi.org/10.1016/j.aip.2009.09.007

Minn. Stat. § 148B.18, Subd. 9 (2001).

Rogers, P. (1993). Research in music therapy with sexually abused clients. In H. Payne (Ed.), *Handbook of inquiry in the arts therapies: One river many currents* (pp. 197–217). London, England: Kingsley.

Trull, T. J., & Prinstein, M. J. (2013). *Clinical psychology* (8th ed.). Belmont, CA: Wadsworth.

Wadeson, H., Durkin, J., & Perach, D. (Eds.). (1989). *Advances in art therapy.* New York, NY: Wiley.

Index

About the Editors

Janet R. Matthews, PhD, ABPP, received her PhD in clinical psychology from the University of Mississippi following an internship at the University of Oklahoma Health Sciences Center. Her postdoctoral fellowship in clinical and neuropsychological assessment was at the University of Nebraska Medical Center. She is a licensed and board-certified psychologist and Professor Emerita at Loyola University New Orleans, where she has been teaching an undergraduate practicum course for 30 years. Prior to coming to Loyola, she was a tenured associate professor at Creighton University in Omaha, Nebraska, where she also taught the practicum course. Her professional activities have included a term on the American Psychological Association (APA) Board of Directors; three terms on the APA Council of Representatives; chair of APA's Board of Educational Affairs, Board of Professional Affairs, Policy and Planning Board, and Membership Committee; President of Divisions 2 (Society of Teaching Psychology) and 31 (Intellectual and Developmental Disabilities); president of Southwestern Psychological Association; and 5 years on her state licensing board. She is a fellow of APA through 9 divisions. Currently, Dr. Matthews is an associate editor of *Professional Psychology: Research and Practice*. She has published over 50 professional articles and over 25 book chapters and books on professional issues. She is married to clinical psychologist Lee H. Matthews, with whom she is a partner in a private practice.

C. (Clarence) Eugene Walker, PhD, received his PhD in 1965 from Purdue University with a major in clinical psychology and minors in experimental psychology and sociology. His psychology internship was completed at West Tenth Street Veteran's Administration Hospital and Riley Children's Hospital, both in Indianapolis, Indiana. Dr. Walker taught at Westmont College in Santa Barbara, California, from 1964 to 1968, where he was an assistant professor and chair of the Division of Psychology, Education, and Physical Education as well as athletic director. From 1968 to 1974 he was an assistant professor, then an associate professor at Baylor University in Waco, Texas. From 1974 to 1995 he was at the University of Oklahoma Medical School in Oklahoma City, where he became director of training in pediatric psychology and cochief of mental health services for Children's Hospital of Oklahoma. On retirement, Dr. Walker was named Professor Emeritus at the medical school and began teaching on the Arts and Sciences campus of the University of Oklahoma in Norman. Dr. Walker has published over 100 articles reviews, and chapters and more than 20 books on research and clinical practice with children and adults.